D1029126

UNITED STATES AIR FORCE

SURPLUS
DUPLICATE

DISCARDED

WIDENER UNIVERSITY

# TAC

*The Story of the Tactical Air Command*

UNITED STATES AIR FORCE

By Leverett G. Richards:

TAC: The Story of the Tactical Air Command
ICE AGE COMING?

# TAC

## THE STORY OF THE

## TACTICAL AIR COMMAND

### LEVERETT G. RICHARDS

THE JOHN DAY COMPANY / NEW YORK

mil
UG 633
.R5

© 1961 by Leverett G. Richards

All rights reserved. This book, or parts thereof, must not be repro-
duced in any form without permission. Published by The John Day
Company, 62 West 45th Street, New York 36, N. Y., and on the
same day in Canada by Longmans Green & Company, Toronto.

Library of Congress Catalogue Card Number: 61-14330

Manufactured in the United States of America

WIDENER COLLEGE
WOLFGRAM
LIBRARY
CHESTER, PA.

117772

MILITARY
COLLECTION

In Memory of Sheila May

# Contents

# CONTENTS

# Foreword

A book about the Tactical Air Command is long overdue. This is one of the youngest commands in the Air Force, but it may well prove to be the most important, certainly one of the most important, in keeping the peace in the dangerous days that lie ahead.

The author has not presumed to write the complete, detailed story of TAC in all its various divisions and functions. But he has captured the spirit of TAC as only a writer who is also an experienced and devoted pilot could do. It is a book about pilots, by a pilot, but not for pilots alone. The author has attempted, successfully, to take the reader into the cockpit, onto the alert pad, and into the command post to show him what TAC is and does.

This is a book that had to be written. As commander of TAC during its formative years I am naturally gratified to see this story told at a time when TAC is playing an increasingly vital role in world history.

GEN. O. P. WEYLAND
USAF Retired.

# Preface

A book should not need a Preface. It should speak for itself. But this is a story without an end. The Tactical Air Command has grown with history even as this story was being written. When Khrushchev threatened to intervene in the Congo, tactical fighters were "repositioned" ready for action. TAC C-130s were used to haul medical supplies into the Congo and to evacuate European women, children and wounded. TAC forces were alerted during the Laos crises and were available for call during the Cuban invasion of May, 1961.

John F. Kennedy in the first months of his term as President emphasized the importance of increased forces like TAC for fighting limited wars with conventional arms. To meet the growing need for speed in any emergency, TAC's tactical fighter wings were concentrated in the 12th Air Force, commanded by Maj. Gen. Karl Truesdell. All troop carrier, tanker and reconnaissance wings were assigned to the 9th Air Force, commanded by Maj. Gen. David W. Hutchinson.

This book has been reviewed by headquarters 12th Air Force, Tactical Air Command and the U.S. Air Force for factual accuracy, and reviewed for military security by the Office of Security of the Secretary of Defense. Such review does not constitute verification by the Department of Defense of factual accuracy or opinion.

This is no history, no official chronical. Rather it is a portrait of the men—and women—of the Tactical Air Command, who devote their lives to keeping the peace. All incidents are true, all characters real, although some fictitious names have been used in Chapters 3, 6 and 12 for the protection of the individuals concerned, or their survivors.

Someone has said: "If you want to destroy the world, call on SAC. If you want to save the world, call TAC." This may not be exact, but it strikes close to the role of TAC.

This book would not have been possible without the aid of able officers and men throughout the Air Force. Special thanks are due to Lt. Col. Jack Giannini, information officer, 12th Air Force; his assistant, Capt. G. A. Knapp, and Maj. A. G. Thompson, former information officer 12th Air Force, both of whom offered inspiration, advice and invaluable aid; Col. Joseph A Stuart, TAC information officer and his staff; Ben Goldman, TAC's director of historical services, and his staff for painstaking research; Maj. James F. Sunderman, chief USAF book program, for special advice and assistance; and above all to Maj. Herbert Prevost and his Tigers who generously permitted me to share their camaraderie, however briefly, on the long crossing of the Atlantic in Fox Able 110. They say I am the first writer to make it nonstop. *Ave Tigris!*

P.S. Thanks to Dorth for endless typing. No one else could read my writing.

LEVERETT G. RICHARDS

# TAC

*The Story of the Tactical Air Command*

# 1. Winged Sword, With Lightning

There is a new sign in the sky—the sign of the winged sword, with lightning. The wings are wings of peace. The sword is the sword of battle. The lightning is the apocalyptic lightning of thermonuclear oblivion.

The insignia is that of the Tactical Air Command, the air force nobody knows. Everyone knows the mailed fist of the Strategic Air Command, holding aloft the terrible swift lightning of total destruction. SAC is a household word throughout the world, has been ever since World War II ended in the atomic fireball over Hiroshima, August 6, 1945. TAC has remained unseen, unheralded and unsung. Yet TAC is equally important to the survival of the free world in this new day of hit-and-run, nibble-thy-neighbor warfare. TAC is the free world's newest weapon in the unending defense against the Communists' strategy of world conquest.

The Tactical Air Command is a new kind of global fire department designed to put out sparks anywhere on earth before they set the world on fire. TAC's aerial fire brigades are ready to go at any time, day or night, whenever the bell rings. Like a fire department, TAC is prepared to dispatch the kind and size of equipment needed for each particular fire—a token force for one-alarm fires; "the works" for a three-alarm blaze.

When the Communists start a fight anywhere in the free world, TAC's job is to get there fast and stop the shooting before the brush fire can become a forest fire.

When Confederate General Nathan Bedford Forrest, famous for his lightning tactics, was asked the secret of his fabulous success he said, "Ah gits there fustest with the mostest!"

TAC gets there "fustest," not necessarily with the "mostest," but with the "bestest." Like good firemen, TAC's strike forces are designed to counter almost any kind of attack with just the right amount and kind of force to put out the fire without wrecking the furniture or tearing down the house.

TAC's commanders are jacks of all tactics, and masters of many. They don't use dynamite when flea powder will do. TAC has a versatility, flexibility and mobility never achieved before. TAC is as near a universal weapon as the world has ever known.

TAC's motto might well be "have guns, will travel." TAC's strike forces can take off on 4 hours' notice, fly halfway around the earth in 17 hours and be ready to fight a few minutes after landing. They can fly reconnaissance at high or low level; intercept and shoot down enemy aircraft with conventional guns or rockets; serve as aerial artillery to provide close support for ground forces, knocking out tanks, troops and gun emplacements on enemy lines; or supply dumps and communications behind the front lines.

Each single-engined jet fighter in TAC's all-supersonic units can carry conventional bombs or rockets. But it is the array of nuclear weapons now available that gives these one-man avengers their awesome power. Each can carry a small nuclear bomb or rocket reduced to battlefield size—or a thermonuclear weapon (hydrogen bomb) which packs more wallop than all the bombs dropped by all the bombers built in all the world before Hiroshima.

To complete the posse, TAC has fast, high-flying turboprop

troop carrier planes able to deliver pentomic troops to back up the airborne atomic artillery.

The Tactical Air Command does not replace or compete with the Strategic Air Command. TAC commanders are the first to acclaim SAC as the free world's principal pillar of peace, bulwark against all-out atomic war for as far as anyone can see into the future. But the hydrogen holocaust is not the only threat to the world today. Unable or unwilling to risk general war, the Communists are trying to devour the free world piecemeal in a series of small bites.

The five years from 1945 to 1950 were halcyon days of American military policy. The A-bomb was our national policy. We had the bomb. No one else had it. We had long-range bombers with which to deliver it. This combination of military might, the most overwhelming in all history, could not be challenged by any nation or combination of nations. This atomic umbrella, held aloft by the Strategic Air Command, was our guarantee of peace. We needed no other. We virtually junked all other weapons and services. The rest of our Air Force, Navy and Army collapsed rather than demobilized in the hysterical stampede to get out of uniform.

The Air Corps had a strength of 2,253,000 on V-J Day, September 2, 1945. Three months later only 888,769 remained in uniform. The Air Corps didn't have enough mechanics left to fuel or "pickle" its planes. The Navy didn't have enough trained men to get up steam.

The national feeling was that we didn't need soldiers or sailors or fighter planes. We had SAC and the A-bomb. There was a feeling that we didn't even need allies. The threat of the A-bomb was considered sufficient in itself to foil any Soviet-inspired aggression.

And this atomic umbrella worked, for a while. When Russian troops marched into northern Iran, the United States exerted pressure through the United Nations Security Council in March, 1946—and the Russians got out of Iran.

March 12, 1947, President Harry S. Truman threw the weight

of the United States behind free Greece and Turkey. "It must
be the policy of the United States to support free peoples who
are resisting attempted subjugation by armed minorities or by
outside pressures," he declared.

The formula varied in each case, but the shadow of the U. S.
A-bomb hung convincingly over the conference tables and the
deliberations of the United Nations.

On September 23, 1949, President Truman announced that
the Russians had exploded their own A-bomb on August 29,
1949—a full three years earlier than the U. S. had anticipated.
It would still be years before they would have effective nuclear
striking power, however.

Then came the Korean crisis. The North Korean Red army
drove across the 38th parallel on June 25, 1950. This was naked
aggression, sheer conquest without any excuse or pretense. This
was an open attack on the free world. This was the first major
test of SAC and the A-bomb. But no threat to use the A-bomb
was made. The Reds rolled on into South Korea.

That day marked the death of the cult of A-bomb worship.
The "umbrella" had leaked. It might still deter the Russians
from direct all-out attack to conquer the free world. But it
would not stop the Communists from fighting "limited wars"
for limited objectives.

Why wasn't the A-bomb or the threat of it used in Korea?
The question is one for historians. Top tacticians on the scene
have said neither the bomb nor its threat would have stopped
the North Koreans at that time in that area. We had nothing
but multi-kiloton bombs then, bombs which could only be
delivered by big bombers against big targets. We didn't have
many bombs, not enough to waste against North Korea, where
no targets existed worthy of this cataclysmic weapon. Political
considerations and the attitude of our UN allies weighed heavily
in this decision.

Five years of complacent reliance on SAC and the A-bomb
had left the United States virtually stripped of other miltary
power. Only one division remained of the Army. The Air Force

had just started to rebuild. All American troops had been withdrawn from Korea in the spring of 1949.

At about the same time Gen. Douglas MacArthur, in a newspaper interview, outlined an American "line of defense" in the Far East which pointedly omitted the Korean peninsula. On January 12, 1950, Secretary of State Dean Acheson, speaking to the National Press Club, outlined a similar "defensive perimeter," from which he also omitted Korea.

"From the standpoint of pure power politics it is easier to explain the Communist invasion of South Korea than the U. S. intervention," as Prof. Robert Endicott Osgood of Harvard University put it in his book *Limited War*.

But intervene we did. "Truman made up the United Nations' mind to intervene," one general explained.

The Korean conflict marked the gestation period of the Tactical Air Command, which was officially conceived March 21, 1946. It also marked the emergence of the father of TAC, Gen. O. P. Weyland. Korea was strictly a tactical war and General Weyland, "Opie" to his friends, was one of the free world's best air tacticians.

General Weyland started his military career soon after the birth of air tactics in World War I and played a significant part in the development of modern air tactics. His first introduction to aerial refueling, one of the mainstays of tactical and strategic air power, came within a few weeks after he had been commissioned a second lieutenant in the Air Service of the Regular Army in 1923 and assigned to Kelly Field, Texas, for flight training. A high light of one of the first air shows to impress the new student pilots was to be a demonstration of the refueling of one open DH-4 biplane by another, employing the method invented that same year by Lts. Lowell Smith and John Richter. As the two wood and linen kites maneuvered into blind formation in front of the crowd the receiver plane nosed up, struck the tanker plane and fell in flames, killing two crewmen in a spectacular crash.

Lieutenant Weyland progressed through the usual schools

and field assignments in the Air Service, rising to commanding officer of the 16th Pursuit Group, Panama Canal Zone, then to Chief of Staff, Sixth Air Force. In November, 1943, as a brigadier general, he went overseas in command of the 84th Fighter Wing to cut his teeth in combat. In February, 1944, General Weyland was given command of the 19th Tactical Air Command and assigned to work with Gen. George E. Patton's famed Third Army in the coming invasion of Europe.

"Initially this was not looked upon as a highly desirable assignment," General Weyland, now retired, recalls.

"General Patton had achieved a reputation as being hard to work with, and he had a rather low regard for air power. However, this was to change rapidly as 19th Tactical Air Command and the Third U. S. Army went into battle as a team.

"General Patton's headquarters, and the subordinate corps and divisions were located in training areas in England, Scotland and Ireland. The veteran 19th TAC combat units, from air bases in the south of England, were engaged in achieving air superiority over the continent, in bomber escort and in the softening-up process prerequisite to a successful amphibious landing and invasion of Northern France.

"I visited Patton's several headquarters and combat divisions to indoctrinate them in the capabilities of modern tactical air power. In turn he visited my combat units at their advanced fields.

"This was something new to him. He watched aircraft armorers load on bombs and refill machine gun magazines; communicators check and tune the all-important aircraft radio; mechanics repair and service the airplanes. The immaculately dressed army commander frequently got oil and grease on his hands and clothes—but he enjoyed it. He sat in on combat briefings before missions and listened to intelligence debriefings after the missions. He quickly achieved a new respect for air power.

"The briefing of an air combat group reflects meticulous planning and a requirement for split-second accuracy. Takeoff, assembly, climb through overcast, navigation to a target three to four hundred miles inside enemy territory, avoidance of flak areas and rendezvous with other air units for co-ordinated action deep inside hostile territory leave little room for error. At first Georgie was incredulous and possibly suspicious at briefing instructions refined to the second. 'Whose leg are you trying to pull?' he once demanded. But when he set his own watch at the time hack and stayed around to see the boys take off on the second, form up and turn on course over the field at the prescribed time, he began to believe that 19th was composed of truly professional crews.

"Thus, prior to the invasion of Normandy in June 1944, the commanders of Third Army and 19th TAC had achieved a state of mutual respect.

"Whereas many ground soldiers still believed that tactical air power should be subordinated to the ground force command, General Patton agreed with me that he would command the ground (Third Army) and that I would run the associated tactical air forces. At the same time we would both lay all our cards on the table, and plan and execute our respective responsibilities in closest co-ordination. And he kept his word. Britain's Air Marshal Tedder and Field Marshal Montgomery had first proved out this relationship in North Africa.

"But General Patton probably was not convinced of the true value of tactical air power until the breakout from the Normandy beachhead. On August first, the Third Army and 19th Tactical Air Command became operational as a team. Air power blasted the German ground defenses at the places Patton had selected for his spearhead attacks. Patton's tanks and infantry poured through the gaps and mopped up disorganized German defenses. Once in the clear, his tanks could really roll. The only hindrance to their rapid advance at times was wrecked German tanks and artillery on the roads. This destruction had been achieved by 19th fighter-bombers operating miles ahead of the American columns.

"A few days after the breakout, our respective headquarters

had advanced also and were set up next to each other in a woods. Late one evening General Patton returned from visiting his forward troop units and called me on our connecting field telephone lines. His voice was high with jubilation as he asked me to come over to his living van. 'I've never see anything like the way your planes have cleared the way ahead of my tanks,' he said. 'Boy, we'll stick together and roll right into Berlin,' he said. 'How about a drink, Opie?'

"Before the evening was over we had laid plans for further refinement and increased flexibility of our co-ordinated operations which was to become a classic in military history; had advanced mutual respect to close personal comradeship and friendship which was to permeate down throughout the members of the 19th-Third Army—and had killed a bottle of excellent Bourbon.

"General Patton was the greatest army field commander I have ever known—and I've worked with a number in combat. He was audacious but sagacious. Despite his colorful language, he was a God-fearing man. He attended religious services regularly, and was not above praying to the Almighty for help when he got into trouble—which was not at all infrequently.

"Being an old cavalryman, Patton believed in open warfare and in attacking when in doubt. His philosophy suited me perfectly, for it enabled tactical air to fight most effectively. When friendly ground forces flush the enemy into the open, tactical fighters can hit them mercilessly with rockets and bombs, and machine-gun strafing. We were agreed that, if at all possible, we should keep the initiative—never let the enemy get set. Keep him off balance.

"Down to the last soldier and airman, Third Army-19th TAC considered themselves the best battlefield team of our time.

"Although some tentative tactical doctrine had been established back home, and many lessons had been learned the hard way in North Africa and Italy, we made and changed our tactics as we went along. New situations required new and quick solutions. We literally threw the book away.

"One of the first innovations in tactics was Armored Column

Cover which 19th instituted soon after the Normandy break-through. We put combat-experienced Air Force pilots in the lead tanks of each column as liaison officers with the Combat Command commander. In each case, this air officer was in radio contact from the lead tank with relays of fighter bombers which were maintained from early dawn until late dusk over and ahead of the advancing armored column. On their own initiative, the fighter-bomber leaders would relay information concerning bridges and road conditions, and survey and recommend new routes if necessary. The same fighters would attack and destroy, or scatter, pockets of resistance prior to the arrival of our friendly tanks. When the advancing armored column bumped into hidden antitank defenses or other obstacles, the Air Force liaison officer in the leading tank called the fighter bombers in and pinpointed the resistance. The fighters would knock the enemy local defense out in a few passes, and the armored column would be rolling again.

"At first it was thought that aircraft should not be used on targets that could be knocked out by artillery. We found, however, that it might take hours for the artillery to deploy forward, get set in firing positions, and finally knock the target out. In our brand of fast-moving combat, this could give the enemy time to regroup and strengthen his defenses. So that bit of outmoded doctrine was ignored. I wanted to keep the Third Army moving, to keep the Germans off balance.

"This type of close air support the ground forces, of course, could see and appreciate. What they could not see, and consequently could not appreciate nearly as well, were the tactical air responsibilities of maintaining air superiority and of interdicting enemy troops and supplies in reserve or rear areas.

"The 8th, 9th and 15th Air Forces all had done a tremendous job of crippling German aircraft and gasoline production. Nevertheless, thousands of German pilots and planes and minimum supplies of gasoline were available. It was one of the 19th's important chores to keep those German tactical air units off the backs of our own ground forces, to keep German air off balance

and ineffective. Whereas American air relentlessly sought out
and attacked German ground forces from dawn to dusk, the
American Third Army operated practically unhindered by German air forces.

"Air Interdiction, or 'isolation of the battlefield,' is the business of cutting enemy lines of communication, of attacking, crippling, or preventing the movement of enemy reserve forces to
decisive battle areas where they are needed. Interdiction also
includes the destruction of enemy ammunition and supplies in
rear areas.

From an early attitude of polite skepticism, General Patton
went to the other extreme. He thought 19th TAC could do anything! In his lightning drive through France from Brittany in
the west, and to Paris in the east, Patton left his southern flank
exposed for some 500 miles, trusting 19th to protect it.

"This we did by daily reconnaissance flights, keeping the
German surface forces under surveillance. When the recc pilots
spotted German formations moving toward the Third Army
flank, they radioed in to 19th Combat Operations Center which
dispatched fighter bombers to the attack—with the recc pilot
pinpointing the target. This was another first, the use of reconnaissance planes to lead fighter bombers direct to the target
without time-consuming picture taking and intelligence processing. No serious attack against the Third Army's flank ever
developed.

"As Patton raced toward the Siegfried Line, other allied
ground forces landed in southern France. The German armies
in the south were in growing danger of being cut off. My staff
intelligence division made a special study of the communication
network in the area, and devised a plan for bottling up the German surface forces by cutting rail lines. This was put into effect
by skip bombing and cutting railroad lines at strategic places.
The Germans tried moving laboriously by highway at night, but
French FFI or guerrillas harassed and slowed them down. Finally
they became desperate and tried to move by day. Our recc planes
spotted the columns, and groups of fighter bombers caught them

in the open and slaughtered whole columns of men and equipment. After a few days the German commander, General Eric Elster, sent through an offer to surrender upon condition the Air Force would quit clobbering him! This was the first time in history that an army had been rendered impotent and surrendered due primarily to air action."

General Elster insisted the American Air commander be presented at the surrender.

It was typical of General Weyland that he jumped in a two-place L-5 observation plane alone and flew down through the combat zone, unescorted, to the Beaugency bridge, site of the surrender. He landed his light plane in a meadow alongside the highway. After the surrender he was jeeped back to his plane and started the engine, only to find he was stuck in the mud. The army commander, Maj. Gen. Robert C. "Bob" Macon, of the 83d Division, and his aide had to rock the wings and push while General Weyland taxied at full throttle over the soft marshy ground, kicked the plane around, still under full throttle, and finally managed to stagger into the air.

"As the war moved on we refined our tactics and developed new techniques for co-ordinating air support for the ground forces," General Weyland said. "Employment of air on the battlefield was a highly complex operation that demanded the closest co-ordination and often split-second timing between high and low level reconnaissance, close support on the battle line, and interdiction attacks on supply dumps, troop concentrations and other targets behind the front. All this was tactical air—knocking out forces in being—in addition to strategic bombing, wiping out the sources of supply and matériel far from the battlefield, which was the job of the bomber wings. It became evident to all concerned in the actual fighting that the air had to be run by an air commander, responsible to air headquarters, in close co-ordination wth the ground commanders, who were only one of our 'customers.'

"As World War Two came to a close, General Dwight Eisenhower, the Supreme Allied Commander, called all the American

senior air and ground commanders together at 12th Army Group
Headquarters and pointed out that the lessons learned in this
war, especially in the best use of tactical air power, should be
preserved for the guidance of future commanders, the Congress
and the President, lest the knowledge gained so painfully be
lost and have to be learned again at greater cost."

General Eisenhower summed up the findings of the conference in an official statement in November, 1947, that has remained national policy ever since: "Tactical air units belong
under the Air Force rather than under the Army."

General Weyland, who had helped write that lesson in the
skies over Europe, was to remember those words vividly when
the Reds rolled into Korea. He had just assumed command of
TAC when Gen. Hoyt Vandenberg, chief of staff, hastily posted
him to FEAF July 16, 1950, to take command of the air battle
as vice-commander for operations Far East Air Forces. In June,
1951, he received his fourth star as a full general and assumed
command of both the Far East Air Forces and United Nations
Air Forces.

The Red attack in Korea was well planned and smoothly executed. But the Reds had made one major mistake in their choice
of a battleground. They had chosen one of the few places in the
world where the U. S. had troops and planes within striking
distance. While the air forces at home were reduced to a skele-
ton of their World War II strength, the occupation forces in
Japan were adequate and ready.

American aircraft were the first United Nations units to
strike at the Korean Reds. F-51s, flying from Japan, harassed the
advancing Red columns. Troop carrier planes landed loads of
American soldiers wherever they could find a landing strip, to
lend support to the retreating South Korean army.

The air forces in Japan had been organized for the defense
of Japan, however. To mold them into a tactical striking force
was General Weyland's job. He had been chosen for the task
because he knew what had to be done and how to do it.

"There wasn't even a field command of any kind," General Weyland recalls. "The war was being run from Japan.

"Our first efforts had to be confined to close support. Trying to slow down the Reds on the battle front, trying to give the ROKs time to breathe, to regroup and make a stand. We even used SAC's B-29s for close support. We did take a few days out to knock out the Commies in the air. That's all it took to get control of the air. And we never lost control from that time on. Without air control, without close support for the troops in those first days, the war would have been over in a few days.

"The Korean war is an old story now. No one seriously questions the decisive effect of tactical air power in that theatre. We did evolve some new gimmicks, such as the airborne forward controllers in AT-6s who directed strikes against ground targets. Our combat rescue operations were something new. Those rescue pilots were the most decorated boys in the war. But mainly we followed tactics evolved on the battlefields of World War Two, although we did have improved communications, electronic aids and bombing techniques.

"We resurrected the F-51s, the A-26s, new B-26s, and the B-25s of World War Two. It took weeks to get them there, deck-loaded on aircraft carriers, and months to get the men and equipment to Korea by cargo ships. It was late in the war before the first wing of F-84s flew over on their own power, refueling en route. We didn't need refueling in Korea as long as we could move our airfields up close behind the lines. But we did experiment with refueling at wing strength in case we lost our airstrips in Korea and had to operate from Japan.

"Korea removed all doubts about the value of jet fighters. There was a lot of talk about jets being too fast to fight or strafe. The F-80 soon proved it could do more damage and suffer less damage in return than the propeller jobs. They didn't have the range we needed, however. The F-84s did, but we were sending them to our allies in Europe instead of to Korea. I had to do a lot of covincing before we finally began getting F-84s. Then came the F-86s and a new phase of air tactics. The Rus-

sian MIG-15 had the advantage of ceiling. It could outperform
the F-86 at fifty thousand feet. It had a 37 mm. cannon firing
explosive bullets that made a gigantic hole, plus two 20 mm.
machine guns. But the cannon had only fifty to sixty rounds of
ammunition and the 20 mms. only two hundred rounds. Both
had a slow rate of fire. The MIG had an antiquated gun sight
and it was of a different trajectory.

"Against this our F-86s had six fast-firing guns with four
thousand rounds of ammo. We could outperform the MIGs if
we stayed down around thirty-five thousand feet where we had
the edge in speed. And we could carry bombs. The MIGs
couldn't. The 86s had range enough to fly up to the Yalu River
and cruise for forty-five minutes or fight for twenty or twenty-
five minutes. The MIGs were short-legged defensive fighters
with limited range. We had better pilots, too, from the start—
although the Chinese pilots became good toward the end of the
war after the Russians came in and began training them," General Weyland added. "American air power met and decisively
defeated the best the Communists could put in the air, whether
North Korean, Commie Chinese, or Russian."

The Korean war proved a prelude to jet warfare. A U. S. Air
Force plane encountered a Communist jet for the first time in
history over Korea on November 1, 1950. The F-80 jet first
drew blood on November 9, 1950, in the first jet-against-jet en-
gagement in history. The MIG-15 bit the dust.

Communist air activity was confined to hit-and-run raids at
night during the first part of the war, but in the final days of the
struggle, while armistice talks were being carried on at Pan-
munjom, Chinese MIG-15 pilots, Russian-trained, became more
aggressive. Rising from their sanctuary beyond the Yalu, where
U. S. planes were forbidden to strike at them, they swooped
down from above the ceiling of the F-80 and the F-86. In September, 1952, 61 MIG-15s were shot down, 7 probably destroyed
and 57 damaged. Despite their heavier weight and lower ceiling, United Nations F-86s shot down more than nine MIGs to

every F-86 lost in aerial combat during the Korean conflict. The United Nations air forces in more than 800,000 sorties inflicted 181,000 casualties, shooting down 1,020 Red planes to 104 for the UN.

Tactical air power had dwindled to a ghost of its World War II strength in the hasty demobilization—more a decomposition—of the air forces after V-J Day. By the end of 1946, the nation's once-mighty tactical air forces had been reduced to six combat groups and 26,810 officers, airmen and civilians under the Tactical Air Command. The newborn Command had become a ghost —a headquarters without aircraft or weapons of any kind—by December, 1948. With the outbreak of the Korean war, however, the Air Force began rebuilding its tactical air power throughout the world. Lt. Gen. John K. Cannon was appointed commander of a reborn Tactical Air Command in 1951, and began training units for duty in the Pacific and in Europe. When General Weyland resumed command of TAC May 1, 1954, he found more of our tactical air strength overseas than at home. About one third of America's tactical air power was stationed in the Far East, now called the Pacific Air Forces; one third was in Europe under USAFE (United States Air Forces in Europe); and about one third was under the Tactical Air Command in the heartland of the United States, mainly in the southern and eastern states. At its peak in 1951, TAC had built itself back to 25 tactical wings and more than 60,000 men. Its strength has remained at about that level ever since and probably will as long as the atomic stalemate continues and Communist aggression is limited to nibbling at small, helpless neighbors along its borders. Current strength is about 60,000 officers, airmen and civilians, plus 1,800 aircraft, of which 1,400 are tactical fighters, bombers, reconnaissance and troop carrier planes. The rest are training and command planes.

While tactical air power had regained some of its World War II stature, it was cast somewhat in the role of the unemployed in the booming, business-as-usual post-Korean era. About half of TAC's aircraft was in the troop carrier business, and business was good. The C-119 Flying Boxcars and C-124 Globe-masters were kept busy hauling Army troops on training missions and carrying cargo of all kinds around the globe.

But what to do with the fighters, now that there was no fighting? Despite the lessons of Korea and Indo-China the general sentiment, even in the Air Force, held that SAC remained the free world's overwhelming shield against aggression, and that TAC was but a rusty dagger to be unsheathed only for minor infighting.

General Weyland set out like a circuit rider full of evangelical zeal to sell his concept of TAC as a global fire department. "We are faced with a new concept on the part of the Soviet's strategy if her timetable of world conquest is to be kept," General Weyland declared in public and in Air Force councils. "It was our tactical air forces that met Soviet air power in Korea, and won. We won so decisively, despite all the restrictions placed upon us, that Communist land armies were forced to dig in and hold ground.

"But the pattern was plain. The Communists, their openly avowed plan of all-out world aggression halted by the threat of nuclear retaliation, had embarked on a campaign of small 'brush-fire' wars. . . . Our problem was to stamp out this military malignancy before it spread over the face of the world."

While he talked, General Weyland also acted. He initiated experiments to see how fast and how light his tactical fighter squadrons could travel. From these tests "FAKs"—Flyaway Kits —were developed, containing the bare minimum of spare parts and supplies needed to support a squadron for thirty days' operations in the field. It took a bit of scrounging to make up the first FAKs. Regular supply channels didn't recognize the project as being legitimate.

To test the "flying fire department" under realistic field conditions, an entire jet fighter-bomber wing was alerted in California and flew with all its combat equipment to North Field in South Carolina. Here the TAC units found a sun-baked airstrip bare of everything but portable fuel tanks, almost identical, even to size and shape, to fields they later used in actual operations overseas. There were no hangars and no buildings, nothing but a landing strip of concrete abandoned after World War II—the kind of scene they could expect to find at a destroyed base overseas in the event of sudden war. For thirty days they slept in field tents, ate out of mess kits, and flew 3000 sorties with live ammunition, the type of missions they would later fly overseas.

Every spare part required to maintain the planes came from the Flyaway Kits. Knowing the ingenuity of the GI at "midnight requisitioning," the TAC officers went to the length of shaking down crew chiefs upon arrival to separate them from any extra tools and parts they might have brought along. Lessons of this drastic test were incorporated in a similar austerity-mobility program for all units of the Tactical Air Command. Each in turn had to pass the deployment test to "Devil's Island," as some GIs came to call the barren field.

To give jet fighters the speed and range required for truly global operations, TAC obtained KB-29 tankers. Later they were replaced by KB-50s, the first being delivered July 11, 1956.

While these training exercises were conducted by squadron and wing, the object was to develop a CASF—Composite Air Strike Force—capable of taking to the air at the sound of the gong, flying halfway around the world, landing, and fighting for thirty days on its own resources.

The CASF—pronounced Casaf—as conceived by General Weyland during visits to troubled Indo-China, Malaya and Singapore, was to be an air force shrunk to pocket size. Spearhead of this packet of power was to be the supersonic tactical fighter-bombers and reconnaissance jets, supported by tankers, troop carrier planes, and a command element. To hurl such a bolt of atomic lightning with the devastating effect desired required a new type of command control.

General Weyland, in July, 1955, chose General Henry Viccellio (General Vic to the troops with whom he worked). General Vic learned the tactical air business during thirty combat missions in the South Pacific in World War II and as Director of Combat Operations for the 12th Air Force in Germany and Chief of Atomic Plans for SHAPE.

To command respect commensurate with the power of the CASF and to operate effectively with theatre commanders anywhere in the world, command of the CASF must rest in the hands of a full air force—the 19th Air Force—not a mere headquarters squadron, General Weyland insisted. The plan was for the CASF commander to become the air commander, responsible chiefly to the theatre commander, in most cases.

General Viccellio's specialized staff not only had to prepare hundreds of detailed plans to meet any emergency anywhere, any time, he had to be ready to leap off with the first elements of the CASF to keep up with the changing situation. The C-130 turboprop transport, equipped with global radio communications systems and almost capable of keeping up with the fighters, became General Viccellio's inflight headquarters. He was prepared to take operational command of the CASF, under the theatre commander, immediately upon arrival.

Like a fire department, the unique value of the CASF lay in speed. Like firemen, the units assigned to CASF duty remained on alert twenty-four hours a day every day until relieved. Every man had to be within reach of a telephone at all times. Tests showed the first fighters could get off the ground within four hours after alert. The first element usually included a single squadron of fighters, half a squadron of reconnaissance planes, a half-dozen tanker planes, and a half-dozen C-124 Globemasters to carry the ground support crews, supplies, and equipment for servicing and maintenance en route. More units were added as needed to meet the particular situation. The last plane could be launched within twenty-four hours of the first alert.

For a three-alarm fire such as the Lebanon crisis of July, 1958, the CASF was headed by two squadrons of F-100s, about 36 aircraft; one squadron of B-57s; one squadron of reconnaissance jets; three squadrons of troop carrier transports; elements of a tactical control system, and a command headquarters. This strike force totaled about 100 aircraft, 1,400 officers and airmen; and 1,662,000 pounds of equipment comprising 2,800 separate items.

Like a good fire chief, General Weyland drilled his units relentlessly under all conditions in California, New Mexico, Louisiana, Texas, and South Carolina to build up their speed. He believed TAC had to get there fast in order to stop the fire in its tracks.

"A single TAC squadron can stop a border war before it starts, if the State Department and the President can give us the order fast enough," General Weyland declared. "Just the sight of a squadron or even a single wave of F-100 Dogs buzzing across their radar screens is enough to give heart to our allies and strike fear in the Commies.

"If shooting has broken out, even a handful of friendly fighters can turn the tide if they get there fast enough, before the aggressor can get set. A fighter squadron in time is worth an air force, plus an army, a navy and a marine corps too late. A task force in two days is worth more than four or five wings in two months."

This kind of speed didn't come overnight. It was born of endless exercises, alerts and deployments conducted with such an air of realism that TAC pilots never knew, when the phone rang, whether it was the real thing or not. At first they developed ulcer symptoms, but like firemen, they learned to live with the sound of the gong. They soon jumped when the bell rang without being "jumpy." In 1959, TAC conducted 13 large-scale exercises with the Army, involving 10,000 hours of flying time, only a fraction of the total exercises conducted on a smaller scale.

With each new exercise the CASF plan was refined. Heavy equipment such as jet engine starter units, cranes for changing engines, trucks, crew stands, and A-frames used for aircraft maintenance were shipped to jet air bases throughout the world, readily available in case of need. Jet fuel, bombs, radar and ammunition were stockpiled at strategic spots in advance. TAC traveled more lightly on each succeeding leap until a minimum of austerity had been reached.

General Viccellio as well as General Weyland and his staff were convinced they had a swift, sure new weapon that could be decisive in turning back the Red tide of aggression at any point on our far-flung frontiers where our allies might be attacked. But they still had to convince the rest of the world.

TAC stretched its wings in its first overseas test of the CASF concept on September 24, 1955, in Operation Mobile Able, when F-84s of the 405th Fighter-Bomber Wing took off from Langley Air Force Base, Virginia, and flew the mid-Atlantic route nonstop to Burtonwood, England, despite loss of four planes on takeoff.

On April 19, 1956, three F-84s, headed by Col. Charles F. Blair, took off from McGuire AFB, New Jersey, on Operation Sharkbait, to pioneer the tough great circle route over the North Atlantic to Wethersfield, England. Colonel Blair, Capt. C. J. Martinez, of the 405th Fighter-Bomber Wing, and Maj. R. C. Tomlinson of Headquarters USAF, flew the 3,145 miles in 6 hours and 50 minutes.

The first test of a full Composite Air Strike Force came with Operation Mobile Baker. This truly composite strike force included 16 F-100s from the 450th Fighter-Day Wing, Foster AFB, Texas; 16 F-84s from the 366th Fighter-Bomber Wing, England AFB, Louisiana; 4 RF-84Fs of the 363d Tactical Reconnaissance Wing; and 4 B-66 twin jets of the 17th Bombardment Wing. C-124 Globemasters from the 63d Troop Carrier Wing airlifted supplies, ground equipment and maintenance crews. The complex maneuver called for the 40 jet aircraft to fly nonstop to various fields in Europe to participate in Operation Whipsaw, a NATO maneuver. By October 9 the whole mobile force had retraced its route to home bases, a convincing demonstration to NATO commanders of TAC's new form of local lightning.

July 5 to 8, 1957, 4 F-100s crossed the Pacific to Hawaii, covering nearly 4000 miles in 5 hours and 15 minutes to test the cruising range of the fighter jets.

July 20 to 25, 1957, a small CASF took off from Foster AFB, Texas, and crossed the Atlantic nonstop to Sidi Slimane Air Base in French Morocco in Operation Sun Star.

November 12, 1957, the first big CASF deployment to the Far East, called Operation Mobile Zebra, tested 19th Air Force plans for meeting any crisis in the Far East, thus accumulating valuable experience that later helped make history in the Formosa Straits crisis.

By this time TAC was becoming well established in its various military trades: strike forces to "show the flag," to make friends and impress aggressors; CASFs on a larger scale, designed not only for show but for business if necessary; training for tactical pilots; delivery of tactical planes abroad; transportation of troops and cargo around the world for all the services; and missile training.

In September, 1954, TAC took over another of Uncle Sam's obligations under NATO treaty agreements—to supply tactical air power to bolster the defenses of Europe against general war. The 389th Fighter-Bomber Squadron was the first "ROT" (rotational duty) squadron to go overseas for six months under command of the United States Air Forces in Europe. Initially stationed at Toul-Rosière Air Base in France, it was moved to Chaumont Air Base in December.

ROT bases in France were closed in 1959 when General De Gaulle demanded control of U. S. atomic weapons.

As a result, ROT squadrons quietly began to stand watch at Aviano, Italy, in 1958.

# 2. Fox Able 110

It all began with a movement order from the "paper palace" alerting the 309th Tactical Fighter Squadron of the 31st Wing, George Air Force Base, California, to take over the commitment at Aviano, Italy, July 10, 1960. This was Fox Able 110—the code name for "Fighters, Atlantic, the 110th crossing thereof."

This was a leisurely operation, no sweat. The 306th TFS, also from George, would hold down the fort until the 309th arrived, backed by the 355th TFS from Myrtle Beach Air Force Base, South Carolina. There was a week to get ready. The 309th could have taken off on twenty hours' notice. Its FAK was all in order, ready to roll. That's the Flyaway Kit—spare tires, cooler turbines, spare engines, tank seals, hydraulic fittings, nuts, bolts, wrenches, crew stands, gaskets, ground power units—1000 items needed to service the men and machines of the squadron anywhere in the world for thirty days. The whole kit is kept in wooden boxes and foot lockers at all times, listed on manifests and ready for loading aboard C-124s of the Military Air Transport Service on a few hours' notice.

The aircraft, too, were ready in a few hours. A few last-minute inspections, a half-dozen test hops, new tires on most of the birds, and they are ready to leap off.

The paper work was the bottleneck. There is an old saying in the Air Force that "when the weight of the paper work equals the weight of the airplane it's time to take off."

There were order stencils to be cut, last-minute immunizations and vaccinations, showdown of clothing for the airmen, check of personnel records, advance per diem payments to be collected, last-minute changes in powers of attorney and wills for the protection of the wives and families who would be on their own for the next four months—great piles of paper work.

Squadron officers spent the Fourth of July pushing the last papers through the mill. Line chiefs made last-minute adjustments. There are no holidays during alerts of the Tactical Air Command. Independence Day is just another day of preparation in the eternal battle for continued independence here and now.

On July 5 the 185 officers and airmen of the squadron attended a final flying safety meeting—a pilot would no more miss a flying safety meeting than a Quaker would miss a Wednesday night prayer meeting. Then they went through the processing line. Each received sets of orders, had his dog tags rechecked, signed out on the squadron roster TDY—for temporary duty abroad—and submitted to a final check of his "shots" record. Tactical Air Command requires all officers and airmen to be immunized against every bug known in any corner of the world, from the usual typhus, typhoid and tetanus to yellow fever, cholera, poliomyelitis and influenza.

Officers and airmen turn in their personal tools and baggage for manifesting and loading onto the waiting Globemasters. It takes five planes to haul the 33 tons of cargo and the ground crews. Two of them have already taken off, to be on hand when the jets land at England Air Force Base, La., and to meet them at Moron AFB, Spain, after the overwater hop.

July 5 is family night. Personal problems faced, finances discussed. No one sleeps long or well this night, neither the half-dozen bachelors in the squadron nor the dozen and a half married men. Rotation tension has already set in.

Alarms begin to ring at 2:30 A.M. By 3:30 the pilots are sitting quietly in the torn-up ready room, waiting for the final briefing before takeoff. The weatherman paints an ominous picture on his charts. Most of the southern states are socked in. Refueling planes can't get off the ground. The jets will have to make the 1,562-statute-mile flight to England AFB, Alexandria, La., nonstop. That is "max range." No help is expected from the wind. It will take almost the last drop of fuel. If the winds are as forecast we'll arrive over the Alexandria omnirange station with 1,530 pounds of fuel, enough for 30 minutes' flight at high altitude, about 15 minutes at low altitude. It can take that long to get clearance to let down in case of a traffic jam. Estimated flight time, 2 hours 50 minutes.

The 21 pilots split into three flights for a final briefing covering all details of takeoff, form-up, navigation across country and emergencies en route.

Now there is a ten-minute lull before "station time," before we load up for the first short leg of the 7,650-statute-mile flight overseas. It is just after 5 A.M., the darkest hour before the dawn, an ungodly hour to launch any endeavor, much less an epic journey one third of the way around the world. Only mad dogs and fighter pilots get up before the sun.

"Do you suppose they take off like this in the middle of the night just to avoid saying good-by?" a TAC wife once asked with forced humor.

If so, the maneuver was a failure. The wives are out in force, shivering in the predawn chill in darkened cars, bolstering each other's spirits. The children are there too—sleepy, but refusing sleep. This is the moment everyone dreads, when the pilots tear themselves away, knowing they will not see their loved ones for months.

The dawn takeoff is a necessity born of the heat and the altitude. The air becomes so thin at midday temperatures and at the 2,875-foot field elevation that it isn't fit for plane or engine.

Even flying light, without wing tanks, the F-100s have little margin of safety at such temperatures.

With three tons of fuel slung under the wings we will need all the help we can get to lift off the 10,000-foot runway. The cool air of dawn packs more power-producing oxygen for the hungry jet engines—and more solid lift for the swept-back wings.

As we taxi out for takeoff, the Joshua trees stand silhouetted against the red haze of the desert dawn like old men with straggly beards. They seem to be shaking their heads as if they have grave doubts of the wisdom of the whole procedure. So have we. All is not quite copacetic with our bird. She keeps popping the circuit breaker in her fuel scavenger pump. A circuit breaker is simply a glorified fuse and when it pops out there has to be a reason. But we taxi on in close trail, sounding like a bunch of snorting grampuses marching nose to tail through the sage-brush.

We take the runway and snuggle up close behind the lead element of F-100Ds.

"Wind eight knots from one fifty, temperature plus nine [Centigrade]. Cleared for takeoff," comes the word from the control tower.

Major Herbert Prevost, squadron commander, and his wing-man release brakes and start to roll. We start counting. Just as the sun bursts over the horizon, bright as the fire cloud from an atomic explosion, an angry cone of flame bursts from the tail of the Colin Alfa Leader and his wingman, with an explosive roar that cracks into the cockpit above the restive roar of our own whining turbine.

We start to roll, with the leisurely pace of a dog sidling down the avenue. Then there is a gentle poof as our own afterburner kicks us in the tail, and our pace quickly becomes urgent. Three thousand, four thousand feet go by as our speed builds up with ever-increasing acceleration.

Lieutenant Lorentzen isn't satisfied, however. He's muttering to himself over the hot mike.

"Sick Dog," he complains. "One fifty. Barely abort speed."

But he lifts the nose off the runway. The heavy plane waddles from side to side like a goose too fat to fly, struggling to get off the ground. Five thousand, six thousand. The 7,000-foot marker has vanished behind the wing before she finally lifts off wearily. Then her speed builds up fast as we bank left and then right to avoid the sleeping settlements below us.

This speed is exhilarating. We are closing the gap with Colin Leader when suddenly we are dead in the air; going backwards, in fact. We are flung forward against the seat belts as if we had hit some hidden barrier. The sudden silence tells the story. We have come out of afterburner. We are up to 350 knots, which is the speed that gives us the best efficiency in a climb. Lorentzen has come out of AB to stop the rapid flow of fuel.

The afterburner pours raw fuel into the hot exhaust of the J-57 jet engine at the rate of about five tons per hour. We will need that fuel later. The weather ahead is not good. The desert below fades into dusty haze as we mount the unseen ladder of the sky, higher and higher, first at 1000 feet per minute, then toiling upward at 500, 300 feet per minute in the thin air of 30,000 feet at Mach .8. We have left Blythe, Calif., far behind before we finally reach 32,000 feet and build up to cruising speed. Now we can see the woolly blanket of clouds that covers the whole of the southern states. Our destination still has 20,000 feet of ceiling. But Tinker Air Force Base, Oklahoma City, is down to 200 feet. Even such old reliable desert airfields as Cannon AFB at Clovis, New Mexico, are down to 100 feet. This is not sufficient for airliners, much less a flock of fast jets. And we may yet have to land somewhere short of England AFB, Alexandria, La. Our form 21a, our howgozit chart, is not looking so very good. This is a sort of fever chart carefully maintained every step of the way by every jet pilot on every flight. And it shows we may be developing a fever.

Our fuel consumption is running above the predicted level for the first two check points en route. At Tucson, Major Prevost calls for a fuel check. Colin Alfa 1-1 has 8,500 pounds, Colin 1-2, 8,600. We have 8,300 remaining. We should have had 8,470.

We steady down, fly more smoothly, quit jockeying throttle, to save fuel.

We have spread out in "tactical formation," with #2 plane about 1,000 feet behind, 1,000 feet to the right and about 500 feet above the leader. In combat he would be in position to whip onto the tail of any enemy pilot who tried to jump the flight leader. Our element holds back about 2,000 feet, riding above the lead element. Our wingman holds off, back and above us in the same manner.

Now the pilots can relax a bit, check their instruments and gauges for trouble, and tune their radios for the next station ahead. But not for long.

"This is Colin Leader. Close her up."

But even before Major Prevost called, his chicks had begun to run for shelter under his wings. They, too, had seen the banks of thin cirrus clouds looming ahead, towering up to 40,000 feet.

As the flight slid into the downy, white cloud we seemed to enter another world. Colin Leader became a gray ghost that changed shape and character with each vagary of light and shadow in the luminous depths of the cloud. The F-100 doesn't look like an airplane anyway. It has the hunchback appearance of a razorback hog rooting for truffles. And in this dream world of opaque ectoplasm it seemed to change shape before your eyes like some mythical monster.

This is an optical illusion, aggravated by the "whiteout" condition, which has confused many an inexperienced pilot until he fell out of formation. Sometimes the wingman thinks the leader is banking when he is not, and gets "the leans." The darker the cloud the tighter the formation the pilots have to fly to maintain contact.

This stuff was thin, however, and did not last long. Our fuel flow was looking better now, but we weren't getting the "metro winds" that had been forecast. We weren't getting the help we needed from tail winds. It was three hours before we were over the Tacan radio station at Alexandria, La. Fortunately we

didn't have to wait for planes below us to get out of the way.
We were down to 1000 pounds of fuel—less than twenty minutes'
supply at this altitude, maybe ten minutes at lower altitudes—
so the controller cleared us for an immediate "jet penetration"
on the radio range station.

Colin Leader called for a radio check, then "Colin Alfa flight,
speed brakes . . . now." And Major Prevost popped out the stout
metal slab which sticks out from the belly of the airplane like
an open cellar door. As the "speed boards" bit into the air stream
we were thrown forward like the passengers in a hotrod when
the brakes are slammed on at full burn. Throttling back, we
stuck our noses down in a steep dive and began descending 6000
feet per minute.

Suddenly the cockpit was filled with streams of thin, white
smoke. Wraiths of white vapor boiled up around our ankles. I
was ready to bail out to avoid being fried alive when Lieutenant
Lorentzen explained this was fog, formed when the moist air,
compressed by the pressurizing turbine, expanded and cooled
as it reached the cockpit. When we reached lower elevations in
the humid Louisiana air, it began to snow in the cockpit.

As we plunged into the warmer air our fuel gauges began to
show a slight increase in fuel quantity, possibly due to expansion
of the fuel. Then it started to draw down at an alarming rate
as we added power to stay in formation. We were down now to
800, 700, 600 pounds. That was not enough to take us around
for another try if we failed to land the first time. As I called off
the pounds of fuel remaining, Lieutenant Lorentzen whipped
the heavy plane over into a steep bank, tucked the turn in tight
and rolled out low in line with the runway, determined to make
good his landing on the first pass. The hot, moist air was turbulent, and we hit a blast of jet wash at the end of the runway
which rolled and tossed us like a canoe in the surf. But the old
tin goose staggered onto the runway comfortably enough.

Once the wheels touched the pavement Lieutenant Lorentzen
pulled the lever to release the ribbon parachute packed just

above the tail pipe. There was a gentle jolt as the drag chute
bit into the air and our speed began to fall off.

"There's that old drag-happy feeling," Lorentzen muttered to
himself on the hot mike. "No sweat now. What do you suppose
happened to all our fuel? Pins in. Canopy clear? Coming open."

So I fumbled around to replace the pins which prevent accidental firing of the canopy or the ejection seat. And the first
leg of another epic was ended.

One of our birds landed with his utility hydraulic system out
of commission, which meant he had one full application of
brakes from the emergency system to stop him on the 9,300-foot
runway, but no hydraulic pressure for flaps or for steering once
he hit the runway. He made it safely, using every foot of the
runway. A tug towed him in to the line. Another lost his drag
chute upon landing and had to use full brakes to bring the
heavy plane to a stop. That automatically meant a change of
tires.

The heat generated by full use of brakes cooks the tires and
can cause tire failure on the next takeoff. The braking action
also burns enough rubber off the tires to require retreading.
Even a normal landing with the aid of the drag chute, coupled
with the high speeds developed on takeoff, tears up tires in
a hurry. Maintenance officers consider themselves lucky to get
12 takeoffs and landings before they have to change tires on a
deployment like this. The narrow tires of the F-100 are dimpled
with pits an eighth of an inch deep in the running surface. When
the rubber wears down until these dimples vanish, the tires
are automatically changed. In addition, a point system is used
to keep track of every tire's health. Two fever points are chalked
up against each tire for every normal takeoff and for every
normal landing at normal weights. Four demerits are tallied
for every takeoff with drop tanks at maximum gross weight of
39,000 pounds or more, and four points for every landing with
more than normal landing weight. When twenty-four demerit
points are chalked up against any tire, it is immediately changed.

"A blowout on takeoff can ruin your whole day," as Lieutenant Lorentzen put it.

There were a number of "squawks" to be cleared on other aircraft as well, minor troubles that showed up on the 3 hour 10 minute flight across country. Major Prevost's Tacan receiver wasn't working properly. His automatic direction-finding radio wouldn't work. Our radios required checking. Our engine wasn't "trimmed" to give full power for takeoff; a dozen other minor difficulties which can be expected to develop in mechanisms as complex as these jet fighters had to be corrected. This is one reason why such deployments are planned with a first short "shakedown" leg over land where possible. Squadron mechanics from the en route maintenance team met the planes as they landed, studied the "squawk sheets" and went to work in the sweatbox heat of lower Louisiana. Their fatigues were wringing wet with sweat. The temperature was 90, humidity 93.

"You should have been here when it was hot," they cracked. The crew chiefs, with their flying store of tools and spare parts, had arrived the day before in their own C-124 Globemaster.

The pilots assembled in the operations building for the "debriefing" that follows every flight.

"There has been a day's slippage," Major Prevost told the squadron. "Matter of airspace," he explained. "SAC needs it more than we do."

A shortage of airspace may seem like somebody's idea of a joke in this space age. But it constitutes a very real problem for military and civilian aircraft alike. Movement of a big formation of jets requires a block of airspace bigger than the New England states.

We would take off and climb in formation on the airways like a single ship. So would the tanker planes. But to refuel in flight would require a block of airspace about 200 miles long, 25 miles wide and 10,000 feet high. Here the tanker planes would orbit in formation waiting for the jets. The jets would have to have room to let down from as high as 35,000 to 20,000 feet to refuel, then climb back to cruising altitude. They would be unable to change course to avoid other aircraft. A chunk of air as big as Florida would have to be blocked off from all entry by other aircraft. Air lines and military commands had to be notified in advance to reroute or reschedule their flights. Three such chunks of airspace had to be blocked on the 5000-mile stretch of busy airway.

In this case, SAC needed the airspace too. And SAC's needs came first. There was no urgency about a routine squadron movement overseas. And so we had a day on our hands.

"Hurry up and wait," has long been the universal gripe in the military. But such delays are in the nature of things in the Air Force. In the Air Force, man plans, but the weather bans.

"Stay loose," is another Air Force aphorism. "The only thing that doesn't change, is change. If you don't like your orders, wait a minute and they'll be changed."

This is fine philosophy. But waiting is still the hardest part of flying or fighting.

Most of the squadron headed for the swimming pool at the officers' club after lunch, although the water was 80 degrees, almost as warm as the air. A few hardy souls tried the golf course in the sweltering sun. Most "sacked out," or "hit the bag," still the most popular indoor sport in the Air Force. By dark most of the squadron was refreshed and ready to go to town, bent on getting as little sleep as possible in preparation for the morrow. A few "sack-rats" prepared themselves by hitting the bag early, intent on rising with the dawn.

How can one mortal man fly formation from nine to twelve hours over water, through storm and dark of night in the strait-jacket cockpit of a single-engined jet fighter without benefit of autopilot; navigate without the aid of a navigator; answer the phone without the aid of a radio operator; keep track of fuel and a score of mechanical systems without an engineer; refuel by day and night in fair weather and foul; keep awake without benefit of a copilot; bomb without aid of a bombardier or radar operator; keep house in a cockpit no bigger than a bar stool sans stewardess, inflight kitchen or indoor plumbing? The answer is something called "crew-conditioning."

"Crew-conditioning is a sort of charm school, with pills and pistols added," in the words of the squadron cynic. It is an attempt to do for the human machine what the mechanics do for the rest of the squadron machinery before launching forth on a flight a third of the way around the world. Every airplane is carefully inspected, "pre-flighted" and given "preventive maintenance" to put it in the best possible condition for the grueling flight ahead. It never occurred to man to do the same for himself until mass military flights became necessary in one-man jet fighters and fighter-bombers nonstop across the oceans. Fighter pilots have to be tough to survive. They have to be in top physical condition to stand the strain of high G pullouts and high-speed aerobatics. They have to be alert. But it is one thing to maintain a peak performance for an hour or an hour and a half, the length of the average fighter mission, and quite another to remain alert and to concentrate on the most exacting kind of flying for nine to twelve hours over water.

The oceans can be spanned without "crew-conditioning." Charles August Lindbergh did it May 20–21, 1927. He flew from Roosevelt Field, Long Island, N. Y., alone in the Spirit of St. Louis to Paris, 3,610 miles in 33 hours 29 minutes and 30 seconds. He did it without sleep, on a quart of water and a sandwich.

Max Conrad, tall rangy father of ten, did it at the age of fifty-eight. In fact, he made Lindbergh look like a piker. Conrad flew alone, nonstop, in a single-engined Piper Comanche from Casablanca, Africa, to Los Angeles at only 100 to 200 feet above the water to set a new world's distance record June 2–4, 1959. He covered 7,700 statute miles in 55 hours 36 minutes. Conrad, an athlete and something of an ascetic, a devout Catholic and a mystic, trained for this and other distance records by gradually weaning himself from sleep for weeks in advance.

Both these men are exceptions. What's more, they didn't have to fly tight formation in rain and storm and they didn't have to refuel in flight over the oceans. And they didn't fly the strait-jacket cockpit of a military jet, which is built like a bomb and flies like one.

TAC not only has to get man and machine to faraway places in the shortest possible time—both have to be in condition to fight within minutes after they land. The "crew-conditioning" to maintain man and machine in this state of readiness really begins in primary training at flight school and it never stops.

Pilots are required to keep physically fit at all times. Calisthenics are about as popular as cod liver oil, but every squadron has its ball team. P. T. (Physical Training) is for cadets. Most jet jockeys log their P.T. on the handball or tennis court, swimming pool, volleyball court, or hunting and fishing. This rather loose system works, however.

There are no fat pilots. Let that antigravity suit start to get tight around the waist and the flight surgeon is breathing down your neck—if the Old Man or the Ops Officer isn't chewing on the other end. Ten pounds overweight and you can wind up eating in the mess hall at a compulsory diet table. If the pounds don't come off, your wings may.

Muscle tone helps fight fatigue on the long hop over water. And good health builds mental alertness. But the human body was never designed for sitting still hours on end in one spot in a strait jacket that includes an airtight rubber oxygen mask and heavy protective helmet. And the sanitary facilities are primitive. The pressurized cockpit is equipped with one pint-sized relief bottle. And only Houdini could contrive to put that to its intended use while flying tight formation through the night in an overcast. Many a TAC pilot has tried it, only to be faced with the embarrassing necessity of filling his boots—which are quite capacious.

The final crew-conditioning is designed to prevent this embarrassment, among other things. Some such program would be necessary if for no other reason than the fiendish hours always chosen for takeoff in all such overseas movements. Our crew-conditioning started at 11:45 A.M. when Dr. A. J. "Jug" Lee, one of England Air Force Base's jolliest flight surgeons, and his armed guards counted the squadron pilots onto a bus and herded us to the chow hall. There we were forced to eat choice steaks, cooked to our order, with potatoes, carrots, peas, salad, bread but no butter, and a single glass of milk or fruit juice—no tea or coffee. This controlled meal provides 920 calories, with minimum bulk. Pilots are cautioned to limit their input of fluids as much as individual taste and will power permits.

The "average pilot," 5 foot 10 inches, weighing 154 pounds, requires 2,400 calories for a normal day's flying. To sustain him for 9 to 12 hours requires only 1,500 calories, the medics estimate. We get the other 600 calories at breakfast. That's enough to keep the fires banked, but not enough to overload the furnace, which would, Doc Lee points out, cut down efficiency and lead to that logy, overstuffed feeling.

This high-protein diet is assimilated slowly and releases energy to the system over a long period of time, when it is needed the most. The flight surgeons have found by experience this sustained energy level is better than the bursts of energy that might be supplied by a diet higher in carbohydrates or sugar. It worked, too, as most of us found out later.

After "dinner" we were driven, still under guard, to the briefing room, where Ops Officer Capt. Don Woske started calling the roll sharp at 1300, with no preliminaries. We knew what we were there for. The weather man unveiled his maps and charts.

"Best I've seen in months," he said. "The whole route looks good. Plus-thirty wind component all the way [meaning a 30-knot tail wind]. Few thunderstorms north of Bermuda. Always is this time of year. Lajes [airport in the Azores] will have scattered clouds at one thousand feet, overcast at five thousand, four miles' visibility, ten to twenty knots cross wind. That's good, for Lajes, any time. Your destination is clear, visibility unlimited."

Dr. Lee mounted the stage, holding a small bottle wrapped with adhesive tape.

"This is England's own go-kit," he explained. "Half pint of water. Can't afford plastic bottles so we wrap them in tape to prevent breakage. Taped to the bottle is a box of APC [aspirin, acetophenetidin, caffeine] and a plastic bottle of nose drops. Take the APCs if you feel sick. Use the nose drops before starting your descent if you have a cold or your nose gets irritated.

"We have a supply of Band-Aids you can put on the bridge of your nose to protect it from the mask. If your mask doesn't fit just right or if you have a nose like mine, that mask can gouge like the living hell after nine hours.

"These red capsules taped to the bottle are go pills—dexedrine, dextro amphetamine sulphate. If you can make it without them, don't take them. But don't hesitate to take them if you need them. They do for the human machine what the afterburner does for the jet engine. Gives you a kick in the pants.

"We used to give them in straight pill form. These are capsules in an enteric inseal. That's just a covering to prevent gut burn. The capsule passes through the stomach to the small intestine where it is absorbed directly.

"When you need one take it an hour and a half *before* you need it. Don't ask me how you make it retroactive. These aren't retroactive pills. The reason for the one and a half hours? Some guys get a high peak of reaction. They're all hopped up at first. Time the pills so this peak is past and you are operating in high, not in passing gear, when you need the lift. Usually you will need one an hour and a half before the first refueling and maybe another an hour and a half before landing. Take one if you have to abort and make your way back to Lajes or Bermuda.

"If you wait too long and suddenly find you need a lift, pull the capsule apart and dump the contents into your mouth. It tastes like essence of old underwear, but it will act immediately.

"The plumbing on this airplane is notoriously inadequate. We recommend you don't drink any more liquids in flight than absolutely necessary. But if you get runaway heat, temperatures can go to one hundred and sixty degrees or higher, maybe much higher. If that happens, drink all your water at once. Don't wait until you feel thirsty. That will be too late. Dehydration will get you. For this reason you should carry an extra canteen of water. You can use it for output, too, as well as input, if you have to. A glass jar will do if you can't find a plastic or metal container. Just wrap the glass with tape to prevent shattering."

Go pills stimulate brain action, help keep a man awake. The flight surgeons have found that they are also anorectic agents, reducing appetite. The effect wears off in about three hours and leaves no aftereffects, as a rule. There are exceptions to every rule, however, and some pilots have taken a go pill in an emergency and found they were still wound up as tight as an eight-day clock many hours later, talking a blue streak and unable to sleep. A few pilots never use them, but most do on these long overwater hops. They have been credited with rousing many a pilot to maintain the alertness and mental vigor needed to save lives in an emergency.

"If you have any complaints, the chaplain will punch your tickets," Doc Lee concluded with a grin.

The commander of the tankers that would refuel us in flight covered details of frequencies, procedures and call signs to be used on refueling. Then the pilots trooped out to stow their spare gear aboard the aircraft. There is barely toothbrush room in a jet fighter. However, no ammunition is carried on routine squadron movements, which leaves room in the ammunition and gun bays for a clean uniform and a shaving kit and that's about all. Removing the external covers and stowing this gear in the merciless sun, tempered only by a humid haze, brought a rain of sweat to every brow. It was a relief to board the bus and return to the barracks. Here the dripping pilots lined up while Dr. Lee scrutinized each closely in turn.

"Fliers are inveterate liars," Dr. Lee confided. "You can't trust them to tell the truth about their health at any time. You just have to know them and keep your eye on them."

As he eyed each in turn he handed out two red capsules while a white-clad orderly marked down the dosage. These were the "no-go" pills, or "stop" pills, as some docs call them—secco barbitol, 1½ to 3 grains. They act like a barbiturate to put a man to sleep. The barbiturate usually wears off in 3 to 4 hours, leaving no chemical aftereffect.

"Aftereffects are usually psychological," Doc Lee explained with a twinkle in his eye. "The pilots get mad at me. Claim they can't sleep on account of the pills, or they can't wake up. Sometimes they claim both. Takes their minds off the overwater hop. That's what we're after."

And so to bed, pills in hand. As we marched down our special wing of the barracks we found the windows draped with blankets. It was a white-hot afternoon outside, but black as night and air-conditioned cool inside. Blankets felt good. Air Police guards were posted in the hall to guarantee quiet. There was nothing left to do but get the eight hours' sleep Doc Lee prescribed.

I took my pills like a good boy and went to sleep before I could get my last sock off. Lieutenant Lorentzen didn't and sat up reading for a couple of hours. Everyone took at least one pill. But not all of them slept. Some were awake hours before the orderlies began beating on the doors at midnight. One pilot never did wake up. He slept right through the commotion of departure. A couple of pilots, who neither smoked nor drank, awoke dizzy and were staggering like drunken sailors from the effects of the sleeping pills. After the 600-calorie breakfast of steak and eggs, however, we were all bright-eyed and bushy-tailed.

The final weather briefing shows the picture unchanged, with ideal weather along the whole route. Long-range B-66 jets have checked the weather in the refueling areas along the route and report everything copacetic. We may have to detour some thunderstorms in the refueling area near Bermuda. Otherwise all is well.

So we file out of the briefing room, each picking up a special inflight lunch for 75 cents as we go. This is the usual embalmed beef sandwich and ham-and-cheese on dry bread. But these are cut into bite-sized cocktail squares for easier eating. You can release your oxygen mask, pop a sandwich into your mouth and slip your mask back on handily. There is also a small can of sweetened concentrated juice, 100 calories, for a shot of quick energy, a hard-boiled egg and the usual flabby dill pickles. Not very appetizing, but relieves boredom on the marathon that lies ahead.

Everyone who can, makes a final trip to the latrine. Then we grope our way out to the line in the blackest hour of the night, 2 A.M., burdened down with go-kit, maps, form 21a, navigation cards, canteen, extra relief bottle, box lunch, cameras, extra candy bars and flashlights. Archie, the cautious type, has two Mason fruit jars wrapped in masking tape. One labeled INPUT, the other OUTPUT. He's taking no chances on the plumbing.

Just climbing into the cockpit ten feet off the ground, clad like a knight of old in cumbersome armor and weighted down with all this gear, is a major undertaking in the dark. Strapping on the airplane is serious business. First the parachute, then shoulder harness, then the seat belt fastened with the lanyard in place which will open the parachute automatically at 15,000 feet. Then the dinghy pack in the seat secured to rings on the parachute. Connect the pressure hose to the partial pressure suit. Connect the oxygen hose to the parachute fitting and plug in your oxygen mask. Plug in the earphones. Fit helmet mask and test for oxygen leaks. Hook the lanyard to the D-ring of your parachute, to open your parachute instantly if you have to bail out at low altitude on takeoff. Now pull the safety pins, which prevent you from accidentally blowing off the canopy or ejecting yourself onto the concrete while parked on the ramp if you happen to hit the "next-of-kin" triggers or ejection controls.

2:15 A.M.: Time to start engines. So far so good.

2:30 A.M.: Time to taxi. Our interphone works, but our radio is dead. We taxi out anyway, still pushing circuit breakers and trying different transmitters. We taxi back to the line. A quick look under the hood and the crew chief has the radio working. We scurry back in line, taxi onto the runway, close the canopy.

Colin Leader, Major Prevost, is calling for ATC clearance—permission from the civil airways traffic controller to take to the air.

"Stand by one," says the tower.

"We're gulping fuel out here," Major Prevost answers sharply.

"Expect clearance at thirty-four," says the soothing voice of the tower.

Tension builds up throughout the squadron. You can feel it in the heavy breathing of the pilots, heard over open mikes. You can see it in the hand signals passed down the line. "Let's go."

Everyone is keyed up for the great adventure. The fuse is lit, the squadron is ready for blastoff, like 18 rockets united as one. Then comes the hollow voice of the controller.

"Colin Alfa flight, return to the line, twenty-four-hour delay."

"Confirm that," snaps Major Prevost.

"Stand by one," comes the voice of Col. W. D. Ritchie, wing commander, on the radio. He has flown out from George AFB to be with the squadron on takeoff.

"Hang loose," Major Prevost orders.

There is a taut silence for two minutes, then Colonel Ritchie is back.

"Twelfth Air Force has shot us down. A line of thunderstorms is moving down from the north into the refueling area off Bermuda."

"Roger, return to the line," Colin Leader orders.

The awkward jets pivot on the taxiway and sulk back to the line like a parade of petulant pachyderms. The pilots unpack their carefully packed cockpits and return to the briefing room for debriefing.

"Watch your taxiing next time," Major Prevost warns. "We had to change two tires just from taxiing out this morning. Remember you've got nineteen tons riding on those wheels."

Now it's back to the barracks at 3:45 in the morning. There is no griping. But the letdown is demoralizing.

What do you do with a day that starts in the middle of the night and ends in the middle of the day? A few sack-rats hit the hay for a quick couple of hours of shut-eye. Most are wide-eyed and moody. They rally round the poker table and chips begin to clink. Some sit down with the nearest paperback.

This is the Air Force. Life is like this, in peacetime and in war. Life is just one fast start and sudden stop after another. It's hard to take and some just can't take it. This squadron is a tight one. Morale is high. There are a number of old hands, captains with a couple of thousand hours, which is a lot of time in jets. A few of them have crossed the Pacific. A few have island-hopped across the Atlantic. But only one or two have crossed the Atlantic nonstop. Now they have time to think about the crossing. Too much time. This is Saturday. Nothing is open on the base but the base exchange and the swimming pool. There is nothing to do but sit and play poker and read . . . and think. The quiet ones become garrulous. There is more kidding and more horseplay than usual. The noisy ones are suddenly quiet, moody. Tension is building up.

"Such feelings prior to flying over broad expanses of water in single-engined jet fighters with all the hazardous possibilities attendant thereto show a healthy realistic attitude," in the words of the only flight surgeon who had made such a crossing with his squadron—Capt. Darrell W. Landrey, of the 31st Wing, George AFB.

"It would be foolish not to be cognizant of the risks involved. . . . The general American public should know what these men undergo prior to such a flight. But they go anyway."

It was not fear of the flight so much as fear of fear that was working subtly on the jet jocks during this long letdown. The younger lieutenants, fresh out of flight school, especially were sweating out the flight—not so much for fear of losing an engine as for fear of goofing up and disgracing the squadron.

The swimming pool finally opened at noon. Just time for a

quick swim. And this endless day began to end—or was it just starting? Once again we loaded aboard the same old bus in the same old way to the same mess hall for the same tender steaks, took the same Seconal and hit the same old sack for a welcome eight hours' sleep, ate the same steak and eggs for breakfast and trooped into the ready room for briefing. The weather looked the same as it had twenty-four hours earlier, maybe not so good in spots. Myrtle Beach, first alternate if we failed our initial refueling, had only five miles visibility in a fog which might get worse. Kindley AFB, Bermuda, had scattered clouds at 1,500 feet and a 25-knot cross wind. But this time we were going.

Sharp at 2:15 A.M. we started engines. At 2:25 Colin Leader called, "Colin Alfa flight, check in."

"One-one—lanyard, dinghy."

"One-two—lanyard, dinghy."

Each in turn acknowledged the radio check and noted his lanyard was fastened to his D-ring for low-level bailout and his seat pack containing his dinghy was fastened to his parachute harness.

"Ground Control, Colin one-zero and flight of eight, taxi instructions." And eight ghostly figures, flashing silver under the mellow Louisiana moon, begin bobbing eerily through the dark, red and green wing lights playing a crazy tune in the night.

Colin Leader pulls onto the runway. His chicks cuddle up close behind him. In the bitter black of the night off the end of the runway a helicopter orbits ominously. Its searchlight probes the ground with a bright finger of light, looking hopefully for any of our birds that may falter and fall in flames on takeoff. A blowout or a flameout at this critical moment can roll an F-100 into a ball of flaming Hell. A team of men clad in heavy asbestos suits is on hand to pull us out of the fire if we fall in flames.

"If she coughs on takeoff, punch out. Don't wait for me or you'll be talking to yourself," Lieutenant Lorentzen says on the hot mike in a last-minute briefing.

"I'll blow the canopy. But you have to eject first in this

buggy, else you may get my feet in your face. If she flames, watch the altimeter and the airspeed. I'll pull her up. When we quit climbing and the airspeed starts dying off, hit the next-of-kin button. Punch out. Be sure your lanyard is fastened. That'll pull your ripcord the second your seat belt blasts loose. Don't wait. Grab the D-ring yourself, and kick free of the seat. You only need a hundred feet of altitude to get out, if you act fast."

The tower cuts in: "Colin Alfa, cleared for takeoff."

Major Prevost's gray ghost and the lights of his wingmen start to roll slowly. Suddenly the quiet of the night is shattered by a double explosion, bright blue and yellow daggers of flame stab the dark as the two lead ships fire their afterburners. Shock diamonds, like hoops of blue flame within the cone of white flame, testify to the speed of the angry fire that shoots out their tails—faster than the speed of sound.

Eight . . . nine . . . ten seconds and Lorentzen releases our brakes and abruptly we begin to waddle slowly down the runway. There is a dull *pow* and we are kicked gently in the tail as our own afterburner lights, shoving us ahead the way a man shoves a boy in a swing. Faster and faster we gather speed through the muggy night, our wheels bumping over the joints in the runway like the wheels of a streamlined train picking up speed as it roars out of the yards. Then the bumps smooth out as we take to the air, pursuing and pursued by torches flaming brightly in the night.

The drowsy Louisiana night is hideous with noise as the gaggle of metal monsters claw their way into the sky, wave after wave, roaring as if the Devil were after them. You'd roar, too, if your tail was on fire, shooting a cone of white-hot flame 15 feet out behind. Stabbed in the pants by this dagger of flame, our 19-ton juggernaut gathers speed, accelerating faster and faster as its speed increases. A jet's power grows with its speed. In a matter of seconds our indicator shows we've hit 350 knots, climbing all the while.

"AB out . . . now," comes the command from Colin Leader.

And we die in mid-air. All of a sudden we seem to stop and back up as the massive thrust of the afterburner is cut off. The pillar of flame is gone. The muffled roar of the blast from Colin Leader, faintly audible even through our pressurized cockpit and foam rubber earphones, dies out. The night is strangely quiet now. As the lights fade and our eyes grow accustomed to the darkness the silver forms of the lead F-100s become faintly visible, like astral minnows swimming up from the depths of the night into the bright moonlight above.

"HOLYS check," Colin Leader cuts in.

That's "H" for hydraulic system. Is it working? "O" for oxygen. Is that fluorescent eye blinking reassuringly at you as you breathe, measuring the flow of oxygen? "L" for lanyard. Is the lanyard disconnected from the D-ring of your parachute? If not, both you and your parachute could be torn apart if you had to eject suddenly at this speed. "Y" is for yaw damper. Is it turned on to automatically keep the aircraft on a straight course when rough air is encountered? Early F-100s were torn apart when the nose yawed too far to one side in high-speed flight. "S" is for the gun sight. No need to turn it on for this flight.

Back to the beauty of the night. The tensions of takeoff are gone. The younger pilots are still working hard to get into formation and stay there in the black of the night. But they're relaxed now. Nothing soothes the anxious spirits of a pilot like the miracle of flight. The air is his element. Flying is his life.

Lieutenant Lorentzen is talking to himself again. Happy talk. "Hmmm. We've got hydraulic pressure. Circuit breaker is staying put. Nice . . . Fuel flowing, or is it? That right drop tank's not feeding."

"Check tanks," Colin Leader cuts in.

"One-three, drop tanks not feeding," Archie answers.

"Check your bleed air," Colin comes back.

"Roger. That's it. Bleed air valve open. Feeding now," Lorentzen replies.

Peace descends on Colin Alfa flight. There is a time of quiet

with nothing to do but keep the direction-finding radio tuned
to the station ahead and watch the Tacan count off the miles as
we swim through the velvet night. We are on airways now, our
eight-ship section flying as one, checking in over each station
like a single airliner. We are at 29,000 feet now, our assigned
altitude. It is Colin Leader's job to navigate and report in. But
we, too, are navigating. We will take the lead if Major Prevost
has to abort. We double check his navigation in case his radios
fail. We have left Jackson, Miss., behind and are closing on
Tuscaloosa, Ala. Birmingham is hard ahead and we turn east
to Augusta. The lights of Atlanta peek through the clouds below—a potful of diamonds spilled on a velvet cloth. A few
rubies and emeralds there, too.

The beauty of the night is fading slowly. The moon is growing old and pale. The sky is getting green in the east—and about
time, too. Here it is 3:30 A.M. and black clouds are looming up
ahead.

"Close up," Colin Leader orders. But his silver chicks have
seen the black wall looming up ahead and are already scurrying
for cover close under his gray wings. He has the only paint job
in the squadron—a light gray—which gives him a ghostly look in
the greenish light of predawn. We penetrate the lazy cloud in
a matter of minutes and are in the clear again. The sky is getting a copper glow to it in the north. That can't be east. Now
the tankers are calling.

"Colin Alfa, this is Shirk one-zero. I have a target southwest
at one hundred forty miles. Squawk three."

Our IFF (identification, friend or foe) is already broadcasting
pattern number three, which should be received on the KB-50J
tanker's radar screen.

"Strangle three and squawk two," Shirk one-zero commands.
And we switch to transmit pattern number two.

"Target confirmed. We are one hundred forty miles northeast of you," Shirk reports.

Now we forget the airways and start following "steers" from
Shirk one-zero.

"Steer one one zero," Shirk orders. "We have you at thirty miles . . . How many chicks in your flight?"

"Eight," Major Prevost tells him.

"Now steer zero six zero," Shirk comes back.

"Who's playing games?" Major Prevost demands. "We couldn't be that far off course."

The tankers are making a wide turn in formation in their holding pattern, turning onto course for the refueling run, Shirk one-zero explains. Their position is changing rapidly, not ours. We stay on course. We are 18 miles out, 15, 12.

"Dive brakes down . . . now," Colin Leader orders. And we start down at 3000 feet per minute.

The sky is blushing a ruddy red. The sun is about to burst into flame at any minute.

"Bogeys at twelve o'clock level," Colin 1-4 reports.

There in the molten rays of the rising sun we dimly make out four flat worms swimming through the red-hot lava of the sky like Manta rays in a red surf. Our flight spreads out a bit, still in formation. Each element of two picks its tanker. Then Major Prevost gives the order to change to tanker frequency. Each pair of jets now can talk directly to its tanker and to no one else.

Their lights flash dimly against the dawn. For night refueling the tankers are lit up like Broadway. Bright lights are directed at the hoses from the tail of the plane, while more lights pick out the hose reel pods. Red and green lights blink like pinball machines on the reel pods themselves to tell the fighter plane when he is getting fuel and when he isn't, when to stand by and when to back off. The tankers, illuminated this way, have been mistaken for flying saucers. The fighters, too, have a bright light that spotlights their probes during refueling.

We are about to be parties to a minor miracle that is the secret of TAC's ability to race with giant strides around the world in any direction, gun in hand. It is called AAR—Air-to-Air Refueling. It's impossible, as any sane civilian pilot will tell you. It's like giving a transfusion in mid-air from a lumbering pelican to a fleet falcon, with your eyes shut. For the fighter pilot's "needle" is behind his back where he can't see it.

Against the ruddy sky the tankers gradually take the shape of flying grasshoppers with their ovipositors thrust far out behind. Upon closer inspection they assume the appearance of medieval monsters with their entrails hanging out, one from each wing tip and one from the tail, streaming far out behind. But these are no pterodactyls. Those are no intestines. Those are long black hoses, 80 feet long, to be exact, trailing 67 feet behind. On the end is a tassel that looks like a feather duster as we come closer. This is the drogue, a wire basket whose steel fingers open up into a funnel shape, held open by a ribbon of parachute silk on the ends of the fingers. But to the pilot of our two-place F-100F they look no bigger than a badminton bird. He is now faced with the obviously impossible task of impaling this elusive bird on the end of the darning needle, called a probe, that sticks out of the right wing of the plane, so far behind the pilot that he can't see the probe he is trying to thrust into the drogue. This game of jet-propelled badminton played at 20,000 or 25,000 feet over the middle of the icy Atlantic Ocean while dodging thunderbumpers at 230 knots indicated (265 mph) could be fun if the stakes weren't so high. The stakes could be life itself.

This first refueling is just off the Atlantic coast. The others will be near islands, in case of an emergency landing. But the margins are necessarily narrow. The slightest bump sets the hose to swinging violently. Even in fairly smooth air it can break a canopy if it hits the considerable expanse of Plexiglas. That not only means explosive decompression, with the sudden loss of cabin pressure, but possible loss of oxygen mask as well. If nothing worse, it means descending to lower altitude to keep warm and get sufficient oxygen. The lower the altitude the higher the fuel consumption, which means the cripple not only can't keep up with the rest of the flight, but may not be able to make land on the fuel aboard. The only solution is to land at the

nearest island, or turn back to the coast if there is still enough
fuel aboard.

Refueling at night or in severe turbulence is like bobbing
for apples, blindfolded. That hose can whip around viciously,
while at the same time the tanker and the jet are being booted
about brutally by rough air.

The trick is to forget that silly bird bobbing about off your
right wing and "fly" the pod on the tip of the wing which houses
the hose reel. First we slow down to 230 knots (265 mph), the
tankers' maximum speed. Then we get down 15 degrees of flaps.
Lorentzen puts the flap switch down, counts ten, then pulls the
circuit breaker to stop the flaps at 15 degrees.

"Look at him. He's leering at me like a shark with a worm
in his mouth." Lieutenant Lorentzen was talking to himself
again. "See—that trap door for the hose is just like a shark's
mouth sneering at me. I'll show him," Lorentzen muttered.
"Little left rudder trim. Little left aileron. Now drive her right
on in."

And he did. With a nudge of the throttle he socked the probe
home into the bobbing drogue. The trick now was to fly tight
formation within five to ten feet of that wing tip reel pod up
ahead while the reel operator on the tanker poured fuel into
our thirsty tanks.

"Valves open. Fuel coming aboard," Lorentzen reported.

"You've got one thousand pounds," Shirk one-two reported.
"Stand by."

We weren't going anywhere without fuel anyway. There
was a two-minute pause while all 8 planes in our flight got
hooked up and took on 1000 pounds of fuel to be sure everything was operating properly. Then Colin Leader gave the
order to take fuel and the tankers started pouring the JP4, life-
blood of the jets, aboard at 53 pounds per square-inch pressure,
about 200 gallons per minute. As the added weight of the fuel
poured aboard, Lorentzen poured on more and more throttle
until his throttle was wide open. Even before that moment,
however, Colin 1-4, on the right wing of our tanker, had reached

full throttle and was starting to fall back, while the reel operator unreeled more and more hose.

"Toboggan, toboggan," Colin 1-4 called out.

And the big tanker gently poked its nose down and began to
go downhill. This not only increased speed, which gave the
heavy jets more lift, but enabled them to tilt their noses down-
ward to relieve the high angle of attack which verged on a stall.
At this new speed and shallow angle of dive with full throttle
they were able to hang on and take the full load, 8,500 pounds
of fuel, precalculated for this refueling.

"You've got eighty-five hundred pounds. Fuel pressure off,"
Shirk one-two informed his two hungry customers.

Then came another intolerable wait while all the ships got
their full load. Holding tight formation on the wing of the
mother ship was harder now, with a heavier load and no margin
of power to play with. Someone was having trouble; we couldn't
tell who. His tanks weren't filling as they should. Finally the
command came to "top tanks," and we took on another 300
pounds of fuel, 8,800 pounds in all. Now all our tanks were
full. We switched back to Colin Leader's frequency. He called
for us to check in, asked for a fuel check and then gave the
word.

"Colin Alfa flight, AB . . . now."

At this speed and altitude the afterburner hit us hard, snap-
ping our heads back against our head rests. In a matter of seconds our speed had built up from 230 knots to 390—climb speed
and then some.

"AB out . . . now," came the word and we were back to normal power for the climb back to 31,000 feet.

We had finished refueling just about on schedule. We were
allowed no more than five minutes to hook up and no more
than ten minutes total to take on our load of fuel and back off
the tankers. If you couldn't get hooked up in five minutes you
would be too far from land and too low on fuel to return and
land at Myrtle Beach, your alternate. Or if you hit "bingo
fuel" any time before that deadline you had to break off and

run for it. "Bingo fuel" is the minimum pounds necessary to reach your alternate for a safe landing.

Our tankers had a "bingo," too. They had to turn around and get back into position to rendezvous with the second wave of eight F-100s at the same spot where they had picked us up. And they had to save enough fuel to give them the same load they had given us. They couldn't give us more if they wanted to, without shorting the second flight and causing them to abort. The fine art of refueling is as complex as clockwork, with wheels within wheels meshing into other wheels. It looks easy when it works but, like a fine clock, it is a mess when it doesn't.

While concentrating on refueling we had passed out of the high clouds around Columbia, North Carolina, crossed the coast and were now floating along in a dream world high above the Atlantic with only a few clouds far below to lend unreality to an already unreal world. Stargazer, the radar net along the coast, fixed our position at 75 nautical miles off the coast.

This came as something of a shock. Here we were floating along far out over the Atlantic, and nothing had happened. In propeller-driven craft the piston engine goes into "automatic rough" the minute you cross the coast. Nothing sounds just right. Every vibration seems suspicious. The compass begins to swing nervously and every quiver of the hundreds of instruments in the cockpit takes on an ominous meaning. Not until you have crossed the wide waters a couple of times without mishap do you begin to relax and enjoy it. But this was our first crossing and everything was quite skosh, maybe too skosh. We loosened up to tactical formation. Pilots rubbed tired eyes, stretched taut muscles and relaxed after the concentration and strain of the refueling.

Colin Leader was calling Picket Ship *Consult,* 360 miles off the coast, and getting no answer. Maybe they were asleep, like the ocean so far below. And then it happened. We had no sooner settled down for a restful flight to Bermuda than my head caught fire. And then the other end. Same thing happened to Lorentzen, and most of the other pilots.

The flight surgeons had warned us this would happen. Always does with leather helmet liners. Purely a physiological phenomenon called "stagnant hypoxia." Weight of the brain bucket resting on the brain box cuts off circulation, induces a fiery sensation that feels as if your head had caught fire. Only way to put out the fire is to rub the hot spot, restore circulation, then shift your helmet liner around a bit. With foam rubber liners, shaped to fit your head, hot spots are not so much of a problem. Same thing happens on the other end. Your pants catch fire, rather suddenly. Feel as if they would burn right on through. Only way to put out this fire is to fidget and shift about and rub your afterburner. Simple enough if you're riding the mother-in-law seat in the back end of an F-100F.

But how do the sprogs alone in the single cockpit of the F-100Ds manage to massage their heads clockwise and their afterburners counterclockwise while flying formation at 30,000 feet, keeping their ears to the radio and their eyes on the fuel flow?

They don't. They squirm and twist as best they can in their suits of shining armor until their fundaments gradually grow numb.

"The first four hours are the worst. Then your pants are dead," the flight surgeon had explained reassuringly. And that's just about the way it is. The longer you sit, the more numb you get until you may become paralyzed from the waist down. Many a fighter pilot has braved the perils of the wide Atlantic in rain and storm, refueling by night and by day in air as rough as a cob, and come through unscathed, only to collapse in a heap when he slid out of the cockpit at the end of the flight onto the unyielding concrete of the ramp, both legs sound asleep.

"Take it easy. Don't try any broad jumps," Major Prevost had cautioned his squadron. "The leg you break may be your own."

Flying formation is necessary. That's the only way a large number of planes can be handled fast in limited airspace. Each can lend support to the other, in peace and in war—up to a point. Some F-100s are equipped with autopilots, but they seldom work and can't be used in formation anyway.

Actually, the ordeal could be worse. Most airplane seats were designed by the inventors of torture racks. They are flat and hard and as far removed from the human shape as possible, with fiendish angles and edges. The F-100 cockpit is as comfortable as a fighter's can be. The seat size and shape is dictated by the amount of emergency equipment that has to be stowed in the hard plastic case attached to the parachute harness. But the humanitarians who flew the early ocean hops attacked the problem with determination. They came up with the "tractor seat," now installed on top of the pile of necessary junk in the pilot's seat. This foam rubber pad is shaped like the tractor seat farmers have found endurable if not comfortable for so many years.

By taking advantage of every opportunity to flex and twist the gluteal muscles and massage his aching afterburner, the average pilot can endure nine hours in the air without screaming. But to maintain a fair level of comfort, something more is needed. Some desperate pilots have tried edresal "to decrease soreness of the buttocks and increase circulation." This drug contains 2.5 milligrams of amphetomine, 2 grains of aspirin, 2.5 grains of phenacetin per tablet. But it didn't seem to do much good. Others have tried rubbing their rears with salve designed to deaden the pain of hemorrhoids. But this is not recommended by flight surgeons.

Flight surgeons have recommended vibrating cushions or roller mechanisms to restore circulation of the blood in flight. These devices have been installed by the Strategic Air Command for use in B-47s, although the three-man crews of these aircraft can relieve each other and move around to a limited extent to restore circulation. No one can relieve the lone pilot of the F-100D. He can't stand up and stretch, or leave his seat. He wears his airplane like a suit of armor and there is no escaping the cramped confinement of the cockpit.

# 3. Too Late, Too Late, Too Late

"Hours and hours of boredom—broken by moments of sheer terror."

That definition of flying is as old as aviation. That's the way it is, flying the Atlantic in a single-engined jet. You float on and on through hazy skies miles above the puffed-wheat clouds, miles and miles above the vague blue backdrop of the ocean. You feel almost out of this world, more a part of heaven than of earth—disassociation, the medicos call it.

Although remote from the world, you are not alone. Other fish swim through this sea of space. In each silver fish you recognize a buddy. The slender thread of the radio binds you all together. If trouble comes, each has his guardian angel. Your wingman will stick with you, come what may. He will call for help and all the world's navies and all the world's air forces will come to your aid. A whole network of ships, planes and 'copters the length of the Atlantic waits below just to help you.

But when trouble comes, that tiny tin cocoon can suddenly become the loneliest place in the world. It is all the more lonely because you are not alone. Your buddy is there almost within reach. But when the chips are down he can reach into your cockpit to help you only with the thin thread of his voice. You have to face your fate completely alone.

That's the way death came to Lt. Bob Beaver. He was flying number four slot in Coco Red flight that lazy April day in 1959, tooling serenely across the pond with the 615th Tactical Fighter Squadron from England Air Force Base, Alexandria, La. Everything was copacetic. The flight, led by Maj. Bill Pattilo, CO of the 615th, had leaped off from Myrtle Beach at the usual hour before the dawn. The weather was fine as frog's hair. The first refueling just past Bermuda had gone smoothly. The second refueling over the Azores was routine. Everything was rosy and the goose hung high. Major Pattilo was relaxing with the satisfaction of another crossing well done.

The first sign of impending tragedy was nothing much to get excited about. Capt. Ronald B. Montague, flying the number five slot, noticed Coco Red 4 falling back a little in formation. In tactical formation your position isn't flown by the book. You "eyeball" it, pretty much. Rather than jockey the throttle and burn excess fuel, you ease the nose down a little and gradually gain speed at the expense of altitude, then ease up slowly to kill off a little speed as you regain your position. But Bob Beaver didn't catch up. (That isn't his name.)

"Better bring her in a little," his flight leader suggested.

Bob did, but a little raggedly. His flying seemed a bit jerky. Bob was usually smooth, steady as a rock. The order was to pass the word but quick if any little thing went wrong in flight.

But Coco Leader finally asked, "Coco Red 4, how you doing?"

"Having trouble with my heat," Lieutenant Beaver answered.

"You got runaway heat, number four?"

"Cabin heat control seems to be out," Beaver replied.

The squadron maintenance officer, winging along in the same flight, cut in to call out the procedures for controlling runaway heat.

"I've tried everything," Beaver replied.

"Can you open your ram air to cool off the cockpit?" the maintenance officer asked.

"Negative," Beaver answered. "But I'm OK."

"Want to turn back to Lajes?" Coco Leader asked.

"Negative," Beaver came back emphatically. "I'll make it."

It was a little late to be turning back. Beaver seemed to have things under control. He was flying good formation now. He had plenty of fuel for the short hop to Nouasseur Air Base at Casablanca, Morocco. He had enough to drop down to lower altitude if necessary to cool off. The flight bored on through clear, bright skies. Beaver complained of low oxygen level, but the routine squadron oxygen check showed he had about the same as the rest of the pilots. The needle indicating the liters of liquid oxygen in the pilot's tank wobbles almost to zero at every breath, then returns to the true indication, which can be deceiving.

Then his flying became a little more erratic. He started to drop back and down. Major Pattilo ordered Captain Montague, Coco Red 5, to stick with Beaver while the rest of the flight pressed on. They were only about 200 miles, a scant 25 minutes, from Nouasseur and safety. Then tragedy began to close in on the two tiny splinters of silver in a sky that began to grow black with thunderclouds that seemed to tower up to the roof of the sky.

Montague, a senior pilot with more than 2000 hours in jets, was deputy flight leader, a veteran of fifty-one jet fighter missions in Korea, a strong man with a compelling personality, a persuasive manner, and a tongue like a whip. He could save Beaver if anyone could. And it gradually became evident that Beaver's life hung on the thin thread of the radio that linked him with his buddy.

At first Beaver said he felt OK as he settled down to fly on Montague's wing. But he kept descending, slowly, erratically.

"How you feeling, Bob?" Montague asked.

"Hot . . . a little woozy. I'm OK."

"Pull the ventilator hose out of your poopy suit, Bob. That'll cool you off a little."

"Roger. I pulled the hose."

More minutes passed as the 100s sped on toward the African coast at nine miles per minute. They were down to about 10,-000 feet now, but with plenty of fuel to make Nouasseur even at this altitude.

The controller in the GCI (Ground Controlled Intercept) station at Nouasseur had them on his radar scope, two blips that showed as one. Captain Montague made radio contact and asked the operator to guide them. Montague was too busy to navigate.

As the two bogeys came within the 60-mile range of his scope, the Nouasseur controller began to record on tape Montague's efforts to talk his buddy in to safety. The record has since been used as a dramatic lesson in flying safety lectures throughout the Tactical Air Command.

At first Beaver flew on Montague's wing while Montague kept an eye on him.

"He almost clobbered me and I had to change and fly on his wing," Montague recalls. "He became erratic and turned sharply into me. I had to duck and skid to avoid a collision. Then I dropped back and flew on his wing so all he would have to do was fly the airplane.

"He kept dropping down lower and lower. He would drop the gear and I would have to persuade him to get it up again. He popped the speed boards and I almost overran him before I could talk him into getting them up again.

"We were still way out there, maybe a hundred miles or more at sea, but Bob kept dropping down and down until we were no more than five hundred feet off the water. Once I think we were only fifty feet above the waves before I could get him to pull up again. Then we climbed back up to about fifteen hundred feet. He would do what I told him and kept saying he could make it. It was hard to tell what condition he was really in. I tried to get him to take his dinghy stabber knife and cut open his poopy suit to cool off.

"We were down where the air was cool. But that cabin pressure air comes off the sixteenth stage of the compressor in the engine at about four hundred degrees temperature. There is a cooler that compresses the air, then cools it down by expansion to any temperature you want it. When the heat 'runs away' it may go to any temperature up to around one hundred and sixty degrees, sometimes as high as four hundred degrees.

"Bob knew this all too well. He had burned the skin off his leg in a similar situation over the States only a month or so before. In fact, the leg was just now healed up so he could fly. In that first case he had insisted on staying with the formation and finishing the mission when his heat ran away. We didn't know what shape he was in until we saw the burn when he took off his flying suit."

"I finally got Bob back up to about five thousand feet. It looked like we had it made," Montague recalls. Then Montague called Nouasseur GCI controller:

"Nouasseur, what's your weather?" Montague asked. "Looks like a line of thunderbumpers up ahead."

"Roger, I have a line of thunderstorms, nearly solid," the GCI operator answered. "Heading one zero five. That will vector you between two thunderstorms."

"Roger. . . . You feel better now, Bob? . . . Okay, let's go. Stay right with me, right straight to Nouasseur. . . . GCI, this is a May Day."

"Roger, understand. Emergency equipment standing by. Squawk May Day."

Montague switched his identification set to transmit the distress signal which blazed forth on the radar scope of the GCI site.

"Roger, squawking May Day. . . . Bob, get up here with me."

"Forty-five miles out, heading one zero five, Coco Red."

"Roger, Bob, we're doing good. Just forty-five miles, Bob. Now get in here with me. You're looking good. Get in here with me. Get in here and follow me, now, boy. . . . Can you hear me? We're almost there. I say we're down to fifteen hundred feet. You got to stay with me, boy, got to stay with me. Pull it up, Bob. Don't get so rough, Bob, don't get so rough."

"Heading one zero three, forty miles," GCI cut in.

"Pull it up, Bob. Pull it up, boy . . . you're doing fine now. Come up now. Get your speed brakes up. Come up now with those speed brakes. Pull it up on my left. Only thirty-nine miles. Speed brakes up, Bob. Brakes up." Montague's voice rose to a pleading pitch.

"That a boy." The relief in his voice was like a sigh as the distressed pilot finally pulled in the speed brakes which had slowed his plane down near the stalling point and would cost him precious fuel.

"Doing fine, by golly."

"Heading one zero five, only thirty-seven miles to go," from GCI.

"Heading looks good. Only thirty-seven miles to go . . . VFR . . . Hurry up, Bob. We've got thirty-seven to go, boy. Pull her up . . . Good job. Doing a good job. Attaboy. Pull her on up. Take it left two degrees to one zero three. Pull her up easy. Hold on to what you got, Bob. Almost there. Only thirty-four miles now. Almost there, boy."

"Coco Red, you're passing the coast now . . ."

"Negative. We're not over the coast yet. I can see it, but not yet. What's the latest heading you've got? I've got a man that's in real trouble."

"Steer zero nine five now, twenty-eight miles, one thousand foot scattered, five thousand overcast . . ."

"Almost there, Bob. I'll get on your wing now. Hold what you got. Bob, watch me." Montague's voice was imploring again as he tried to lead the sick pilot in over land.

"Coco Red, the runway will be seventeen."

"Roger, seventeen. . . . Back off on the power a little, Bob. Back off a little. Back off on it . . . pull it up. Pull it up. *Easy!*"

Montague shouted a startled warning as Beaver erratically jerked his stick back, nearly hitting Montague's plane.

"Pull up. *Pull up, Bob.*"

Montague's voice now cracked like a whip, interspersing sharp, imperious orders with his wheedling, cajoling, imploring efforts to keep his buddy in the air.

"Easy does it, boy. Pull up. Pull it up, Bob, just a little bit. Here I am. Look out the right and you can see me now."

"Twenty-four miles to go, dead ahead, zero nine five."

"Roger, GCI . . . Ease it down here with me, Bob. Ease it down a little. Around left just a little bit. That's OK. Now listen to me. Listen to me, Bob boy. Just hang on. You got it made . . . Come on down here with me, buddy. Come on down here . . . Do you feel better now, Bob?"

A muffled "Negative."

"What?"

"*Negative, negative,*" Beaver answered harshly, but strongly.

"Fifteen miles," GCI chanted.

By now the parboiled pilot was down to about 1000 feet. But it was beginning to look as if he might not make it. He was wobbling erratically, but then would steady down and fly smoothly. He had blown his canopy off as he came across the coast, which would cool and tend to revive him. But he was responding more slowly to commands. Maybe he wasn't getting the word.

Montague had to decide whether he should bail Bob out or not. Beaver couldn't bail out at sea. Now he might make the field, or could he?

"Bob, you've got your gear down. Get it up. Pull up, *pull up . . . pull up, pull it up! Get that gear up!*"

Montague was shouting with all the urgency he could muster. Beaver was holding a steady course now, but descending slowly, porpoising slightly as he overcontrolled on the elevators.

"What's our heading Operator?"

"One zero five."

"Come around left, Bob. *Come around to the left!*" There was desperation in Montague's voice now.

"Pull around to the left. Pull her up, Bob. Pull up and bail out. Pull up. Listen, pull her up and bail out. Pull up and out of that thing, Bob—"

"Only twelve miles to go," GCI cut in, like a Greek chorus offstage.

"How many? Twelve? . . . Pull up. Get that gear up, Bob, pull up and go around in that thing. Bob, *pull up.* Pull up and bail out of that thing!"

Montague's voice broke hoarsely as he put all the power he had over Beaver into that one last despairing command.

But Beaver didn't pull up. He left his gear down. He continued his slow descent, power on, as if determined to land his awkward aircraft on the desert, airport or no airport. He had complained earlier he couldn't see the runway. Every F-100 pilot in his right mind knows you can't crash-land a Dog and walk away from it, gear up or gear down.

The tortured pilot set in a passable landing on the hard floor of the desert, but the F-100 bounded into the air, struck a great clump of gnarled cactus and flew apart.

"Too late . . . too late . . . too late," Montague murmured into his hot mike, like a requiem. Came a long moment of silence, then:

"Mark your pigeon one hundred ten degrees ten miles," the crisp voice of the controller cut in.

"Roger, that's where he is," Montague said hoarsely.

It was two and a half hours before crash crews from the base could make their way to the spot where Beaver had crashed. His body was still hot inside the heavy rubber anti-exposure suit. The investigating board found dehydration was the cause of Beaver's death. In fact, doctors on the spot doubted if he could have survived had he succeeded in landing or bailing out. Once the water content of the body is reduced below a certain level, the tissue of the brain is affected.

The pilot may experience painful headaches, blurred or double vision, general weakness and loss of power to think and act.

Many a TAC pilot pointed the finger at the poopy suit Beaver wore as contributing to his death. The insulated suit is dehydrating in itself and prevents normal cooling by evaporation when the cockpit heat runs away, some pilots and flight surgeons say.

The poopy suit has saved the lives of many a pilot who had to bail out over water, however, others declare in its defense.

# 4. Miracle of Blackfoot Charlie

Poopy suits in the Tactical Air Command are like beards in the Antarctic. You are either for them or against them. You either believe they are indispensable, or impossible. Either you swear by them, or at them.

The poopy suit is a suit of rubber armor that weighs about 25 pounds with all accouterments and it costs about $1000. It's listed in supply catalogues as the MD-1 Anti-Exposure suit. Pilots universally call it a poopy suit, probably because by the time you succeed in putting it on you are too pooped to care whether you survive or not.

TAC pilots flying over water in tactical jets have in the past been required to wear the anti-exposure suit at all times. More recently the decision to wear or not to wear the suit has been left to the pilot or the squadron commander. The general rule has been to wear the suit when flying over water colder than 59 degrees. The theory has been that the suit is not needed in water warmer than 59 degrees.

Houdini himself couldn't get out of a poopy suit, much less get into one, without maid service. You don't just step into a poopy suit as you would into a suit of coveralls, although there is a superficial resemblance. There is a rigid ritual that begins with removal of everything down to your dog tags.

Then you don long winter underwear, preferably waffle-weave cottons, next your flying suit, then winter socks and high leather flying boots laced eight inches up the leg. They don't snap off like oxfords if you have to bail out and are good for walking out.

Now you lace on the antigravity suit, or G-suit, tightly fitted to your legs and abdomen with bladders which are automatically inflated in turns and pullouts to apply pressure, prevent blood from rushing to the legs and abdomen, forcing it to the brain to prevent blackouts.

Next you slip into a rubber vest that covers your chest and back. Only this one is full of pinholes and worth about $200. This is your aid conditioner. Air under pressure from the aircraft heating-ventilating system is pumped into this vest through a hose at your navel. As it squirts out through the holes it provides cooling air. A one-way valve in the poopy suit lets the air out but won't let water in. Without this forced ventilation the suit is a perfect sweat box, leaving the body no means of cooling itself by evaporation. You now don a second heavy suit for insulation.

Now you are ready for the poopy suit. It looks like an old-style deep-sea diver's suit. You lay it out on the floor, find the right opening and force your combat boots into the heavy rubber boots cemented to the suit itself. You can log ten minutes P.T. after this workout.

Now you stand up, if you are still able, and thrust your wrists through sleeves so tight they would choke a snake. You can't make it if you forgot to remove your wrist watch.

Next you crawl into a long rubber snood like the tunnel entrance to a mountain tent, thrust your head through a hole made for a rabbit, and pull the hole in after you. If you found the right hole and didn't get claustrophobia en route you are now draped in what feels like a hangar for a blimp.

That long rubber tunnel you crawled through is hanging

down your front like the umbilical cord of an elephant. Your squire of the bedchamber seizes it manfully and ties it into a huge knot, then tucks it into the pouch on the front of the suit and zips up the flap.

He pulls the hose from your ventilating vest and from your antigravity suit through a plastic navel in your rubber armor and you are clad in full armor, like Don Quixote. But don't try tilting at windmills. You can walk, ponderously, but not run. Every movement starts the sweat running. The watertight neckband is so tight it chokes you. Your squire has to insert a rigid plastic ring in the collar to hold the neck open so you can breathe. He inserts similar plastic retainers at your wrists to keep the wristbands from cutting off circulation to your hands.

Now you can try on the waterproof hood which fits over your head and down around your shoulders, and the waterproof mittens, both carried in pockets on the legs of the MD-1, together with a survival knife, and any other survival items you choose to carry.

Now you don the new "Mae West," life preservers which are held under your arms in pockets the size of big bars of soap by a strap harness. Your parachute goes on over these life preservers. You are ready to struggle up the ladder to the cockpit. It will be quite a struggle. You have not only gained 25 pounds of weight, or more, but you feel like a feather bed. The cockpit of an F100 was tailor-made for the "perfect 38." You have to slip into it with the aid of a shoehorn at best. Put on 25 pounds of weight and strapping on the airplane is liking forcing a size eight foot into a size six shoe. It can be done, but the bulging balloon hampers your every movement.

"This suit certainly is not the answer," to quote a flight surgeon who used it in a double crossing of the Atlantic in winter. "It is too heavy, cumbersome, and presents numerous difficulties in the cockpit. It might even be considered a flying safety hazard, as its bulk can contribute to mishaps, such as accidentally striking the emergency speed brake handle, as has happened on several occasions.

"It should be investigated. The Navy has developed a suit weighing only seven pounds that may be worn over a partial pressure suit and still permit the pilot to swim, it is so flexible."

The poopy suit is supplied with zippers in all the right places for personal sanitation. But to operate one of these zippers, and then untangle the foot-long folding flaps necessary to answer calls of nature is a major feat meriting the award of the DSC— Distinguished Sanitation Cross, or OPP—Order of the Purple Plumbing.

But nothing you could say would lessen 1st Lt. Robert Picht's faith in the poopy suit.

"It saved my life," he will tell you earnestly.

Lieutenant Picht is a sharp-eyed, alert, athletic man who could pass for the ideal fighter type. He had 1,800 hours in his log-book, about 550 of it in F-100 fighters, on March 15, 1959, when he started out across the implacable Atlantic with the 309th Tactical Fighter Squadron of the 31st Wing, George Air Force Base, California.

"Never shake hands with a flight surgeon. That's what did it," Picht declares with a grin. "Twice I shook hands with Doc Landrey, our flying flight surgeon, at Myrtle Beach just before taking off across the drink. Twice I had to abort. The third time I refused to shake hands, and look what happened.

"I was flying number two on the wing of Colonel Robert W. Stephens, CO of the 31st Wing, in Blackfoot Charlie flight. We were an hour and thirteen minutes out . . . Thirteen may be unlucky after all, come to think. . . .

"Everything was routine. We were cruising at thirty-one thousand, just a hundred and ten miles west of Bermuda. The night was black as the pit. The F-100 Dog was running smooth as syrup. I had just emptied my wing tanks and checked the instruments, when bingo, that old Dog died.

"It got awful quiet up there. The silence was deafening. My lights went out right away. I found my flashlight and checked the instruments again. RPMs were zero, fuel flow zero. Everything said—'frozen engine.'

"I tried an air start, but there's nothing you can do with a frozen engine. I trimmed her up, jettisoned my wing tanks and went into a glide at two hundred and twenty knots and began cleaning house. When my lights went out the guys lost sight of me. The flight had to press on, but Captain Jack Bryant, flying second lead in number five slot, closed in to try and fly cover for me. He couldn't see me, so he stayed a couple thousand feet above me and throttled back into a glide to match my airspeed. I would read off my altitude as I went down so he could stay above me and not run into me.

"I turned off my SIF identification radio and Captain Bryant took over the radio calls. He put out a May Day call and squawked May Day to give the boys at Bermuda a chance to spot me as I went down.

"We went through several layers of cloud, but it was so dark you couldn't really see the stuff. Besides I was busy. I had just thirteen minutes to clean up the cockpit ready for bailout. In that time I figured I would glide about sixty miles closer to Bermuda, which was all to the good.

"I kept my mind on the manual and all the training we had had over the years. I took everything loose in the cockpit and shoved it behind my head to give me plenty of room when I fired the ejection seat. There have been plenty of cases where the guys couldn't get at their ejection handles because of stuff stuck alongside the seat, or junk hit them in the face when they blasted-off the canopy.

"Then I took everything out of my pockets I didn't need and put my .38 pistol in my pocket. I figured I might want it for signaling. Our squadron had a rule that we carry a couple of small hand flares in the pocket of our flight suits just to supplement the flares in the seat pack, and I made sure I had them in the pocket of my poopy suit. That saved my life.

"You often wonder what you would really do if you had to bail out. These things always happen to the other guy. You wonder if you'll freeze and forget everything you know.

"But when the time came I punched out without any more

hesitation than diving off a high board, less maybe. When the altimeter hit five thousand feet by the light of my flashlight, I put away the light, socked my heels back in the stirrups, pressed my buns against the back of the seat, tucked in my chin and my elbows and pulled up sharply on both canopy release handles at once, just like I had done a dozen times before in the trainer at the base.

"Then I reached down for the ejection handle and pulled it. I don't remember anything more until the parachute canopy opened. I could just barely sense it dimly outlined against the clouds above. Evidently the seat had fired out like it was supposed to. The seat belt had blasted loose a second later, pulling the rip cord to my parachute. Since I was below fifteen thousand feet, the chute had opened a second later about the time my forward speed slowed down. I got a good jolt when it opened. But if it hurt it felt so good I didn't notice it. I still had plenty to do as I floated on down, although it was so dark I didn't feel like I was falling.

"I unfastened my helmet and got rid of that right away. I got busy pulling the plastic retainers out of my poopy suit at the wrists and neck. I wanted that mother to be watertight when I hit the drink. I reached down for the strap that fastens the one-man rubber dinghy to the parachute harness. The strap was there all right. I started hauling it up, but it felt awful light. The dinghy was supposed to be hanging down there somewhere in the dark thirty feet below me.

"But all I could find was three feet of cord. The seat pack that held the dinghy was ripped open all right, but the dinghy was gone. . . . Must have ripped out of the pack, inflated and torn loose during bailout.

"Talk about bailing out of the fire into the frying pan! Looked like I didn't have much chance. Then I quit thinking and went back to work. I had no idea how far I had fallen and I still had to inflate my water wings.

"I gave the left one a sharp pull and the bladder inflated and slapped me in the face. I shoved it under my arm out of the way.

"It was about this time I saw the plane hit the water and explode with a roar and a flash. That's the first I knew I was down under the last of the clouds.

"Then I opened the canopy release cover on the left shoulder of the parachute, ready to dump the air from the canopy the minute it hit the water, so it wouldn't smother me in about one hundred yards of nylon. I unfastened the chest strap on my parachute, sat way back in the straps and got ready to slip out. I also remembered to remove the personal survival kit from my parachute strap and fasten it to my life preserver harness. I was thankful for that, too.

"I was ready for the water. I no sooner had the thought than I hit. I don't know what I expected, but it was like hitting a trampoline. I seemed to go in only about two feet and then I bounced way out of the water again and came down with a plop, like a balloon. The suit was full of air and so buoyant I was floating around on my back, waving my feet in the air. I lay back and inflated the other water wing, then tied them in front. This gave me more buoyance around the head and my feet stayed down where they belonged.

"Then I began looking around for lights or flares. I couldn't hear Bryant over head anywhere and figured he'd had to go on in to Kindley [Air Force base, Bermuda]. It was still dark as pitch. I figured about an hour to daylight yet.

"I was pretty comfortable for the first half hour. I was dry and warm and floating high. I guess I knew what a spot I was in, but I felt real lucky that I had the poopy suit on. I wouldn't have lasted long without it. I know that now.

"There was nothing to do now but wait. No use firing any flares until they had time to get some search planes in the air. Waiting wasn't easy. But I never lost hope.

"Then I began to feel wet around the waist. I checked the valves to the G-suit and the ventilator garment there and they were as tight as I could get them. But the water kept seeping in. I kept getting wetter and wetter. First my waist and then my legs. Then I could feel the water squishing around in my boots. They were filling up, slowly.

"It was like the Chinese water torture you read about. The water kept rising higher and higher in my poopy suit and I kept sinking deeper and deeper into the salty brine.

"If it hadn't been for the water wings, I would have sunk right away. The cells were holding me up now. But all the time I was sinking deeper and deeper into the water.

"The temperature of the water was sixty-one degrees, the weatherman had told us, maybe a little warmer than that, close to Bermuda. That was supposed to be warm enough for survival without an anti-exposure suit. But I was getting chillier and chillier. Pretty soon I was so cold I thought I couldn't stand it. The waves were slapping me in the face by now. I was gradually being pulled under by the weight of water in my suit. It was up to my lower chest by now. But the cold even took my mind off this Chinese torture.

"I was shivering all over now, like you do when you're caught out in the rain and soaking wet. Just miserable. Then I began to jerk and shake like a man with an epileptic fit. I thrashed around uncontrollably until pretty soon I was puffing and panting. That seemed to warm me up and I felt better for a while.

"Doctors tell me this is the same kind of uncontrollable 'secondary shivering' that has saved men's lives in the cold country when they were caught out without enough clothes on. Nature won't let you freeze. She resorts to such violent exercise you warm up in spite of yourself.

"I thought I had bought the farm this time. My hands were shaking so I couldn't even adjust my collar or wipe the water out of my eyes. And all the time I was sinking deeper and deeper. It was getting harder and harder to hold my head up. I remember cussing whoever had 'modified' the life preservers. They used to come together and form a regular collar under your arms and in front of your face so if you got groggy or became unconscious, the life preservers would hold your face out of the water. That is a principle you find in a lot of Navy and Coast Guard life jackets, too.

"But no, someone had decided this was annoying. So they had changed the design and cut a Vee out of the water wings so your head could fall down into the Vee and allow you to drown in comfort when you got too tired to hold your chin up above the water.

"And that's the spot I was in. The water was up to my chin now. Ever try to hold your head back and your chin up for an hour while shivering and bouncing around in the waves? You can't last long.

"There was one ray of hope by now. It was getting light. Off on the horizon I thought I could see a red light moving back and forth. My eyes were so blurred and battered by the salt water that I wasn't sure for quite a while. Then I was sure.

"I put my thumb through the ring and tried to pull off the top of the canister to fire one of the two flares I had in my pocket. But it was wet and the ring tore out. I tried the other end, which contained smoke, but it wouldn't work either. My hands were so numb I couldn't hold on to the canister and I lost it.

"I did manage to get out my .38 pistol and fire a couple of shots. I thought there would be enough flash from the shot to be visible, but that didn't work either.

"I knew I was in a spot now. I knew how hard it would be to see anything so small as my pumpkin head floating down there among the waves. I had tried to keep close to my parachute canopy all through the darkness. I knew it would be visible, although drifting under the water a couple of feet.

"I kept my eyes glued to that red light. Now I was sure it was a plane, weaving back and forth, flying a search pattern low above the water. I figured this was my last chance. And that was a slim one. I had to wait until he got close enough to see me, but not too close, because the visibility from most of these airplanes is mighty limited, especially straight down.

"I had my last flare in my hand. I had my thumb stuck through the loop and I figured I might as well break off my thumb in a last-ditch effort to fire that flare. Nothing would matter if I didn't manage to fire it off.

"I was straining now to keep my chin up and treading water part of the time. I kept my eye on the flashing red light and when I figured he was about a thousand feet away I gave a mighty jerk. The top came off and fired the flare, a bright, blinding red fountain of light. I held is up as high as I could, pointed at that plane.

"I never knew until long afterward by what a slender thread my life hung at that moment. That red light was the anticollision light on a MATS C-121 Constellation transport that had been diverted in flight to join the search. The copilot just happened to be looking out his window at right angles as they made their sweep almost over me. He thought he saw a red light flare up, then disappear under the wing as the plane sped on over me at about one hundred and eighty knots. He wasn't sure, but he took the controls and banked around where he could keep the spot in sight, and sure enough he picked up my flare and kept it in sight until it burned out. By that time he had me spotted.

"All I knew was that fuzzy light changed course and began to circle, even after my flare died down. They were down low and I could hear their engines. The sun came up fast from then on and the C-121 was soon joined by a couple of Air Rescue SA-16 flying boats. They kept circling me, but they weren't doing anything. Here I was slowly sinking into the salt water. The waves were slopping over my head now. I was treading water like mad and I think I was hollering at those mothers to do something. Why didn't they land and pick me up? Couldn't they see I had just about had it? I had dumped out some yellow sea-dye marker. That was the last thing I had on me and that was all the poop I had left in me.

"Then my answer came drifting over my head like a miracle out of Heaven. I looked up a little and right in front of my face was a loop, a sort of sling. It was dangling from a helicopter.

It had sneaked up from behind me, from downwind, and I never even heard it.

"I hollered some silly thing, asking if they were going my way and stuck out my thumb in the universal sign of the hitchhiker. All the time I was grabbing that loop with one hand and tucking it under my arms.

"Then they gave a yank and lifted me out of the water. My poopy suit was swelled up like a pumpkin with all that water and they had to exceed their manifold pressure to yank me out. I couldn't crawl into the 'copter door, but managed to roll halfway in. Then I sat there on the edge of the doorway and cut open my suit to let the water drain out before they could pull me inside. Funny thing, my flight suit was soaked almost to the neck. But my cigarettes in my sleeve pocket were dry as toast.

"They wrapped me up and poured on the heat. I felt better right away. But my body temperature was still down four degrees when they finally got me into the hospital.

"Boy, was I ever glad to see that 'copter. They acted awful glad to see me, too, but also astonished. They said they had lots of business out here, but hardly ever got anyone out alive and kicking.

" 'Why not?' I asked.

" 'Sharks,' they said. 'We were waiting for the last pilot that bailed out here. Saw him go down just twelve miles off the end of the runway and picked up his parachute within two or three minutes. But no sign of him. Just sharks, swimming around.'

"That thought never entered my mind, or it probably would have scared me to death, on top of everything else.

"I guess you would have to call this a five-way miracle. Without the poopy suit I would have been a goner. Without the flares I didn't have a chance. If that copilot hadn't been looking where he did at the exact second he did I would never have been found. If the sharks had found me I wouldn't be here. And if that 'copter had been five minutes late I wouldn't have been hitchhiking.

"Me, I got out without a scratch, unscathed. A hot shower and a shot of old Mgug and I began to warm up. They put me to bed, but I was out chasing the nurses around, talking my head off. Couldn't sleep for twelve hours. Full of adrenalin, the Doc said. Just couldn't simmer down. Sleeping pills did no good. It was twelve hours before I finally fell asleep. Then they couldn't wake me up.

"Give up when the waves started slapping my face? The thought never occurred to me. I was too busy thinking of ways to survive. I could have passed out easy enough during those hours just before dawn. Actually I was only in the water ninety-two minutes. It just *seemed* like hours. But I was full of the will to survive. I guess it's all in the mind. No, I'm not a Christian Scientist. Catholic. But I never counted any beads. Never thought of it. I was too busy fighting to stay alive.

"Two things I learned. I wear that poopy suit when I go over water. And I'm never without a couple of flares in the pocket of my G-suit, any time."

# 5. Four-Engine Ocean

It would be hard to contrive a more complex and hazardous operation than these Fox-Able movements. To permit 18 one-man jets to fly the 5000-mile route, 4000 miles of it over water, requires the split-second co-ordination of 18 other aircraft and three ocean vessels. Success depends not only upon perfect timing and skill on the part of every air crew, but upon the right weather at half a dozen bases over a third of the globe.

Flights of four tankers must be able to take off from three different bases along the route on schedule, find enough air space clear of clouds at the right time and place for two successive refuelings, and still have time, fuel and weather to permit return to their bases. Three long-range planes must be able to take off from three different bases en route and take up positions along the route to serve as "Duckbutts," on which the fighters can home by radio and rely for navigation and other emergency assistance. Before the fighters take off, pathfinder planes, usually WB-66 twin-jet Weather Reconnaissance Aircraft, must be able to fly to the refueling areas and make sure the weather will be good enough to permit refueling when the fighters arrive. The weather must remain good enough to permit both Duckbutts and weather planes to return to land at their own or alternate bases.

In eight years of such ocean-hopping, more than 6000 single-seated jet fighter and fighter-bomber planes have crossed the Atlantic or Pacific, refueling in flight. This does not include crossings by the Strategic Air Command or TAC multi-jet bombers with more than one pilot. The safety record has been incredibly good. Exact figures have not been compiled, but only about a dozen pilots have been reported lost over water in the past ten years. The worst losses have occurred on takeoff at night. A flight of three taking off in formation disappeared without trace at Myrtle Beach, S. C., in July, 1959. An F-104 disappeared without trace after taking off at night from Bermuda under a low overcast in 1960. The losses on the actual ocean crossing are less than .002 per cent. Statistically, you are safer crossing the ocean alone in a jet, refueling in flight, than you are crossing the street in Hometown, U.S.A., or driving your convertible down the freeway.

These statistics are comforting as you swim serenely high above the cobalt blue of the Atlantic in your aluminum and titanium shark, keeping one eye on Colin Leader and the other on the fuel gauges, oil temperature, hydraulic pressure and clock. But, human nature being what it is, it is the exceptions and not the general rule that fill your thoughts.

When Colin Alfa 1-4 reports that he smells fumes in his cockpit, stomach muscles tighten in seven other cockpits of Colin Alfa flight. They're remembering Lt. Bob Beaver.

"Smells like the cooling turbine," Lieutenant Terbet reports.

"Feel any vibration?" Colin Leader asks.

"I can hear her whine right behind my head," 1-4 replies.

"Keep me posted," Colin Leader answers.

There is nothing anyone can do about it. The cooler turbine is mounted in a compartment just behind the pilot. If it runs out of oil, burns up, throws its blades, or gets hot and freezes, he'll know it soon enough. His heat will run away and he'll be in deep trouble.

It is 0613 hours. Major Prevost has already contacted the tankers. They are 40 miles north of course. Thunderstorms have moved into the scheduled refueling area. We will have to do some ducking and dodging of towering cumulus. They will be at flight level 250 (25,000 feet) to get above the worst of the clouds.

It is 0620. We are scuttling through cloud canyons between towering cloud castles that seem to pierce the sky. Suddenly our speed seems to pick up as we dart past massive pillars of alabaster.

"Colin Alfa. This is Shirk two-zero. We have you at nine miles, heading one hundred."

Sure enough, there were the tankers, looking like dreadnoughts plowing through the valleys of the clouds with anchor chains dangling from wing tips and tails.

The hookup was quickly accomplished and we waited for the signal to take on fuel. With a full load at this altitude we couldn't stay on even by tobogganing. Looked like we might have to use afterburner to catch up and make the hookup, which isn't easy, because you have an excess of power. But we finally made it and topped off our tanks. Someone else was having trouble, however. We hung on past the scheduled bingo time. Finally Colin Leader came on the air and ordered the flight to break off and "press on."

It was 0643. The refueling had taken 18 minutes. Major Prevost called for a fuel check; then, "Let's get out of here," he ordered and we went into afterburner to pick up climbing speed. We were just about on time, but 40 miles off course. The tankers gave us a corrected heading to Ocean Station Echo, our next check point, a surface rescue vessel, and we settled back to relax, stretch cramped legs and rub our hot spots. Those who could, took off helmets to rub burning heads. We broke out the bite-sized lunches and had the embalmed beef, hard-boiled eggs and small cans of sweetened juice. This was the critical leg of the flight. We had passed Bermuda somewhere under those towering cumulus clouds before No. 2 AAR, the second refueling. It was about 1,800 nautical miles to Lajes air base in the Azores. We were passing the PSR for Bermuda—the point of safe return. There was a long PNR—point of no return—here. If we ran into trouble there was nowhere to go but down. We couldn't return to Bermuda or go on to the Azores. Weariness and lethargy were beginning to set in now.

The cumulus clouds that threatened us like clenched fists had dwindled away. We were wafting along now between the blue bowl of the sky and the equally blue bowl of the mid-Atlantic, with no more than a few tufts of lamb's wool far, far below to lend unreality to the scene. Even the ocean seemed to drowse in the afternoon sun, for the day got later by an hour every hour as we swam against the sun, turning the clock ahead an hour every 15 degrees of longitude. So they hadn't got us up in the middle of the night just for "discipline." We really did have to take off at 2:30 A.M. in order to land in Spain during the last hours of the waning day. Going back we would overtake the sun, turn back the clock and regain all those lost hours. Colin Alfa 1-6 was still having turbine trouble, but his heat remained under control. All was well, so far.

Far up ahead clouds covered the ocean. That would be the Azores, mother of storms. Her volcanic peaks were always cloud-capped. Lajes was the bane of tanker and fighter pilot alike. She spawned low ceilings, rain and cross winds, winter and summer. Now a single black cloud, like a pyramid, took shape below. That was no cloud but the tip of volcanic Ilha da Pico itself. We were diving down to meet the tankers for our third and last refueling.

The air was calm, the tanker steady, but Lieutenant Lorentzen was having his troubles trying to hook up. He was cool. He was confident. He was missing only by an inch or two. But he was having his troubles. The fine art of refueling is like the game of golf—some days you're in top form; other days you can't hit par. On the fourth try Lorentzen goosed the throttle and made a determined stab. He caught the edge of the drogue, but slipped off. Our momentum carried us another ten feet. The heavy hose, stiff with fuel under pressure, wrapped around the probe and sneaked up over the top of the wing. An inexperienced pilot could have torn off a hose, or a probe, or both. Lorentzen slowly eased off his throttle. The hose caught on the eyebrow flap on the leading edge of the wing that popped in and out with every change of speed and altitude at this critical angle of attack, then reluctantly let go and uncoiled itself from the probe.

We made it on the next attempt, just in time. Everyone was hooked up now and ready to take fuel. But others were having trouble, too. Colin Alfa 1-7 could only take on 11,700 pounds of fuel, 2000 short of his full load. His tanks weren't feeding as they should. Colin Leader finally ordered him to back off the tanker and press on. This was the short leg of the flight. We didn't need a full load of fuel. As he backed off, the source of the trouble could be seen hanging from his probe. A two-foot length of parachute silk from the tanker's drogue was stuck in the valve at the end of the probe, holding the valve open. He was losing a little fuel. His oil pressure was also dropping and the oil supply to the bearings of the main rotor, which spun 9000 revolutions per minute, was getting low. This could be non-habit-forming. Loss of oil meant overheated bearings and a frozen motor. Shades of Lt. Robert Picht crossed the minds of his buddies.

Later Colin 1-7, Lt. Pete Bowles, found he had lost all hydraulic pressure to his utility system. That meant only emergency brakes for landing, no hydraulic steering of the nosewheel. The 307th squadron had lost an airplane that way five months before. With no nosewheel steering, the pilot had lost control in a cross wind, left the runway, hit a raised manhole and broken his bird into small pieces. He wasn't hurt.

The end of the long traverse was in sight now. That odd-shaped shadow on the water was the coast of Portugal. It was 1100, not a cloud in the sky, and the castles of Spain could be seen close beyond. Most movements had been required to detour Portugal, but we were cleared to cross the dry hills of this peaceful land and let down direct to Moron Air Base near Seville,

Spain. Major Prevost, whose number one hydraulic system for actuating the flight controls had failed, took the two other crippled birds and high-tailed it direct for Moron. Lieutenant Terbet's cooler turbine was whining like a banshee now, but held together until he hit the runway. Then it went to pieces, leaving a trail of broken bits. Bowles set his bird down gently, popped his drag chute successfully and rolled to the end of the runway under control. There he shut down the engine and was towed to the line.

The remainder of the flight, their flagging spirits revived by the sight of land, whipped into a tight echelon formation and gave Portugal a show as they went by. As they approached Moron they pulled into a tight five-ship diamond and skimmed low over the alabaster castles and whitewashed cities that stood up above the hills like fortresses. Buzzing low over the broad Andalusian plain they clung to their formation like burs despite rough air boiling up from the hot fields below, using speed brakes and afterburners to burn up excess fuel. By 1200 noon, Central Standard Time, the last shark-tailed Supersabre was parked on the concrete ramp of the Spanish base. It was 1900 (7 P.M.) Franco time and the sun was fast setting in the copper sky.

As the whine of the jet engines died out, the traditional beer brigade was swarming up the ladders passing out cool cans of beer to the pooped pilots. Fox Able 110 was history. The 110th crossing of the big waters by squadrons of lone fighter pilots had been accomplished without loss of a man or a plane, covering 5000 statute miles of land and water in 9 hours, 10 minutes, an average speed of 545 miles an hour.* All 18 birds had made it, no spares required. Three birds were "bent," but not broken. Mission 100 per cent accomplished, Major Prevost reported.

"Boy, is my tokus twitching," one pilot proclaimed as he cautiously eased his paralyzed pants down the ladder to the concrete ramp.

---

* This doesn't include hundreds of individual-delivery "High Flights" and many CASFs and other operations.

"When we came to Bermuda, I figured that was far enough."

"That's an awful lot of water. Too much for any old stove-pipe."

"My buns are dead."

"I've had it."

"These oceans are for the birds."

"If I'd wanted water I'd have joined the Navy."

The comments were caustic and irreverent as the pilots gathered around Bowles and his probe, festooned with scraps of nylon, to rub their backs and exchange banter. In a matter of minutes aching tailbones were forgotten. Song and chatter filled the barracks. The ocean-conquering pilots, dressed in their best civvies, were off to see Seville. Only the old hands who had made the big leap before hit the bag. Briefing for tomorrow's hop to Aviano was set for 0900.

It's thirty Spanish miles from Moron to Seville, an hour and a half's jolting ride in a bus, dodging unlighted carts, mules and donkeys, a journey in many ways more hazardous than the five thousand miles over the Atlantic. But most of the fighter jocks were eager to brave the perils of the night for a look at the ancient cathedral city with its gracious parks graced by bright Valencia oranges and its gay flamenco dancers. The pride of Seville is its flamenco, danced with a fire and ardor that embodies the very poetry of motion. To see and hear the flamenco artists at the Christina Hotel is an experience never to be forgotten. And the fighter pilots never forgot it, although they came dragging back to the base "flying low and smoking" at the darkest hour before the dawn.

Reveille came at 0700, breakfast at 0730 and briefing for the 1100-statute-mile flight to Aviano, Italy, at 0900. A cold front was moving in off the Mediterranean. Broken clouds were forecast, with a plus-30 wind component, running up to 65 miles tail wind at times. That made it only a two-hour flight. No refueling required.

Two planes were left behind for minor maintenance. The first wave of eight took off at 1100. The runway temperature

was already approaching 100°. The air was rough on takeoff.
The fields and olive groves looked parched and white with the
heat and the prolonged drought as the humpbacked jets snorted
for altitude. Castles in Spain dominated many a hilltop, with
whitewashed houses huddled close around as if for protection.
Fields, both large and small, radiated out from the castle like
spokes from the hub of a wheel. The New Economy could be
seen in the pattern of the fields around the bigger cities, the
tiny farm plots of past days joined into bigger fields for better
use of modern machinery. As we left the plains and soared
over the higher hills and into the mountains the fields became
smaller. Every square foot of land was cultivated by the industrious Spaniards. Even steep slopes were terraced for trees and
vines. Now and then the monotony of gleaming white houses
was relieved by a village pink or brown or red. The color of
the soil, from which the houses were made, seemed to determine
the color of the city. At flight level 290 (29,000 feet) Colin Alfa
flight leveled off and trimmed for cruise flight at .84 Mach.
    "Be advised. Stranger at twelve o'clock, thirty miles," Siesta
Control warned. Looked like a flight of F-104 Starfighters from
Moron out for practice intercepts. We were soaring over the
mountains now, with Valencia dimly visible on the shores of
the Mediterranean. Great Barcelona sprawled in tight circles
of masonry ahead, ringed by clouds. As we crossed the bay
toward Marseille, a babel of voices kept the radio humming—
Italian, French, Spanish, and English with a blend of accents.
Pedro Control didn't answer. Neither did Jerry. Now we were
over a radiant white undercast, with now and then a glimpse of
the French, Swiss, and Italian Alps through a hole in the
clouds. Through a broad rift in the clouds Lake Garda could
be seen, looking like a pool of ink at the bottom of a cleft in
the mountains. Sixty-eight miles out of Aviano.
    Time to start getting clearance for letdown. What had the
briefing officers had to say about this letdown? Tricky. Aviano
stood like a dagger pointed at the vital southern flank of the
Red line, just 40 statute miles from the Yugoslav border on

the east and 45 miles from neutral Austria on the north. This southern flank of the Communist fortress is strongly fortified. NATO planes which had come too close were greeted by flights of Red fighters, plainly visible on Italian radar scopes.

The instrument letdown into Aviano was tricky at best. The radar had long been unreliable. After many experiments, electronic engineers finally built a chicken-wire fence at the right angle to prevent descending planes from disappearing off the face of the scope during critical phases of their letdowns. The radio homing beacon was good enough. But there was nothing to prevent the Commies from sending out a stronger signal on the same frequency and luring unsuspecting friendlies across the border, or into the mountains that rimmed the field on three sides. There is suspicion, but no proof, that this may have happened to some of the planes that crashed on those mountainsides.

To guard against any such hazards of the cold war, every flight first tuned Treviso radio, thirty-two miles southwest of Aviano, and homed over this station as a double check on its position before starting descent into Aviano. Overshoot your letdown and in two minutes you would be into restricted border zones—or into the mountains, which rise up to eight thousand feet within twenty miles of the airport. Landings are nearly always made to the north. All turns on instruments must be made to the right. The foot of the mountains lies just four miles off the airport to the northwest. Instrument weather prevails at Aviano about 90 per cent of the time. Heavy clouds, heavy rain and low ceilings can be expected any time in the year.

That's what gives the Po Valley of northern Italy its breathtaking beauty. Seen from the air it looms up like a lush, green paradise of orchards, vineyards and grain fields, dotted with picturesque towns and villages, each with its cathedral spire and high-walled homes. We checked over Treviso, started our descent, hit Aviano homer and popped the speed boards and afterburner to burn off more fuel before landing. The boys tucked in tight to put on a good show for the rival squadrons

on the base as we bored through the clouds and broke out over
the airport. In fact, we could almost read Major Prevost's wrist
watch as we rolled into a 60-degree bank over the airport in
muggy, bumpy air that once again bred a snowstorm in the
cockpit. Lorentzen greased her on for a smooth landing and
we rolled the length of the concrete runway and started an
extended cross-country journey through the maze of concrete
taxiways to the hardstands, or "Marguerites" as the Italians call
them, where the planes are parked for maintenance and refueling.

Each jet was met by a wildly cheering group of eager pilots
from the 306th Squadron, also from George Air Force Base. The
fact that they could take off for home now that their replacements had arrived may have had something to do with their
eager enthusiasm. Instead of the traditional "tall cool one" they
ran up the ladder to the cockpit with a crystal goblet in one hand
and a bottle of what looked like rare champagne in the other. It
tasted like distillation of old overshoe. It is the *vino paisan*, the
lowliest wine of the countryside.

The rotating squadron "sets 'em up" at the club in the quiet
village, but the pilots and mechs of the 309th pause only long
enough to write up any discrepancies in the Form 1s before
going into a huddle with the base commander. Within forty-
eight hours they will "take over the commitment" of the 306th
at Aviano. It could be done sooner, but there are two other
squadrons on the field able to stand the alert until the 309th
has been briefed on the local situation and had time to study
target folders.

The 309th has completed its routine squadron deployment
in six days, covering 7000 statute miles in fourteen hours flying
time without accident or incident. The two birds delayed at
Moron are flown in two days later, giving the squadron its full
complement of 16 F-100Ds and two F-100Fs. Within twenty
hours of the 309th's arrival, the 306th is on its way back to the
States over the same route, bag, baggage and flyaway kit.

# 6. Victor Alert

Italy is a proud, independent nation, seat of ancient civilizations. She is a member of the North Atlantic Treaty Organization, an ally of the United States. We have mutual defense treaties which pledge us to defend Italy if she is attacked. These treaties make her defense problems our problems. They extend our frontiers to the Adriatic and the Alps. It is our national policy and our pledge to stop the Red tide of aggression at the shores of the Adriatic and the passes of the Alps, just as we have helped to stop the Red tide at the China coast and at the 38th parallel in Korea.

The Italians believe us when Uncle Sam signs his name to such treaties of mutual defense. But America is a long way off. The Communist menace is as near as the sunrise. Italy lies with her back against the Iron Curtain, her ears assailed by Red threats. Her cities are vulnerable to artillery and short-range rockets.

The authority of the Italian Government is further challenged by an active Communist Party, with a fourth of the seats in the House of Deputies. Those who live on the razor's edge learn not to squirm. But to keep up their moral courage and to convince the government that American support is real and

ever ready, Uncle Sam is committed to supply certain armed
forces to the NATO commanders in the theatre. That's where
the TAC squadrons come in. They are assigned to 17th Air
Force, a NATO command with headquarters at Ramstein Air
Base, Germany. They take operational orders from the commander of the 7227th Support Group at Aviano. They are available for any duty required of them in the theatre. While
standing by they continue their endless round of training in
instrument flying, gunnery, bombing with conventional practice
bombs, rocket firing and simulated delivery of "special
weapons."

But the "commitment" at Aviano, the duty that sobers the
most exuberant of these modern fighter-bomber pilots, is the
Victor alert. Each of the three squadrons takes turns standing
alert for a week at a time not only at Aviano but at Grosseto,
another NATO field owned and commanded by the Italian
air force on the west coast of Italy 90 miles north of Rome, 210
miles from the Yugoslavian border.

It is hard to believe that we live in the shadow of a Red menace when one sits on the front porch at Keokuk, Iowa, and see
nothing but jetliners and light trainer planes coasting across
the sky. But the imminent possibility of atomic oblivion becomes as tangible as the threat of fire or flood when you see four
shark-tailed F-100D Supersabres crouched behind makeshift
barricades of steel and rock at the end of the runway, ready to
retaliate against enemy attack faster than most firemen can
respond to a fire alarm. The alert stands are removed as far as
possible from prying eyes, but the world well knows that these
war Dogs, dedicated to keeping the peace, "have nuclear and
thermonuclear capabilities."

The hours every TAC pilot spends in perfecting delivery of
simulated nuclear or thermonuclear bombs by LABS maneuvers
(Low-Altitude Bombing System) suddenly take on new signifi-
cance when squadron pilots spend a week at a time on alert,
married to their silent planes, sleeping and eating in trailers
alongside their weapons. Each TAC pilot, like pilots of the

Strategic Air Command, has a target assigned behind the Commie curtain. He has plenty of time to study and memorize the target and the route from all possible angles during his days and nights on alert.

"The days of the Hell-raising, happy-go-lucky, trigger-happy flyboy is gone," one commander, a veteran of World War II and Korea, put it. "TAC can't afford cowboys in the cockpit any more. This is a serious business. And believe me, they take it seriously. If this doesn't sober them down, sitting alert out there with plenty of time to think, then we get rid of them. This is too great a responsibility to place in the hands of any but trained, professional pilots of proven character. And believe me, you've got to have character. You've got to be tough and dedicated to do this job.

"It vindicates your faith in America to see how this assignment makes men out of kids. They don't talk about it much, but these earnest young officers know the Reds have them zeroed in. They know that only the boys on alert would have a chance if the bell ever rang. The alert planes would get off before the base was 'atomized.' The rest of the squadron is always on two-hour alert. Many times during the tour the bell rings and they dash to their planes in the dark of night, never knowing whether this is it. But if it were, most of these fatalists wouldn't expect to get as far as the flight line."

One thing that worries field commanders is the security problem around these alert pads, a problem apparently inherent in the mores of the country. At Aviano, while the alert pad is removed from other base activities as far as possible, it is still within a stone's throw—or a hand grenade's throw—of the hayfields around the base. Farmers standing on their loads of hay can look down into the alert pads, although details of the plane's armament are hidden by makeshift shields. Farmers also harvest the hay alongside the hardstands where the planes are repaired and refueled before going on alert. They have cut the grass with hand scythes, raked it with wooden hand rakes and loaded it with wooden pitchforks for generations on this spot and they continue to do so, because every stalk of cow feed is important to the local economy. But they could plant bombs or commit sabotage without moving from their labor.

At Grosseto a surfaced rural lane runs along the edge of the air base, hard against the cyclone fence. A saboteur could toss a hand grenade or more powerful explosive over the fence and into the alert stands as he drove by on his tractor or hay wagon. He could do even more damage with high-powered rifles or machine guns. Yet efforts to get this rural road closed during the night hours were abandoned in the face of a political situation that is one of the hard facts of life in Italy today. There are about seven million Communist Party members in Italy today. They held about 22 per cent of the seats in the House of Deputies in 1960. They hold the majority in some sections of the country. The mayor of the town of Grosseto, just outside the air base, is a Communist. Khrushchev, in propaganda beamed into Italy from behind the Iron Curtain, has demanded the removal of U. S. aircraft and support forces from Aviano and from Grosseto. He calls these forces a "provocation."

He well knows what they are there for and knows their capabilities. These aircraft on Victor alert vastly increase Russia's problem should she try an all-out atomic attack on the free world. Not only is the number of targets she would have to wipe out vastly increased and dispersed, but the nature of her attack is complicated. If she attacks the watchdogs close along her borders, she gives precious minutes of warning which enables U. S. and NATO aircraft and missiles at more distant bases to be launched. If Russia launches all-out atomic attacks first on SAC bases and other prime military targets in the U. S., England, and Greenland, she gives the agile one-man bombers with their deadly loads time to dart in under the radar net, under the fighter screen, under the defending rockets, find major military targets and wipe them out—in some cases before SAC's big bombers could even get off the runways.

TAC's alert pilots know this—and more. The Reds know this —and more. They know and understand far more than the

Americans at home, who foot the bills but never see where their money goes.

The Italian people know well enough where these flying dragons come from and what they are here for. They have been invited to see for themselves on open house visits to Aviano—which of course didn't include views of the alert pads. They know what weapons the planes carry. They don't even ask any more. The Italian press doesn't even note the arrival of new squadrons any more. For the first year the "changing of the guard" was worth a couple of paragraphs. Now it has become so routine there is not a line about it in the local press or on the radio.

The thunder and roar of foreign and domestic planes is nothing new to the *paisanos* of Aviano and the countryside for miles around. Aviano is one of the two or three oldest airfields in Italy. It was first used by the Italian army in 1910 as a training field because it was on a broad, flat plain relatively free of fog. The Italian air force was separated from the army by 1923 and Aviano became one of its major bases. The army continued to use one side of the airport, however, and still does, for a tank unit. Italian eagles exercised their wings here in both fighters and bombers until 1940, when Aviano was used as a base for bombers launched against Yugoslavia in World War II. Most of the present hangars and other permanent buildings were constructed by the Italians during World War II.

The Germans occupied the base late in World War II. Taxiways and parking stands protected by U-shaped revetments were built miles from the base operations area. Many of them can still be seen in the fields surrounding the base, along with a few bomb scars, mementoes of Allied attacks. Everything is dispersed at Aviano. The air base consists of seven separate installations spread over a five-mile area. Jet fuel and gasoline are stored a quarter mile from the base. Headquarters offices are in a separate cantonment on the narrow country road that leads to Aviano, four miles from the base. The officers' club, gymnasium, hospital and officers' quarters are located in a walled compound in Aviano itself, a town of 3000. The base exchange, theatre and airmen's quarters are located in a separate compound a block from the officers area. Maintenance shops and supply storage is on the outskirts of Aviano, and the railhead for the base is in still another part of town.

The air base, named Pagliano e Gori, after two Italian heroes, is a NATO base, commanded by an officer of the Italian air force. The Italians maintain no aircraft or personnel on the field, however, except an administrative staff. The base is operated by the 7227th Support Group of the U. S. Air Force, under the command of 17th Air Force, a NATO command, with headquarters at Ramstein, Germany. The U. S. Tactical Air Command bases two squadrons of F-100s at Aviano at the invitation of NATO and the Italian government. Major expenditures on construction come from NATO funds, but U. S. funds are used directly for most of the routine renovation work. This is the pattern of U. S. aid to its NATO allies in many parts of the world.

About 1000 U. S. Air Force officers and men are stationed at Aviano for three-year tours of duty to operate the base, "keep house" and provide supplies, such as fuel, and services such as housing to the squadrons which rotate here for four months' duty. The two squadrons together add about 400 to the base population during their rotational tour.

Introduce 1,300 Americans into a rural village of 3000 proud Italians, heirs to the accumulated culture of an ancient civilization, stir well, season with Communist propaganda, and you have the kind of a stew that can cause international indigestion. This is the kind of stew that bids fair to be the major dish on the Free World menu for as far as the eye can see in the future. To their multiplicity of other duties and responsibilities, TAC air crews now have the additional duty of ambassadors at large.

Most Americans find Aviano an attractive overseas assignment. The Italian people are warm, human, friendly, forgiving, easy to get along with. They are naturally inclined to like the *Americanos,* not for their money or for any financial aid the homeland may have received from the U. S. treasury, but because they are *Americanos*. Many Americans become fast friends with the Italians, especially those Americans who make an effort to learn enough of the Italian language to exchange social pleasantries. Nothing warms the heart of an Italian like the adoption of his language. This is true in most foreign countries. The Air Force has long recognized this simple human trait and has long encouraged those assigned overseas to learn the national language in GI schools on the base.

Americans who spend even a few days in Italy quickly acquire a new respect for their Roman allies. The Italy of tumbled-down shacks with dirt floors, burlap curtains and chicken-coop walls portrayed in the movies is belied by the immaculate apartments and ample homes of the middle-class Italians. In fact, their walled homes with well-kept gardens, terraces, balconies and marble or tile floors would be considered elegant even in Hollywood.

While the pace of life is different and the afternoon siesta gives an appearance of indolence, the Italians are industrious hard workers. The farmer and his wife are up before the sun, riding their tiny wagons, drawn by the family cow, out to the fields. The big, mouse-colored cows amble amiably along, chewing their cuds, unhurried but untiring, while the *paisano* and his family rake the hay and load it by hand. Then the cow ambles back to town, where she is thriftily stabled under the bedroom to provide heat for the farmer and his wife, and the hay is stowed in the yard under cover.

At Aviano, as in all of Italy, Americans come face to face with avowed Communists, often for the first time in their lives. If they expect bewhiskered Bolsheviks with lighted bombs in hand, they are bewildered to find smiling, cordial *simpaticos* who show every sign of liking their American guests. This is one of the confusing aspects of life in Italy. There are those, like Marcello Bertogna, veteran of the Italian campaign in Africa and now interpreter for the Americans at Aviano, who say most Italian Communists are not Communists but dissidents who vote the Communist ticket as a means of registering a protest against any one of a number of things.

Bertogna, a devout Catholic, like most Italians, says much of the Communist vote—6,700,000 in 1958—was a protest against some aspects of the domination of the national life by the Church of Rome. Criticism of the clergy is common in Italy, but even the Communists never miss a mass, Bertogna and other informed observers say. They don't seem to see the impossible contradiction. Their idea of Communism is not Moscow's idea of Communism. Many Italians who vote communistic don't trust the Russians, especially since the ruthless suppression of the Hungarian revolt. Many vote for Communism as a protest against the wide gap between the rich and the poor, especially in Southern Italy. Others support the Communists as a protest against the national government. Regional loyalties are still strong, possibly a hangover of the old city-states, which weren't united into one nation until 1870.

Whatever their reasons, the Communists in Italy are an active element with which every American has to learn to cope. The hammer and sickle adorns many a village wall, but not in Aviano. Parades and demonstrations are common, especially on May Day, but Americans are not personally heckled in Aviano nor in Pordenone, the nearest city of any size—30,000. Even where the Communists predominate, they paradoxically welcome the Americans.

J. D. Zellerbach, U. S. ambassador to Italy, was asked to dedicate a workers' housing project in a Communist stronghold when he was administering Marshall Plan aid in Italy. He accepted reluctantly, expecting to be heckled. As he entered the town he saw the hammer and sickle flag waving from every house. There were the usual rude inscriptions inviting Americans to go home, in not quite that kind of language. But the whole populace lined the streets, smiling, cheering and waving American as well as Italian flags. The Communist mayor, in full regalia, was there beaming and smiling to welcome him—

blissfully unaware of the paradox of Communists welcoming
the chief foe of Communism.

Communism in Italy is no comic opera threat however, informed NATO sources agree. "Not all people who vote Communist may be 'real' Communists," an official USAFE (United
States Air Forces in Europe) briefing warns, "but the people
they vote for are."

The Communists in Italy and behind the Iron Curtain consider the Americans in Italy a major target, which they would
wipe out with propaganda if they could. Big guns in this barrage of propaganda include 110 hours of radio broadcasts per
week beamed into Italy from the USSR and Czechoslovakia.
Soviet and satellite films are shown in film clubs and other Italo-
USSR "cultural" groups. Street fairs, festivals, beauty contests,
summer camps and relief efforts are fostered by the Commies.
Millions of dollars of Russian money are spent annually to convince Italians that the Americans are monsters bent on grinding
Italy under their heel, seducing their women and poisoning
the air with atomic and hydrogen weapons. They picture
the Americans as fat bankers, trying to buy Italy with dollars.
When persuasion fails, the Reds rattle their rockets. TAC's
thermonuclear-capable jets at Aviano and Grosseto have been
Krushchev's principal target, but in 1959 he hurled one of his
major threats against the Italians if they permitted the United
States to establish rocket bases on Italian soil. Training of Italian soldiers in nuclear warfare has continued, however.

Any incident involving Americans in Italy is prime ammunition for the Communists' propaganda guns. When four jet
fighters crashed in as many months at Grosseto air base in 1960,
Communists in the house of deputies demanded the immediate
removal of the American detachment on the grounds that they
were a menace to the peaceful countryside and incompetent to
be trusted with modern high-powered aircraft and armament.
Fortunately, leaders of the majority Christian Democratic party
were equal to the occasion.

"Is the honorable deputy aware that three of the four planes that crashed unfortunately were aircraft owned and flown by the Royal Italian Air Force?" the government's floor leader demanded.

That spiked the Commies' guns.

The Italians are a most forgiving people. They expect *Americanos* to be a bit strange. They are a demonstrative people, but full of dignity. They love their wine, but they respect it, too. They never drink enough to forget their manners.

They resent *Americanos* who get roaring drunk in public. It is hard for them to understand the peculiar power of the local wine—which they drink like water—to knock out unsuspecting Americans like ether and leave them completely oblivious to their actions. Italian police arrest any GIs they find roaring down the village streets in the dark of night, but turn them over to U. S. military authorities as quietly as possible. There have been no trials of American servicemen under Italian law in the Aviano area except for hit-and-run driving.

This is another offense that is hard for any host country to understand or forgive. But the Italians are incredibly *simpatico*. Take the case of the GI who married a local Italian girl only to find she had tuberculosis. While she was in the hospital the GI drowned his sorrows in country wine on New Year's Eve. Next morning he hit and killed an Italian pedestrian with his car, then ran from the scene of the accident. In court he testified he didn't remember a thing. The Italians felt sorry for him. Even the Communists ignored the incident.

More typical of Communist treatment of news involving Americans was an incident involving a navigator of the Military Air Transport in July, 1960. The MATS crew, finding no space in the Aviano barracks, were driven to Pordenone, twelve miles away, the nearest hotel. About four o'clock the next morning the body of the navigator, Lt. Jack D. Maytag, a jolly, happy-go-lucky youth, was found in the street outside his fourth-floor window. The Office of Special Investigations spent a week investigating the mystery, but never released its findings.

*Messaggero Veneto,* the independent newspaper at Pordenone, reported the incident as follows:

> It appears that during the night Lt. Maytag had a nightmare in which he imagined himself on board an aircraft in emergency. This would explain the fact that he had donned his flying suit, thrown out his personal effects and then jumped as if bailing out. He must have awakened when he hit the electric cable, but by then it was too late to break his fall.

The right wing *Gazzettino* of Venice, one hundred miles to the south, added the following explanation:

> It is not known what made the officer take such drastic action: it is presumed, however, that he was suffering from a type of sleepwalking disease. This is supported by the fact that he had put on his flying suit before taking the jump.

But *Unita,* the Communist newspaper which covers all Italy with more than a million circulation, had the following unfriendly explanation:

> The officer was under the influence of alcohol.
> Although the Hotel personnel insisted that he present his identity documents, he did not so do. Besides throwing out his personal effects before the leap, he threw out also a bottle of Scotch. The causes of the incident are unknown; it has been ascertained, however, that he had been awake all night.

Grosseto is a new airfield built since World War II for the Italian air force. A squadron of F-86s supplied by the United States is based there as part of the Italian Air Defense Command. Commander of Baccarini air base at Grosseto is Lt. Col. Mario Mecatti, a brilliant Italian ace who shot down 22 Allied planes in aerial combat during World War II. He is quick to add, however, that he was shot down seven times by Allied planes. One of the pilots who shot him down over Sicily was an American, Billy Irving. The two later became fast friends. Irving was later killed in a crash.

Colonel Mecatti's fondness for Americans makes easy the job

of the commander of the detachment of 125 American officers and airmen stationed at the base. Their job is to "keep house" for the TAC pilots who stand the Victor alert on this sun-baked seacoast, 210 miles from the Iron Curtain. Four planes, with pilots and supporting ground crews, come down from Grosseto to spend a week at this outpost opposite the island of Elba where Napoleon spent his exile.

Sometimes they feel as if they, too, had been exiled. Airmen based here have written letters to their congressmen complaining of hardships beyond the call of duty. It is true here, as in many spots on the far-flung outposts in this hot-cold war, the job has called for Spartan measures. The alert planes are parked in the open, exposed to the sun and the rain, protected from the eyes of the curious and the bombs of saboteurs only by makeshift barriers of pierced steel planking, rock and barbed wire. Here, too, the planes are within fifty feet of a public road which runs along the perimeter fence. The pilots spend their week in a trailer van alongside their planes. Air police live in an adjoining shack within a fifty-foot sprint of their posts of duty day and night. The base fire and crash crew shares the same type of Spartan accommodations in the hangar. The crews are tied to their posts during their week of duty. But when they are not standing alert they can jeep two miles across the field to a seaside resort under the pines with all the charm of California's Monterey peninsula. In this area, called the Marina, the Italians have built as handsome a living area as any American air bases could boast. From their ample masonry barracks the airmen can amble across the road and through the pines just a block or two to one of the most attractive beaches in Europe. Here the warm waters of the Mediterranean lap at golden sands that curve away as far as the eye can see in both directions.

There are no bathing beauties except at the summer resort of Marina, a few miles up the coast, but there is the sea and the sun, and fun to be had in the surf winter and summer. Here under the pines, behind the towering dunes, the Italians have built an officers' club of native stone that would be called magnificent anywhere in the United States. This they cordially share with the Americans, just as they share their noncommissioned officers' club, hospital, mess hall and other accommodations in the cantonment area.

"We couldn't ask for more cordial co-operation from the Italians," the U. S. detachment commander declared. "They will go to any lengths to give us anything we want, if it is within their power. I only wish we could get that kind of co-operation from our own people on some of the bases where I've been stationed. We work together here as if we belonged to the same service. Actually, we do. We're both under the same NATO command. We're all working for the same thing. Our only problem is communication. I haven't been here long enough to learn very much Italian. We have to use an interpreter and that is clumsy."

The life is not an exciting one for the airmen. But it is a job that has to be done. The accommodations are not as plush as a few of the private rooms for senior airmen at American bases; but airmen who complain of hardship in sunny Italy should see the boxlike barracks which cling grimly to the bare rock of Simiutak, one of our communications outposts on the coast of Greenland, cut off from all human contact by raging sea and impenetrable ice during nine months of winter.

The language barrier is a very real handicap, especially in coping with Communist propaganda in an outpost like Grosseto. But American ingenuity and "can-do," coupled with the old frontier help-your-neighbor spirit, sometimes scores a victory that surmounts the language barrier. Two GIs from the permanent party at Grosseto scored such a victory one sunny day on the 21st of May, 1960.

Airman Second Class Robert B. Johnson of Charleston Estates, South Carolina, and Airman Third Class Paul D. Hopkins of Charlotte, North Carolina, were enjoying the golden sands of the beach this Saturday morning.

An Italian fisherman was digging for clams, wading out with a cumbersome stick-and-net arrangement hip-deep in the pounding surf. Suddenly he stepped into a deep hole and disappeared. As the wave subsided he came up choking and screaming for help.

Airman Johnson jumped to his feet and raced for the floundering fisherman. Diving into the deep hole he seized the struggling *paisano*, who was unable to swim. Although half drowned and unable to help himself, the fisherman would not let go of the morning's haul of clams and the heavy apparatus used for flushing his quarry. Johnson had to haul both fisherman and clams through the treacherous surf to shore, where he administered first aid.

The fisherman slowly regained his strength and trudged homeward with his catch, thanking his American friend with many an eloquent gesture for saving his life. Neither could speak the language of the other, so the grateful man's name was never learned.

This was a day to be remembered, a day when the Mediterranean smiled its mellowest and beckoned all lovers of beauty to the beach. Among those who succumbed to the charms of the deceptively gentle surging of the surf was an Italian airman— Giovane Gianfranco—who was supposed to be on duty in the Italian compound under the tufted pines. The first the American knew of Giovane's presence was the excited shouts of his two companions. Looking down the beach the Americans saw two Italians helplessly shaking their dripping comrade and screaming hoarsely at him as if to shout him back to life.

Airman Hopkins sprinted to the scene, took in the situation at a glance and went to work with the assurance of long training. The Italian airman was as blue as the Mediterranean. There was no sign of pulse or breath. But Hopkins cleared out the Italian's throat, then laid him down and immediately began administering artificial restoration, with Johnson's aid.

It was many minutes before life began to flow feebly back into the nearly drowned Italian airman, while his Italian friends stood by, shaking with anxiety. Finally he was able to resume breathing on his own. His color improved and he regained consciousness. By that time the Italian Air Police had been called and carried him off, wrapped in blankets.

Nothing further was heard of the incident for about three weeks. The American airmen said nothing, although word of their exploit did reach the ears of their commander, Capt. John S. Andrus, through the grapevine. The Italians, for their part, kept quiet for fear they would get their buddy in trouble for yielding to the lure of the beach during duty hours.

There is a system of communications in every military organization of whatever nation, however, commonly known as "latrine rumors." In the Italian air force this *"radio fante,"* or "bootcamp broadcast," finally reached the ears of Colonel Mecatti. He sent a letter of appreciation, couched in gracious Latin phrases, thanking Captain Andrus for the quick and selfless action of his airmen who risked their lives to "bring back to life, with much skill," the Italian airman, who "appeared to have drowned."

No word of this feat of American "can-do" appeared in the Grosseto press, which is dominated by the Communists, but it was spread far and wide by the "Voce Di Popolo," which, in the words of the old Italian saying, is "Voce Di Dio"—"The Voice of the People Is the Voice of God."

Such spontaneous acts of American courage, competence and inbred instinct to answer calls for help at any cost do more to combat the Communist hate campaign than millions of dollars of economic aid or thousands of idle words.

# 7. Unsung Heroes

"Flying the pond is a fifty-fifty proposition," the tanker pilot observed wryly. "We do all the work and the jet jocks have all the fun."

That's the lament of the tanker pilots, the unsung heroes of the Tactical Air Command.

"We roll out of the sack while the fighter jocks are still sawing wood, baby-sit them all the way across the drink, find them when they're lost and wipe their noses when they get in trouble. Then by the time we land they've copped all the medals, eaten all the steak, drunk all the liquor and got all the girls dated up. I think I'll join the Foreign Legion."

There may have been times when tanker pilots really felt that way. But not any more, not in TAC. They are pretty proud of their jobs. Some call it *esprit de corps*. They know it takes a team to win any game, especially the tactical war game. They know the man on the flying trapeze gets the hand as he flies through the air with the greatest of ease. But they know, too, that he is no better than his anchor man. And the "truck drivers" of the tanker corps are the anchor men of the aerial artists that constitute TAC's strike forces.

Their job looks easy, but it requires special skill, endurance,

experience, cool judgment and command ability. His hands on
the controls of the tanker plane must be as strong and steady as
the hands of the anchor man on a team of aerial artists. He must
have the endurance to maintain a smooth, steady course for a
half hour at a time. He must be man enough to take off and land
in the roughest sort of weather when his chicks are in trouble.
He must have the experience and the tough-minded judgment
to make decisions and make them right. For the tanker commander is in command of the formation during the critical minutes of refueling. And it is he who must decide when and where
and whether to attempt refueling in rough weather. It is the
tanker commander who must call bingo on pilots who are unable to make their hookups in the narrow strip of time and
space allotted.

Finally, he must, when the chips are down, decide how much
of his own fuel to give to the distressed fighter pilot, weighing
the lives of his crew of eight against the lives of the jet pilots.
Now and again, at the end of a daylong mission, as he drags his
B-4 bag wearily into the barracks at some strange base after
weeks away from home, he casts envious eyes across the field at
the sleek silver SAC tankers, powered by bellowing jets that fly
high and fast, up among the jets they service, up where the air
is smooth, up above the weather, where hookups are a picnic.

Captain R. W. Kapfhamer, of the 622d Aerial Refueling Sq.,
England AFB, is typical of the breed. He stands both tall and
broad, has the hands of a truck driver, but the icy blue eyes of a
pilot who has lived in the sky for more years than he cares to
recall. He was flying tankers when refueling was a fishing expe-
dition as complex as a Chinese crossword puzzle. That was 'way
back in 1948, in the 509th Aerial Refueling Wing of the Strategic Air Command; not exactly the horse and buggy days of
refueling, but the Model-T days. The pressure was on to develop a usable system for refueling bombers in flight. Bombers
meant the Boeing B-29 Superfortress in those days, powered by
four Wright R3350 engines, developing 2,200 horses each. The
tanker plane had 300 feet of hose and about 300 feet of cable,

all wound up on a reel, with a 50-pound hunk of lead on the end of the cable to make it hang down. The receiver had a light cable with a kind of a wind sock to pull it out straight behind the B-29.

"The tanker had to fly loose formation on the left wing of the receiver plane, above, to the left, and behind just enough so you could see the receiver plane out the nose of your tanker," Kapfhamer recalls. "Then you slid slowly across to the right side of the receiver plane. As you did so, if you judged your altitude and distance right, your cable, with that fifty-pound weight dragging it down, would tangle with the cable extending straight out the tail of the receiver. There was a grappling hook on the end of the tanker's cable, like you use to drag for bodies, that would catch the receiver cable. Then the reel operator in the receiver plane would reel in the cable, pulling the hose from the tanker along with it until he could get hold of the end of the hose and connect it into the coupling leading to the fuel tanks on the receiver plane.

"When he had the hookup completed we would open the valves in the tanker and the fuel would flow by gravity through that three hundred feet of hose into the receiver. You had to fly pretty steady formation. It wasn't an easy position to fly. It was awkward to see the receiver plane even by day and not easy to judge the right distance. It's harder to fly formation this far apart than it is closer, of course.

"We could transfer 4000 gallons of avgas that way, by gravity, in 37 minutes, including the hookup and the breakaway—after we got a little practice," Kapfhamer reminisced. "The normal breakaway was made by the reel operator on the receiver letting the cable out about one hundred and fifty feet, then we would back off and a weak link in the cable would break and we would reel in the hose and the remaining cable.

"The reel operators had to work in an open bay, which was pretty rugged. In 1950 off Labrador we were practicing refueling at thirty-five below. I've seen it down to sixty below. The reel man had to wear a felt face mask and goggles and of course heavy arctic clothes to keep from freezing.

"We got the B-50s in 1954. The B-50 looks like another B-29, but it is seventy-five per cent new inside and out, with bigger engines, bigger fuel tanks, much longer range. And then they hung the reel pods on each wing and one in the tail. By 1958 we had hung a jet engine under each wing of most of our KB-50s, making KB-50Js out of them. With this 14,000 horse-power from our four-piston engines and 9000 pounds of thrust from two jets we are really in business. We can get off a 6000-foot runway grossing 180,000 pounds. That gives us 42,000 pounds of avgas and 30,000 to 38,000 pounds of JP4 for our jets and for the fighter boys—depending on the length of the mission.

"With this kind of a load we cruise at 8000 feet as long as we can to burn off fuel. As we approach the refueling rendezvous we start climbing to 20,000, 25,000, or as high as 29,000 feet for the refueling. At this altitude we cruise about 190 knots indicated [208 miles an hour true airspeed]. We fly a race track course in V or echelon formation waiting for the fighters. The navigators on the tankers sweat out the position of the fighters and our own rendezvous times. We can transmit radio signals on which the fighters can home with their automatic direction-finding radio. But mainly we rely on our own radar. The navigator keeps his eyes glued to the scope. He can pick up the bright blip of the fighters' IFF or SIF radar identification transmitters 150 miles away. To make sure he has the right planes on his scope he asks them to change the pattern of their blips. Usually they are transmitting on channel one or two, and we ask them to squawk three for positive identification. Then the navigator notes their direction and distance and tells them to steer a heading to inter-cept us. All the actual chatter is carried on by the tanker com-mander to the fighter commander to cut down confusion. It used to be a major operation to make a rendezvous like this. Even a tanker formation is a small speck in an awfully big sky. But this works well, day and night.

"Once the fighters have us in sight and are letting down, we push the RPMs on the props up to 2600 and open the throttles up to METO power (maximum extended takeoff power). Then we fire up the jets and turn them up to ninety-eight per cent of full power. That boosts our speed up to two hundred and twenty knots indicated [225 miles an hour true airspeed] to give the jets better control. Usually we descend one thousand feet to pick up our speed and spread out the formation until we are flying nose to tail but about 200 feet between wing tips. This gives us room to move up and down, fore and aft, as necessary during the refueling. We have to time this speed-up pretty carefully as we are about doubling our fuel consumption when we draw this much power, and fuel is the critical item in this whole operation. We burn twelve thousand pounds per hour at METO power.

"Once the fighters are ready to hook up, the fighter commander gives the order and each jet switches to the frequency of his particular tanker so he can talk to his tanker and no one else. It used to be a mess when everyone was talking on the same frequency and no one knew who was who, or what was what. Once the hookup is made we shoot 500 or 1000 pounds to the fighters to see if the system is working right. Then each tanker reports to the tanker CO. We wait until all fighters are hooked up, then the tanker CO reports to the fighter CO and the fighter leader gives the order to take fuel, which is passed on by the tanker CO. Everyone thus starts taking fuel at the same time. As the jets get full they usually have to call for a 'toboggan,' especially at higher altitudes, and we nose the tanker down into a slight descent to increase the airspeed by ten knots or so and improve the angle of attack for the fighters.

"As each fighter gets a full load the tanker engineer reports to his CO. The jet jockey isn't the only one that has his hands full on a refueling. The tanker pilot has to hold a steady course, trying to stay clear of the rest of the tankers in the formation and dodge thunderbumpers. The navigator keeps a close eye on our course and position. The reel operators check their equipment, then open the housing on the pod that houses the hose and pay out sixty to sixty-seven feet of hose. The hose is eighty feet long. The right wing reel operator sits in the right blister with his remote controls in front of him; the left operator in the left blister; and the tail reel operator in the waist. He can't see his hose, but is guided by his instruments.

"The hoses are reeled out as we pour on the power. They add a lot of drag, cutting down our speed about ten knots. The engineer controls the fuel flow from the cockpit console. He pumps enough fuel into the hoses to fill them once they have been extended. This stiffens them and adds weight so they won't whip around so much. Makes them a little better target for the hookup. When the reel operator sees the pilot make his hookup he reels in the hose as the fighter moves up, until about 24 feet of hose remains off the reel. Then he opens the valves to the hose and gives the engineer the word to start pumping. The fighter pilot has opened his valves before he makes the hookup. These are in addition to automatic one-way valves in the couplings to prevent fuel loss during accidental disconnects. The reel operator reels the hose in and out, playing his fighter like a fish as the fighter moves forward or back.

"The engineer can put up to one hundred twenty pounds of pressure per square inch on the hose. But this would blow up the fighter's fuel tanks like a blowout on a kid's bicycle tire. There is a valve at the reel operator's station that cuts the pressure down to 53 PSI maximum, and the reel operator can cut it down further for topping off the tanks. This is enough to pump fuel aboard the fighter at fifteen hundred to two thousand pounds per minute, two hundred to two hundred eighty-five gallons per minute. The fighters may take anywhere from seven thousand to ten thousand pounds of fuel, which only takes four to six minutes for a single fighter. But someone always has trouble. It takes ten to twenty minutes to refuel the usual flight of eight fighter-bombers, depending on the type of jet. F-101 Voodoos and F-104 Starfighters take fuel faster, and have less trouble hooking up. Their probes are mounted right in front of the pilot in the case of the F-101 and easily visible in the case of the F-104. If the refueling goes by the book it takes about ten minutes, during which we travel about fifty miles on course."

Nothing stops a tanker pilot. He's like the postman. Neither rain nor sleet nor dark of night will keep him from his appointed rounds. His sense of urgency is that of a mother hen. Once the fighters are launched and past the point of safe return their lives depend on the tankers. Without that airborne transfusion their minutes are numbered. Keeping that preplanned rendezvous on time is often a matter of life and death. Usually one spare tanker is provided for every four in case one has engine trouble or has to abort for other reasons. In Operation Quick Span, demonstration tour of the Middle East by a TAC strike force in February, 1960, there were no spare tankers. All three hoses were required to refuel the formations as they skirted the Great Salt Desert between Iran and Pakistan.

As the clock in the cockpit clicked onto 0740, SE time (time to start engines), number three engine began to turn reluctantly on all three KB-50Js, then grumbled, smoked and burst into throaty roars. Then number two, number one and number four engines coughed and smoked to life. All fans were turning now but one—number four engine, outboard on the right wing of 447, number three in the tanker formation, wouldn't budge.

"Starter dead?" Capt. E. E. Morgan of the 427th Squadron, Langley AFB, Va., asked his engineer.

"Dead. Circuit breakers checked. She won't turn."

It was time to taxi. Takeoff time was 0800. To find and fix the trouble might take hours, if it could be done at all in the field. Captain Morgan called the formation commander, Col. Hollis B. Tara, "Pull off the ramp a little, Colonel. Give me room to get in behind you."

Briskly, but carefully, Captain Morgan maneuvered his high-tailed monster out of his parking place, taxiing on three engines to a position squarely behind Colonel Tara's tanker. He eased forward until the nose of his plane was only five feet from the tail of the CO's. The crippled KB-50J shuddered slightly in the propwash from Colonel Tara's four fans.

Then Captain Morgan's engineer feathered the propeller on the dead engine. Captain Morgan called for full power from number four engine on Colonel Tara's aircraft. As the propwash struck the crippled tanker she rocked and swayed like a sailboat in a gale. The engineer began unfeathering the prop on the dead engine, gradually exposing more and more blade area to the gale of propwash.

Slowly the blades began to turn, then faster and faster. As the engineer poured on the prime the engine began to fire, came to life with a cloud of smoke and settled down to a quiet roar. Colonel Tara taxied off, Captain Morgan close behind. By the time numbers one, two and three engines had been run through their pre-takeoff check, number four was warmed up and ready to roll at precisely 0800.

The same problem faced the tankers when they landed at Teheran, capital of Iran, on the long flight from Karachi, Pakistan, back to Incirlik air base at Adana, Turkey. There, on Mehrabad airport, there was no place to stir up a hurricane of propwash without stirring up a dust storm that would hide the runway and interfere with airline traffic. But Captain Morgan taxied out anyway, with the propeller on number four engine still feathered. When the CO gave the order for takeoff he took off, with one propeller feathered, the other three fans clawing the air furiously, and both jet engines putting out their 9000 pounds of thrust. When he reached 1000 feet above the airport and had a safe 150 knots, Captain Morgan passed the word and the engineer started unfeathering the propeller. As it began to turn under the force of the 150-knot wind of flight, the engineer completed a "routine start," and old 447 quickly pulled up into formation.

The crowds who watched the strike force take off at Karachi and at Teheran little noted nor long remembered what they saw. But the skilled professional pilots of the Pakistanian air force at Karachi and the polished veterans of the Imperial Iranian

Air Force at Teheran exchanged animated remarks in their own languages as they watched the crippled tanker waddle out and keep its scheduled takeoff. They knew what was going on. They knew one dead engine out of four was too much. No one would think of taking off in the face of those odds, except maybe in a war emergency.

If the purpose of Operation Quick Span was to demonstrate the skill, ingenuity and can-do spirit of the American pilot as well as the peace power of his equipment, the demonstration was a success. The pilots and commanders of the air forces which are our allies in the critical Middle East got the point. *Nothing* stops a CASF from fulfilling its mission, in peace or in war. They are still talking about that three-engined takeoff in Teheran. No one had to explain it to the Shah.

He is a pilot himself, with a fleet of airplanes of his own, including a twin-engined Fokker turboprop like the F-27 Fairchild airliners used by local service airlines in the United States.

The job of a tanker commander goes beyond observing schedules and following orders, however. Any plan made by man can be unmade by Mother Nature. Metro winds, no matter how accurately forecast, can shift suddenly as storms move in from the unobserved wastes of the oceans. Jet movements from the United States to Europe and Asia rely on tail winds averaging from 25 to 100 knots. Sometimes the winds suddenly switch and blow from east to west as storms move across the air routes. This can spell disaster for unwary fighters who have no means of checking the winds until they are too far from land to turn back. By that time it is usually too late to alert the tankers and get them into the air ahead of schedule, or divert them from the planned rendezvous point if they have already taken off. Alert tanker commanders have saved many a fighter by keeping a trained eye on the weather and moving up their own take-off times, or changing the rendezvous points at the risk of their own tankers.

Lajes Airport in the Azores has a delightful climate—but the weather is foul. The Portuguese inhabitants live there only

# Unsung Heroes

because they were born there and can't get away. The islands are inclined to be rugged, fit more for sheep than for airplanes. Hills stuffed with rocks tower hundreds of feet in the air alongside the runway, which lies on the floor of a valley. Nevertheless, Lajes has served as an oasis in the salty wastes of the Atlantic ever since the first planes flew over that ocean. There was no crossing of the Atlantic without the Azores until comparatively recent times. The same is still true for TAC's lonely fighters. Lajes is the first stop on the island-hopping flight back from Europe or Asia. Without a transfusion of JP4 over the Azores the Europe-bound fighters, flying nonstop, would be sucking wind before they reached Spain. Without the Azores there would be no nest to shelter the tankers—and the cripples who fall out of formation for one reason or another.

The eastbound fighters usually rendezvous with the tankers directly over the Azores, riding the prevailing westerlies on the long, lonesome leap from Bermuda.

"But sometimes the westerlies go West without prior notice," Major Bud English, of the 427th Squadron, recalled as he sweated in the jungle heat of Langley Air Force Base.

"We were sitting at Lajes on the first F-104 crossing in November, 1959, just to fly emergency cover in case anyone ran short of fuel and needed a sip to make his landing. No refueling was planned on the island-hopping route from Bermuda to Spain.

"The Starfighters had been given a plus-twenty-four wind component, which would bring them in with a minimum fuel reserve. But after listening to the Duckbutt aircraft reporting their winds and checking with PIREPS [pilot reports] from MATS planes on the route, I figured the boys actually had a minus-ninety, a direct head wind instead of a tail wind. It didn't take more than a turn of the E6B computer to figure they would run out of fuel two hundred miles from the nearest land.

"There was only one thing to do, rout the boys out of the sack and get 'em in the blue. Only there wasn't any blue. The clouds were down on the deck and the wind was howling directly across the runway. It always is when you have a howler at Lajes.

"By the time we had the fans turning she was kicking up thirty-five knots with gusts to forty, a ninety-degree cross wind. That's too much for the KB-50Js. But we got 'em in the air without losing any pieces and went out to meet the 104s. We caught them three hundred and eighty miles west of Lajes and made a rendezvous on a collision course. They were glad to see us. They were running about forty minutes behind their flight plan and beginning to pucker as they watched those fuel gauges unwind.

"Back at Lajes the weather was really getting nasty. By the time we had refueled the second wave of fighters, visibility was down to half a mile. The cross wind had reached sixty knots. The field had been closed. The SAC bombers had taken off for Africa. SAC tankers always hold back enough fuel to get to Africa if Lajes socks in. We can't. Time we load up with jet fuel for the fighters we can't carry enough avgas for ourselves to go anywhere. Santa Maria, our only alternate in the Azores, was socked in tight. We had no choice but to land back at Lajes. Cracking that two hundred-foot ceiling on GCA was hairy. We were cocked about sixty degrees to the runway when we saw the threshold lights. We all managed to set down, with full throttle on two engines and full reverse on the other to hold them against the cross wind. We blew a couple of tires and had to reline some brakes. But we were lucky not to break any birds in a wind like that. It was a case of weighing eighteen fighters against five tankers, eighteen men against forty. Those are the decisions that make you old in a hurry. We were lucky that time."

"I figure I can thank Colonel Tara for saving a whole flock of my chicks on one of the roughest crossings I've ever had," says Lt. Col. Frank Emory, commander of the 356th Tactical Fighter Squadron from Myrtle Beach, South Carolina.

"This was Junex 3, a test of the northern route for fighters. The weather is worse there, but the tankers can take off from land bases in case the island bases should be knocked out in time of trouble. We were supposed to fly the route over the

North Atlantic past Maine, Newfoundland, and the Great Circle Route to England in June, when the weather is best. But it was October before Junex 3 got off the ground. Actually this was the second crossing over the route.

"The weather was a witch's brew the whole way. There was a nasty line of thunderstorms lying in the refueling area off the coast of Maine, but we managed to find the tankers in the sticky dark of the night. I was leading and I was just about to tack onto the lead tanker, flown by Colonel Tara of the 450 Air Refueling Wing, when there was a big burst of flame from number two engine. Fire, smoke and sparks flew out of that pot like a fireworks stand on the Fourth of July.

"We fell back, expecting the whole wing to blow off. But Colonel Tara caged the prop, cut off all the juice to number two engine, poured the extinguisher to her and finally smothered the flames, or else they burned out. I expected the colonel to abort and head for home base. But pretty soon I heard him on the horn, as calm as a judge.

" 'Had a little two-bit fire there,' he drawled. 'Got her cooled off now. Go ahead and tack on.'

"That was no two-bit hole in the nacelle. It looked like the Grand Canyon to me, although I couldn't see too well. But Colonel Tara knew the spot we were in. He didn't have a spare tanker and we didn't have a place to light. Our alternate fields along the coast were all socked in, but tight.

"So he held that lame duck of his at 230 knots [265 miles an hour] and we took on fuel as fast as we could. Then he turned around and went back to pick up the next wave of fighters. By that time it was getting light and Colonel Tara's crew began to get a good look at that hole in their wing.

"Next thing we could hear them hollering May Day and an Air Rescue plane took off to meet them. They greased in that landing like they had eggs on board. If they had hit hard the wing might well have fallen off. The main spar was burned half through. It's a wonder the fuel tanks didn't blow or they didn't shed a wing over the ocean in all that turbulence.

"But that fuel saved our necks. We forged on through the night, with the weather closing down at Argentia and Gander as we went by. We just did make it to Lands End, England, where we took on another five thousand pounds of go-juice. By that time all primary fields in that end of the Islands were down to six hundred and one [600-foot ceiling and one mile visibility]. But the British radar picked us up seventy-six miles out with a cheery 'Welcome, little friends,' and vectored us down to a safe landing. Then everything socked in."

Hardest decision for the tanker CO always is when to call "bingo" when the fighters are in trouble. If he waits too long, if he carries the limping fighters too far along his flight path, he may carry his own crew too far from his own base and imperil the lives of all.

The closest shave in ready-room lore is the tanker commander who carried a formation of fighters 100 miles beyond the limits of their refueling area to give them range enough to buck a head wind into the Azores. Then he cut and ran for Bermuda, with a bare margin of safety—which vanished as shifting winds and sour weather stretched out his flight time. The last tanker finally made his instrument letdown and landed with one minute's fuel supply left, just enough to clear the runway, with engines conking out right and left for lack of fuel.

These are the missions that try men's souls but never make the headlines. No medals are struck for devotion to duty like this, no commendations are posted. But the tanker crews tell the story with a quiet pride.

Over land, where alternate airports are available, the tankers, with their 2000- to 2500-mile range, seldom have any such sweat. Working in relays, the flying filling stations once kept a forlorn fighter aloft for eleven hours over Europe while he watited for the weather to improve sufficiently to permit a safe landing.

The tanker crews have won most of their medals for such saves over the oceans or the deployment routes, but they get most of their gray hairs on training missions. Jet pilots fresh out of flight school have to learn the fine art of refueling in their advanced training out of Nellis Air Force Base, Las Vegas, Nevada, and way points. The tanker crews can only cringe helplessly as the green pilots come charging at the hose like baby hummingbirds, wobbling and porpoising, rocking and rolling as they overcontrol.

Nervous tyros have been known to charge the tanker like a bull with a barb in his neck and tear off long chunks of hose. Landing with ten feet of refueling hose trailing back over his right wing can make the best of pilots nervous. But it can be done. One of the prized fixtures in the ready room of 307th Tactical Fighter Squadron at George Air Force Base is a huge ashtray fashioned from a drogue torn off a tanker. List price on this twenty-pound piece of plumbing in supply catalogues is about $1,200. The tanker crew that lost this one tried by every means short of civil war to get it back. But the fighter squadron figured they had earned it.

Many a probe has been broken off in the course of refueling practice, but usually without damage to the aircraft. Many a canopy has been broken by hoses flailing like whips in rough air—especially in the earlier days of refueling when metal "funnels" were used to guide the probe into the drogue. Air currents tended to deflect these metal shields, especially after they were bent in the course of rough hookups. The metal was hard and heavy enough to crack a canopy and often shatter it completely. Such "incidents" were inconvenient and usually forced the jet pilot to drop out of the flight and land at the nearest alternate airport, if any. But few reportable accidents have been charged to refueling.

The worst was a training accident which, fortunately, happened over land, out of Cannon AFB, Clovis, New Mexico, in September, 1957. The overeager fighter pilot lunged at the hose with a jab of the throttle that caught the drogue squarely, but closed up the normal 60-foot gap between the fighter and the wing of the tanker at too great a rate. To avoid hitting the tanker, the fighter pilot pulled up and over the wing, wrapping the hose around the tanker's wing. Then he backed off, tearing the hose out of its reel pod and loosing a flood of fuel.

The fuel caught fire and wrapped the wing tip in flames. A fire fed by JP4 jet fuel will melt aluminum in a matter of minutes. There was no way to put out the flames. They quickly burned into the fuel tanks. The crew of the tanker bailed out just as the wing burned off and the KB-50J spun down, trailing streamers of red fire and black smoke.

Only one tanker has had to ditch at sea, so far as the records show, and that is one the tanker troops would rather not talk about. "Faulty navigation," is the lost ship's laconic epitaph.

The Atlantic is a four-engined ocean, as the multi-engine pilots are forever reminding TAC's Lindberghs. But the Pacific is a six-engined ocean. The Atlantic is a big, rough ocean, but it does have islands that serve as steppingstones. The Pacific is far from pacific, and it is almost as empty as the Antarctic. Islands are few and far apart.

This disquieting thought was running through Lt. Fred Bowles' mind one bright June day in 1960 as he settled down for the long crossing from California to Hawaii at 30,000 feet. The squadron had leaped off in the brassy dawn on the first of June for the Far East, in Operation Mobile Yoke. President Eisenhower was planning a trip to Japan, Indonesia and way points where the Commies had been busier than usual of late. TAC just happened to be going that way in advance of Ike's visit.

This was one of those days—perfect. The winds were as forecast. Fuel flow was normal. Everything was going by the book. Halfway across the big leap—longest overwater air route in the world and without a speck of land—the tankers showed up like squids in the distance. The air was calm, the hookup was a piece of cake. The refueling was routine.

Lieutenant Bowles broke off, kicked in the AB and joined formation. As they settled down for the long climb back to cruising altitude the flight leader called for a fuel check. The right wing tip tank was down already, although it had shown full when he broke off. Lieutenant Bowles, husky, bronzed young athlete with arms like oak limbs, made a quick check of switches and circuit breakers. Nothing wrong here.

Then he looked back at his right wing. A white spray was flowing off the wing. It looked like fuel pouring out behind the wing. Some seemed to be blowing up over the leading edge and back over the top of the wing as well. Looked like a massive leak. His wingman confirmed his estimate.

Bowles reported to his flight leader. Then he checked his map and form 21a, spun his computer with his free hand, and figured he could lose all the fuel in the leaking right wing tip tank and still have plenty to make Hickam Air Force Base, Honolulu. If it looked close he might be able to go into Hilo, about 100 miles east of Honolulu.

Could be the seal was leaking where the tank attached to the wing. But there was a check valve that would prevent loss of fuel from the rest of the system. Lieutenant Bowles relaxed. He was inclined to be annoyed when the flight leader reported the incident to Honolulu control and asked Honolulu to scramble a tanker. The tankers from George had yielded up their fuel and were long gone, well on their way back to base. He didn't need any help. Why make a federal case out of a little leaky valve or seal, or whatever it was?

The next fuel check showed the left wing tip tank draining, too. The book said it wasn't possible for fuel to be siphoned out of the whole system through one leaky tip tank. But that's what was happening, Lieutenant Bowles reluctantly concluded. The system was designed to burn out fuel in the wing tip tanks first, the fuel being forced under pressure from the tip tanks into the main tanks in the fuselage. The fore and aft main tanks would show full until both tip tanks went dry. Then what? The check valves on the wing tip tanks would prevent more fuel from pouring out through the leaky tip tank, according to the tech orders. Both tip tanks were emptying on the double. Bowles could almost see the indicators move. That 900 gallons should have lasted for near two hours; it was gone in less than half that time. But there was no sweat. When the tanks ran dry the check valve would prevent fuel from draining out of the main system.

When the tip tanks ran dry, Bowles blasted off the tanks to reduce the drag, save fuel and stretch his range. He still had 7,728 pounds of fuel (1,189 gallons) in his fuselage tanks, enough to make Hickam, if all went according to the howgozit chart. The tip tanks are not attached directly to the underside of the wing but to a connecting "pylon" of aluminum from which bombs or rockets can also be hung. An explosive metal bolt, fired by an electrical impulse, cuts the tanks loose from the pylon. But Bowles had no sooner reported "Tanks Away" than his wingman reported fuel still pouring out of the right wing. The automatic check valve was not checking the flow of fuel from the connection to the missing tank. After consultation with his flight commander, Bowles pressed the switch which blasted off the pylon itself, leaving the wing clean. But still the fuel overflowed in a white streamer behind the right wing.

A surge of pressure during the refueling operation evidently had ruptured the seals where the tip tank connected with the pylon and the pylon with the wing. At the same time the check valve apparently had been put out of commission. Now fuel was siphoning out of the main tanks at an alarming rate. As the minutes bled by, Bowles could see the JP4 draining away at a rate that was hard to calculate. It looked as if he might have enough to flame out about 50 miles short of Hickam. He might glide to safety, if the weather was CAVU. And he might not. He might go into the municipal airport at Hilo, 100 miles east of Hickam, if the weather was clear. But it wasn't. And the runway was short, with obstructions to add to his difficulties. It looked as if the "incident" which had started out as a minor annoyance was building up to a bailout at sea.

But back at Hickam the first precautionary call to scramble a tanker had been taken in dead earnest. The tanker crew on alert had made like fighter pilots, running to their high-tailed KB-50J and firing up as they taxied out. Cutting short their check list they rolled onto the runway and were off at full power. Now they were boring through the blue, still at wartime power. Better to burn up a couple of engines—which they did—than splash one fighter.

Picking up the flight of fighters on their radar screen, the tanker began vectoring Bowles and his wingman down to the flying fuel farm. The leaky Supersabre was still 45 minutes out, with fuel for 45 minutes—or less. Bowles sighted the tanker going all-out 365 statute miles from Hickam. He had 1,900 pounds of fuel aboard, just enough to make Hickam at the normal rate of 3000 pounds an hour, enough to get about half-way there with the hungry leak in the right wing devouring as much fuel as he burned in his jet engine.

The stubby Supersabre latched onto the smoking tanker like a long-lost suckling pig onto its mother's vest. The hookup was deft and sure. It had to be. There was no time to waste. As Bowles' wingman passed word to the formation, the tension that had built up over the past two hours vanished. The formation bored on in to Hickam while Bowles and his leaky cripple lagged behind, enjoying a life-giving transfusion of precious JP4. Bowles was content with 4000 or 5000 pounds, but the tanker shot him a full load, 7,700 pounds, enough to stay aloft for an hour or more, even with the hole in his fuel system.

A half hour after dropping off the tanker, Bowles was over Honolulu. After sweating out a dwindling fuel supply for two and a half hours, he found himself suddenly embarrassed by an overdose of fuel. He had to pop his speed boards and cut in his afterburner to burn off his fuel load to the allowable maximum weight before he could grease in a landing.

It took a while to make out the required reports, in septuplicate. Then Lieutenant Bowles hit for the officers' club to buy the tanker boys a beer. He figured they had earned it.

Ever since that day the tankers have reduced the pressure on their pumps when they top off the tanks on the Supersabres.

# 8. Two Days to Swim

Captain Robert P. Barry, of Panama City, Florida, is a rugged, happy pilot type with a supersonic smile and a disarming air of unconcern. He would rather be a fighter pilot than President. With his contagious smile and engaging manner he could be both. He has the air of a playboy without a care in the world.

But the experiences he has had would turn the hair of a lesser man white overnight—especially the events of May 8, 1959. The bare report of that day's "incident" reads like Poe's "The Pit and the Pendulum."

This nightmare began casually, as such incidents so often do in supersonic jets, where minor malfunctions can start chain reactions that snowball until the lone pilot finds himself in deep trouble. An "incident" in Air Force jargon is "an accident going some place to happen."

This was TAC Strike Whiskey, another routine operational test of the ability of a squadron of Supersabres to get there "fastest with the bestest." "There" in this case was to be Okinawa, via Hawaii, Guam and Wake. The 308th Tactical Fighter Squadron blasted off the runway at George Air Force Base at 1000 hours on this misty morning, on schedule, swung on course and climbed to 30,000 feet. At 550 statute miles off the coast, over the cloud-shrouded Pacific, the last wave of six F-100Ds of Tomahawk Red flight rendezvoused with three tankers of Headburr flight of the 622d Air Refueling Squadron, England AFB.

The hookup was routine. Captain Barry throttled back, extended his dive brakes and descended to the 20,000-foot level of the tankers. He dialed in the right amount of trim, then reached down, pressed the flap lever down, counted ten, then pulled the circuit breaker on the flap circuit. He only wanted fifteen degrees of flaps and that was the only way to get it. The flap-control lever would only bring the flaps full up or full down. Fifteen degrees was just right. It reduced stalling speed and gave better flight control without increasing the drag enough to require much extra throttle for slow speed flight.

The hookup was easy for a pilot of Captain Barry's experience. Some of the other pilots had a little trouble, however, and the flight was about 650 miles off the coast, 750 miles from George AFB, when Tomahawk Red Leader gave the order to break off and reform for the climb back to cruising altitude. Headburr commander gave the order for the tankers to return to base. They were down to bingo fuel for their own piston engines, with just enough JP4 fuel remaining for their jet engines on the long haul back to George, where they were serving on temporary duty with the 4505th Air Refueling Wing Detachment. Two spare F-100Ds of the 308th turned back at the same time. Everything was skosh, Maj. Stewart Laurie, squadron CO, reported. The spares wouldn't be needed.

As the spares peeled off to overhaul the tankers for the return flight, Captain Barry's waggish mind was doing some fast calculating. Just to kill time he confirmed his mental arithmetic with a quick spin of the dials on his E6B computer.

"It would take two days to swim back over the distance we cover in every minute of cruising flight outbound," he mused with a grin. "So who wants to swim?"

His wingman, Lt. Gale Mecham, rudely shattered his reverie.

"Looks like your flaps are still down, Bob," he reported.

Captain Barry made a quick check. Circuit breaker in. Flap

handle up. Utility system hydraulic pressure normal. Those mothers should be up, full up. But of course he couldn't see them himself.

"No sweat," Captain Barry reported to Tomahawk Red Leader.

Ten or fifteen degrees of flaps wasn't fatal. It would drag down his cruising speed maybe 20 or 30 knots and increase his fuel consumption. But there was still a chance of getting them up. Barry warned his wingman, slowed up, then popped his gear down and his speed board out to drain the hydraulic pressure on his utility system, hoping air pressure at 300 knots would force the flaps up. But it didn't.

He pulled up his gear, tucked in his speed boards again and waited for his speed to build up. The flaps hadn't budged. They were still cutting about 30 knots off his cruising speed. There was only one thing left to try. There was a separate emergency system for operation of the flaps. Putting the flap lever in UP position, Captain Barry hit the emergency flap extension lever.

Barry was thrown against his seat belt with a sickening lurch. His wingman skidded off to the side and overshot him. It was the same sudden deceleration you get when you pop the speed boards. The flaps were stuck full down. Captain Barry was in deep trouble.

"You got full flaps now," his wingman cut in laconically. As if Barry didn't know it. He had full power, but his speed had fallen off to 220 knots. That is minimum. You don't go below 220. He couldn't stay in formation now. He couldn't even hold altitude.

"I'm aborting," Barry notified Tomahawk Red Leader. He began a slow turn and pointed his nose toward the California coast, which lay somewhere in the mists of the distance. His wingman stuck with him, throttling back to a slow glide. Captain Barry's crippled bird couldn't maintain altitude, even with full military power. She was sinking slowly, 300 feet per minute, toward the blue bosom of the Pacific far below. Barry switched to the tanker frequency and called May Day.

"Headburr Leader, this is Tomahawk Red one-five. Wait up. I'm aborting. Flaps full down, descending from flight level two nine zero."

Headburr Leader rogered the call and ordered a slowdown.

"We're cutting back to one seventy knots," he told Tomahawk Red. At that speed the F-100 should easily overhaul the tankers. But no one had much experience trying to cruise a Dog with flaps full down. The cruise control charts don't contemplate such a desperate condition. Captain Barry was making history, however reluctantly. But a quick calculation indicated he wouldn't be making much more. He was about 700 statute miles from the coast when his flaps finally went full down and he had to turn back—there was no choice. Hickam lay a full 1,650 miles to the west. Seven hundred miles was a scant hour and fifteen minutes at normal cruise. But the situation with Tomahawk Red 1-5 was hardly normal. He was stuck with full flaps and full power and going down, down, down, 300 feet per minute. From 29,000 feet he was dragged down to 20,000, still with full throttle. Even in the heavier air of 20,000 he couldn't hold altitude. If he went lower his fuel consumption would increase rapidly.

Captain Barry notified his staggering wingman and then kicked in the afterburner. The AB was a fuel hog, nearly tripling fuel consumption. But, booted by the doubled power, the ruptured Dog began slowly climbing back up to 29,000 feet, still at 220 knots, 255 miles an hour.

Another twirl of the E6B computer showed Barry he was getting nowhere fast. He would run out of fuel an hour and a half from the coast, about 380 miles out in the Pacific, if he didn't run out of luck before that. Troubles have a nasty way of pyramiding, although it was hard to see how he could be in any deeper trouble than he was now.

"Let's see now, three hundred eighty miles at four point five miles per day. That's about an eighty-day swim. Heck, my TDY will expire before that," Barry figured whimsically as he struggled to get the last pound of performance out of the Supersabre. "And I couldn't collect per diem either. Air Rescue would play hob finding me in all that chop down there. They couldn't land if they did. And it's too far out for a chopper."

Barry decided on one last desperate attempt to shake off the great expanse of flaps which stuck out below the wings like barn doors, dragging him down, down. Sticking the nose of the shark-mouthed plane almost straight down, he tried to build up speed enough to tear off the heavy flaps. Then he pulled out as hard as he could, building up all the G forces he could. But nothing happened. He couldn't build up more than 400 knots of speed in a vertical dive with all that expanse of flaps holding him back. And that wasn't enough.

The maneuver cost him a lot of altitude and again he fired up the afterburner to climb back to altitude. There was nothing left to do but sit and think and fly as smoothly as he could to save fuel. His only hope now was the tankers. And that wasn't the lead pipe cinch it might seem.

The air was alive with chatter. Headburr flight had stop-cocked their jet engines to save fuel for Barry's limping bird. They were loafing along on 50 per cent power on their recip-rocating engines, at a mere 170 knots indicated. But Tomahawk Red wasn't catching up very fast. The tankers had him on their radar scopes now, still 150 miles out. He had been homing on their radio signals with his ADF, automatic radio direction finder, but the needle had been hunting uncertainly. Now they could vector him on a direct course.

But once he caught them, his troubles wouldn't be over. They only had 6,500 pounds of jet fuel among them and that wasn't enough to make land, by Barry's calculations. It was a whole lot better than nothing, though, Barry thought with a grin. No matter how bad things may get they can always get worse, he thought.

And sure enough, they got worse. Three times now Barry's sick Dog had staggered from 29,000 down to 20,000 feet. Three times he had poured on the afterburner and climbed back up. But the fourth time he hit 20,000 and kicked in the AB he felt no comforting kick in the pants as fire shot out the tail with explosive force. He tried it again and again. The afterburner just plain wouldn't light.

"Looks like I've really bought the farm and all the livestock this time," Barry muttered. Then he got on the horn to Headburr.

"Wait up, you guys. I'm fresh out of afterburner."

The words sent a chill through all the far-flung network of pilots who were listening, spellbound, to guard channel, the emergency frequency over which all distress calls are broadcast. Air Force and Coast Guard rescue squadrons, ships at sea and all the scores of aircraft that churn up the airways along this Lincoln Highway of the Pacific turned up the volume and sat glued to their headsets.

Headburr Leader ordered his tankers to orbit where they were, although they were getting low on fuel themselves. It was obvious Tomahawk Red could never catch them now. The shark-shaped 15-ton tin monster was designed to cruise never slower than 220 knots. But in a last-ditch effort to hold altitude Captain Barry slowly raised the nose, increasing the angle of attack, giving the butterfly wings more and more lift. As he did so, drag increased and speed fell off, 200, 195, 190, 180 knots. And still the stubby plane descended, like a lead glider, 19,000, 18,000, 17,000 feet.

He was closing the gap. He was catching up on the tankers. But still he settled lower and lower, into heavier air where he burned more fuel and made even less ground speed. And the fuel was draining fast away. It had taken only an hour and a half from George to the first refueling rendezvous. He had already been fighting his way back for two hours against those infernal flaps and he was still 200 miles off the coast.

He was down to 15,000 feet and a scant 2000 pounds of fuel when he finally sighted the tankers on the dim horizon. The problem now was to hook up. He was staggering along at 165 knots trying to hold altitude. That wasn't flying speed. It was barely maneuvering speed. That was the minimum speed for a normal approach for landing. It was no speed at which to tackle the complex job of stabbing that flailing drogue with a probe you couldn't even see. The controls were sluggish and response was slow. The eyebrow slots on the leading edge of the wing were fully extended, allowing air to flow behind them and up over the wing. That was all that prevented an all-out stall and spin.

A hookup didn't seem possible. But if the impossible had to be done, one couldn't have picked a better pilot than Captain Barry. He was one of the first half-dozen pilots to crack 1000 hours in tactical jets. And all of that time was in the F-100. He had engineering experience and had been chosen to test new tactics with the F-100. He was one of those who had zoomed the F-100D to flameout altitude, using an experimental "moon suit," and lived to keep still about it. The project was restricted at the time.

Now he needed all his skill and experience. After two hours of fighting those flaps he was down to 1,900 pounds of fuel. Barry played it cool and hooked up on the first try. He had full throttle and no margin for maneuvering. As he started to fall back he had to call for Headburr #1 to slow down. He couldn't afford to lose any more altitude.

It didn't take long to drain what little JP4 was left in the tanks. Then he broke off and tried Headburr #2. He had more load now. With full flaps and no afterburner he couldn't catch up with the big KB-50J, although she was loafing along, nose-high, her props ticking over so slowly you could almost count the blades. He managed to struggle up within twenty feet of the wing. Then the reel operator skillfully allowed the hose to unreel and dropped the drogue back fast enough to make contact with the Supersabre's probe, which stuck up at a ridiculous angle, due to the near-stalling speed and high angle of attack.

It took the thirsty fighter only a few minutes to drain Headburr #2's tanks. A glance at his gauges showed Captain Barry he still couldn't make land. He was still 150 miles offshore.

The added load of fuel cut down his speed still more. He

hung onto Headburr #2 as long as he could. Headburr #3 was
still lagging behind, coming up slow. Barry figured he didn't
have enough power now to make another hookup. So he blew
off his drop tanks to reduce drag and improve his performance
somewhat.

Then he dropped off the tanker. He was still on the verge of
a stall and still losing altitude. For the umpteenth time he
jabbed the throttle into afterburner, on the off-chance it would
light off.

It did! There was the comforting sound of the kickoff bang—
then the empty whine of a compressor stall. For some obscure
reason the air was eddying turbulently, jamming up in the jet
engine, robbing it of its power. The surge of power died off and
Barry took her out of AB. Now he was back where he started.
There was nothing to do but try another hookup without AB.

Headburr #3 came up slowly from behind, dropped down
and began to inch over in front of the helpless fighter. This one
wasn't in the books. Barry, with throttle already wide open, was
unable to maneuver his logy fighter. It was up to the tanker
crew to hook up with the fighter. Guided by the reel operators,
the pilot did just that. While Barry held his altitude and heading as steady as possible, the big awkward tanker eased down
and back until the fighter was cradled between wing tip and
tail. Then the reel operator began fishing for the probe with his
drogue. It took a while, but he finally dropped it skillfully over
the thirsty end of the probe and pumped all the jet fuel left in
his tanks after supplying two waves of fighters 540 miles back
along the course to Hickam.

Headburr #4 accomplished the same feat. But his tanks, too,
were nearly dry. Another quick calculation showed Barry he was
still doomed to get his feet wet. After draining all the jet fuel
aboard all the tankers he still couldn't make land.

"I figured I might be able to bail out on the coast of San
Clemente Island," Captain Barry recalled. Every detail of his
harrowing experience is still sharp in his mind. "Then I figured
I could take on a little avgas from the tankers and try burning

that. That would take me to the north coast of Santa Maria Island where I could bail out. Air Rescue had been keeping track of me and I told them that was what I would try. That was better than dunking my buns in the Pacific, which looked mighty cold and agitated. I could see it all too clearly by now."

Then came one of those last-minute reprieves which only happen in Hollywood.

Back on guard channel a tanker by the unlikely call sign of Nutbutter 361, en route to Hawaii, had lost an engine about 100 miles off the coast and 100 miles north of San Clemente Island, and was turning back to land at George Air Force Base when the crew heard May Day talk. Listening in, Capt. John R. Barr heard Headburr Leader reckoning that even if he succeeded in taking on all the fuel remaining in Headburr flight, Tomahawk Red still couldn't make the coast. *Nutbutter 361* got on the horn.

"We've got thirty thousand pounds of JP4 we can't use. We're coming on down. Give us a steer," Captain Barr announced.

Captain Barr poured on full military power and came trucking on down the coast as fast as *Nutbutter's* three props and two jet engines would carry her. She closed the 180-mile gap in a little more than half an hour and joined the refueling formation.

"Boy, was I glad to see that mother," Captain Barry recalled with a grin.

"There was the same business of faunching around until the tanker could drop her drogue over my probe—a neat trick any time, especially at stalling speed.

"Once I latched onto that hose I wasn't about to let go. We staggered all the way to George together, letting down as we came. The sight of the dirty brown smoke from the cement plant never looked so good. I carried power all the way to the runway and had no trouble stopping the Dog.

"That desert never looked better. I'd seen too much water for one day, and enough slow flight to last me a lifetime.

"It only took about one and a half hours to reach the refueling area outbound. I had logged four hours and twenty minutes by the time I shut her off on the line at George. That's the longest four hours I've ever lived through."

There was a big blast at the officers' club that night as Captains Barry and Barr sat around a table covered with tall cool ones. The fighter and the tanker crew posed for pictures on the ramp. Captain Barr wrote the complex story of the save for the *Journal*, George Air Force Base newspaper, and won an award for the "Best News Story" of the year in the Tactical Air Command.

Thirty-five days later Captain Barry was leaping off again, this time over the Atlantic on Fox Able 110, his supersonic smile undimmed.

# 9. Probe and Drogue

Cut off Air-to-Air Refueling and you cut off the legs of TAC— and SAC. Without refueling, neither would have the global range which is the secret of their power to prevent attacks. AAR, as the military calls it, has become as American as hamburger, as vital as blood plasma. An AAR hookup is being made about every two minutes around the clock, around the world. Aerial refueling is one of those developments that are inevitable in the very nature of the airplane. It is only surprising that its adoption as SOP (standard operating procedure) took so long. It was thirty years after the first successful demonstration of aerial refueling that SAC adopted this vital invention and became a giant overnight.

Captain Lowell Smith and Lt. John P. Richter had no thought of giants when they began tinkering with valves and hoses in their open cockpit DeHaviland DH-4s back in 1923 at Rockwell Field, near San Diego, Calif. They only knew that the Spads they flew in World War I conked out for lack of gas after twenty to forty minutes of combat flying.

"I had to fly nine sorties on the day the Saint-Mihiel offensive started," Richter, now a retired colonel, recalls. "We all wished we could refuel somehow without having to return to our bases just when the action got interesting."

It was some six years later, when Richter and Smith were stationed at Rockwell Field, near San Diego, under Maj. H. H. "Hap" Arnold, base commander, that they were able to do something about it. On June 25 they took off in their DH-4BM, pulled up under and behind a sister plane flown by Lts. Virgil Hines and F. W. Seifert, and grabbed a 40-foot rubber hose, reinforced by steel cable, as it was lowered down to them. Within two minutes the hookup was completed—the first refueling in flight by hose in the history of aviation.

It was called a stunt. On August 27 and 28, 1923, the same team broke the world's endurance speed and distance records, staying aloft 37 hours 15 minutes. This, too, was called a stunt. They didn't have to refuel. They weren't going anywhere anyway.

On October 25, 1923, the same team took off from Sumas, Washington, on the Canadian border, and flew to Tia Juana on the Mexican border, 1,200 miles nonstop, to set another new speed and distance record and demonstrate the military value of AAR in dramatic fashion. Refueling planes, one of them flown by Capt. R. G. Ervin and Lt. O. R. McNeel, were based at Eugene, Oregon, and Sacramento, California.

This first refueling was strictly an open-air operation. The begoggled "vendor" sat in the open cockpit of his DH with the hose coiled around his feet. He horsed it over the side by main strength and awkwardness. A steel cable lashed to the rubber hose prevented it from tearing under its own weight. Rubber was soft in those days. The "vendee" reached up into space to seize the whipping hose by the nozzle and held on for dear life while he fed it into a "manifold," or maze of plumbing in his crowded cockpit. Richter got his start as a locomotive test engineer with the Santa Fe Railroad and knew his way around the mess of pumps, tanks, valves, and gauges. He had rigged a hand pump which put pressure on the receiving reservoir mounted behind the rear cockpit and thus forced the gasoline to the plane's gas tanks. He could also receive water, oil, and food by the same aerial special delivery system—which is more than can be done by any modern aerial refueling system.

Richter had installed shutoff valves at both ends of the 40-foot hose, which had to be operated by hand. There was no time to shut off the valves, however, when the two planes in blind formation ran into rough air. Neither pilot could see the other plane. When the "formation" hit a bump, the hose was frequently jerked from the receiver plane, drenching Richter with the raw gasoline. It looked, for a terrible moment, as if they might set themselves on fire. The 90-mile wind of flight, however, was always sufficient to blow the fumes away before they could catch fire.

General Mason M. Patrick, Chief of the Air Service, recognized the military importance of this aerial achievement and officially commended the fliers. In November of the same year another team of pilots tried a similar demonstration at an air show above Kelly Field, Texas. The planes collided, killing the crew of one plane. This was the first of only two fatal accidents charged to aerial refueling on Air Force records. It was also the end of aerial refueling in the U. S. for six long years, although the French experimented with it the same year.

In 1929 Maj. Carl "Tooey" Spaatz, Capt. Ira C. Eaker, and Lts. Elwood "Pete" Quesada and Harry Halverson set out to break the old record. Using almost the identical equipment first employed by Richter and Smith, they circled Los Angeles for 150 hours 40 minutes—a new record—before engine trouble forced them to land. They burned 5,205 gallons of gasoline and 202 gallons of oil, covering 11,000 miles at an average speed of 70 miles an hour.

Necessity on this flight was the mother of one "invention" still used by fast TAC fighters forced to refuel from slow tankers. The trimotored Fokker C-2 monoplane *Question Mark* tended to stall out trying to stay behind and below the slow biplane. As the *Question Mark*'s load increased, the tanker plane had to nose down and increase speed to prevent the *Ques-*

*tion Mark* from stalling and falling off the hose. Recalling the frequent showers of gasoline suffered by Richter and Smith, the crew of the *Question Mark* came equipped with raincoats, storm hats, and rubber boots. They, too, recommended development of a valve at the receiving end of the hose that would automatically close when contact was broken.

The flight of the *Question Mark* started a refueling fad that spread to France, Germany, and England. Civilian pilots joined the race, each outdoing the other until Dale "Red" Jackson and Forest O'Brine in a monoplane named *Greater St. Louis* set the incredible record of 420 hours 21 minutes and 30 seconds, which stands to this day, although all such records are unrecognized by the Federation Aeronautique Internationale. Again, however, the U. S. Army failed to take refueling seriously. It remained for the British to develop Air-to-Air Refueling beyond the "stunt" stage. Squadron Leader Richard Atcherley of the Royal Air Force came to the National Air Races in the United States in 1930, where he saw demonstrations of aerial refueling. He returned to his squadron and by 1932 had patented a Rube Goldberg sort of cable-and-hose method of gravity refueling essentially the same as used by Captain R. W. Kapfhamer from 1948 to '50.

Sir Alan Cobham, a civilian pilot who had pioneered the Empire air routes to Africa, Australia, and India, watched S/L Atcherley's experiments with no idle interest. By 1932 Sir Alan was experimenting with two DeHaviland DH-9s, using a line weighted with a paint can filled with lead shot. The fearless young man in the open cockpit of the receiver plane would reach out and grab the line with the crooked end of a cane, then haul on the line to unreel the hose.

The lead-filled paint can, swinging wildly in rough air, almost proved a lethal weapon. It finally fouled an aileron in flight. Cobham replaced it with a thin rubber bladder filled with water, which burst harmlessly when it struck the receiver. With this rough-and-ready system Sir Alan took off with the first production model Airspeed Courier approved for 3,700 pounds gross weight at takeoff, but 5,050 pounds after being re-fueled in flight. This was Sir Alan's primary interest in refuel-ing. In his years of pioneering around the globe he had acquired many a gray hair as his DH9, groaning under a full weight of fuel, waddled the length of the turf before staggering over the inevitable hedge at the end of the field on takeoff.

Why not take the hazard out of the takeoff, he thought, by leaving the fuel behind, then picking it up in flight after the climb to altitude, when only half power is required for cruising?

The plan worked. Once at cruising altitude, Sir Alan took on a full load of fuel and headed for Malta on the first leg of his projected flight to India. Over Malta he was refueled again, without difficulty. Then, just as he was topping off his load, a pin fell out of his throttle linkage, leaving him with little more than idling power. He managed to glide to land for a gear-up landing.

But Sir Alan didn't give up. He organized Flight Refueling Ltd. in 1934 and continued work on commercial use of inflight refueling. By 1937 the scramble was on to establish transoceanic air routes. Flying boats were the only aircraft with long range and none of them could fly the Atlantic nonstop. Catapulting and piggy-back takeoffs were tried. But air refueling proved the answer. P. R. Allison, one of Cobham's associates, had patented an automatic cutoff valve to prevent fuel spillage. This enabled the company to get an airworthiness certificate on their refuel-ing system. On August 5, 1939, Imperial Airways started a series of sixteen nonstop crossings of the Atlantic from Shannon, Ire-land, to Botwood, New Foundland, refueling twice in flight. About 1000 gallons were passed in 16 minutes. Actual refueling took less than eight minutes, with five minutes for hookup. Despite the complicated cable-and-hose system, commercial air-line refueling was a success. Service between Southampton and New York was assured.

Before this experiment could make its mark on commercial aviation, World War II broke over England. But Flight Refuel-ing Ltd. remained the dominant force in the field. When the

United States entered the war in 1941, the U. S. Army Air Force called on the company to install its equipment in a B-24 tanker plane with a B-17 as a receiver. The Yanks, typically, added a powered reel to do the heavy work of handling the hose. Higher speeds made it impossible to manage by hand. Again the project never got beyond the prototype.

In 1944, the British Air Ministry called on Sir Alan's company to convert 600 Lancaster bombers as tankers and 600 Lincolns as receivers to permit Tiger Force to bomb Japan from Southeast Asia. The company no sooner had its production lines rolling than Uncle Sam offered the British an island base within unrefueled reach of Japan. Then the A-bomb was dropped at Hiroshima and the show was over.

The British Government, however, recognized aerial refueling as commercially practical and financed the only postwar air-line refueling projects on record. Experiments over the English Channel in 1946 showed that air-line pilots could refuel with a minimum of training at altitudes up to 20,000 feet, while flying on course at cruising speed. In 1947 the British made a series of twenty-two crossings between London and Bermuda in converted Lancaster bombers, refueled by Lancaster tankers. Only one flight was not completed—because of engine failure. The tankers were based on the Azores Islands and made their rendezvous with the aid of very high-frequency radio, and the Rebecca radio beacon invented by the British during the war.

Weather was no problem on the Bermuda run. Because of the success of the Bermuda trials, the British decided to experiment on the stormy North Atlantic route from London to Montreal. British Overseas Airways Corp. modified a Liberator 2 as a receiver, and Flight Refuelling Ltd. bought four Lancastrians for tankers, basing them at Shannon, Ireland, and at Gander, Newfoundland, and Goose Bay in Labrador. Fifteen flights were made, with two inflight refuelings on the westbound flight against the prevailing winds and one on the return flight, helped by tail winds. One refueling was 500 to 600 miles west of Shannon, the other about 100 miles out of Gander westbound. One refueling about 200 miles east of Gander gave the Liberator a full fuel load for the eastbound flight. Although the trials were conducted in the worst weather of the winter, between February and May, of 1948, only three refueling contacts failed, none of them due to the refueling equipment. No paying passengers were carried on any of these trials, but scores of observers, technicians, and press people made the flights.

The British Government was impressed with the commercial advantages of refueling, but did nothing further about it. By this time, however, the United States Air Force was convinced. Twenty-five years after American pilots had proved refueling in flight was possible, the Strategic Air Command decided it was necessary if SAC bombers were to be able to reach any target anywhere in the world. A B-29 was sent to Flight Refuelling Ltd. for conversion as a loop hose tanker. Equipment was ordered to convert 100 B-29s as receivers and 60 B-29s as tankers. Boeing Airplane Co. was given the contract to install the equipment. At the same time, in October, 1947, Wright Field was ordered to develop an American refueling system, based on the British system—and just in time. This was at the height of the competition between the Air Force and the Navy for custody of the A-bomb.

Events moved faster than the Air Force anticipated. Wright Field's system wasn't ready for testing when, on March 24, 1948, the word was flashed that refueling had to be demonstrated within three days. The next day Lt. Col. Walter P. Maiersperger, of the directorate of Research and Development, headquarters USAF, and his crew reported to Boeing's plant at Wichita. The B-29 tanker and receiver took off Sunday afternoon and, after 52 minutes of fishing with cable and hose, managed to make a hookup and transfer 440 gallons of antifreeze. The test didn't set any records, but it convinced Congress. During congressional hearings the next week, the Air Force was given the prime responsibility for delivery of the A-bomb. Refueling would give SAC unlimited range, the Air Force contended. To prove this point, the *Lucky Lady II,* a Boeing B-50, girdled the globe in

February, 1949, refueling four times in flight. She covered 23,-108 miles in 94 hours 1 minute. Taking off from Carswell AFB, Texas, February 26, 1949, she flew 3,800 miles to the Azores, refueled; flew 5,200 miles to Dhahran, refueled; flew 4,900 miles to the Philippines, refueled; then to Hawaii, 5,300 miles, for the final refueling, landing back at Carswell on March 2, 1949.

While the glorified fishing tackle invented and built by the British worked well enough as an interim measure, it was not satisfactory at speeds of 190 miles an hour, which was minimum for the heavy B-29s and B-50s. And the cable and hose couldn't be used in one-man fighter planes. Here, SAC and TAC took separate paths. At the time the Air Force ordered Flight Refuelling Ltd. equipment, a contract was signed with Boeing for design of a better system. The result was the flying boom, now standard equipment on all SAC tankers. Heavy aluminum pipes mounted in the rear of KC-135 jet tankers can be flown into place in the receptacle of the jet bombers by means of a pair of wings activated by the slipstream, or wind of flight. More fuel can be transferred faster and at higher flying speeds. The system has some disadvantages, especially in rough air, due to the rigidity of the boom. The pipes can telescope like a trombone, but can't bend like a hose. Only one boom can be mounted on an airplane. Only one plane can be refueled at a time.

The first Boeing flying boom equipment was in operation by 1949. But by the end of 1948 the Air Force had asked Sir Alan Cobham's Flight Refuelling company to come up with a better system for fighters. Sir Alan was already thinking along these lines and by early 1949 had developed the first probe and drogue installation, although the origin of the idea is still a mystery. The Air Force sent two B-29s to England, one to be fitted with a probe mounted above the cockpit, the other to be fitted with hose reels in the tail and a reel pod under each wing tip. Two F-84s were fitted with probes on the left wing for the test program. Meantime, to prove the probe and drogue system, Flight Refuelling Ltd. on August 7, 1949, set a new endurance record for one-man jet aircraft, keeping its Meteor 3 aloft for 12 hours and 3 minutes, with 10 refueling contacts.

It was a brilliant World War II fighter ace who tipped the scales toward the probe and drogue system which ultimately gave TAC's one-man, one-engined fighters a reach almost as long as SAC's bombers. Colonel Dave Schilling, commander of the 56th Group, Selfridge Field, Mich., took the 61st Squadron to Europe in 1949, immediately after its conversion from propeller-bound F-51s, to F-80s, the first jet fighters. Colonel Schilling, after an outstanding career as a pilot and officer, was later killed in an auto accident. With him on this first whirlwind tour of Europe was Lt. Col. W. D. Ritchie, now a colonel, commander of the 31st Tactical Fighter Wing at George AFB.

The tour was intended as a show of force to impress our European Allies with the might of our modern jet air force. But the flight was no faster with jets than with propeller planes. There was only one way to get there—island-hopping from Presque Isle, Maine, and Goose Bay, Labrador; across Davis Straits to stormy Bluie West-1, Greenland, then Iceland and Prestwick, Scotland, waiting out storms for days en route. Then the whole uncertain process had to be repeated on the return trip.

"We could see that wasn't the way to do it," Colonel Ritchie recalls. "We figured there had to be a better way if we were to get jet performance out of jet fighters."

Upon their return, Colonel Schilling was transferred to the Pentagon and was sent to England where he saw Sir Alan's probe and drogue system of inflight refueling. He wrote a report recommending that the possibilities of this fast, flexible system be investigated immediately for Uncle Sam's new jet fighters. He and Colonel Ritchie were placed on loan to the director of research, assistant chief of staff for development, and told to investigate. Colonel Schilling ferried one of two F-84Es to England for modification and went to work.

The British had been using just one drogue on a tanker. It was Colonel Schilling's idea to refuel three planes simultaneously from a single tanker. The British had been using a valve in the probe of their receiver planes which permitted gasoline to spill onto the planes' canopy when contact was made or broken. Colonel Schilling spurred them to devise a hydraulic valve in the probe which would be closed at all times except during refueling, when the receiver pilot would hold it open by a switch on his control stick. This valve worked fine during a dozen test flights at many altitudes and for times as long as seven hours, but it nearly cost Colonel Ritchie his life later.

By September, 1950, Colonels Schilling and Ritchie were ready for the final test. Up to now all refueling had been in fine weather within sight of an emergency field. On September 22, 1950, the two eager young colonels took off from Manston, England, for the final test—Fox Able 4, the first nonstop jet fighter flight across the Atlantic, refueling en route.

The first refueling, from a Lancaster just off Prestwick, Scotland, was duck soup. The Lancs were able to hold 220 miles an hour for the hookup, which was a comfortable speed for the F-84 with partial flaps. The probe was set midway of the left wing, a little higher and a little further forward than the probe of the F-100Ds. It took only about ten minutes to make contact and fill the two 230-gallon external tip tanks and the internal tanks. A full drink was good for 1,300 to 1,400 nautical miles under no-wind conditions at the Hog's cruising speed of 450 knots, 518 miles an hour. The second hookup out of Keflavik, Iceland, was routine. Both pilots got a full load. The weather was fair. Trouble was brewing, but neither pilot was aware of it until they had skirted the nightmare tip of Greenland, where great glaciers slice deep cuts in the black primordial rock of the mountains, and were well on their way across the icy waters of Davis Strait, where no aviator has ever survived a bailout. There, near Ocean Station Baker, they met the lone B-29 that had been converted as a tanker with a single drogue and stationed at Bluie West-1, terror of ferry pilots, for the flight.

Colonel Schilling had to make the first hookup, and fast. Just beyond the Point of No Return for Greenland he had found that one tank was not feeding. He was down to a few minutes of fuel in the other main tank when he met the tanker. Colonel Schilling took on just enough fuel to be able to make Goose Bay, if necessary, then backed off to let Colonel Ritchie take on his load. Colonel Ritchie had no trouble ramming his probe home into the metal funnel of the drogue on the first pass. He pressed the trigger switch on the control stick that should have opened the valve in his probe, and hung on, flying tight formation with the limber hose. But nothing happened. The gas gauges showed no fuel coming aboard.

He backed off and tried again. Still no fuel. He tried opening his valve first and making smart contact with the drogue with his valve open. Still no fuel. There was nothing that could be done. It was months later before Air Force engineers discovered that the long steel stem on the fuel valve contracted with the cold and jammed after prolonged exposure to low temperatures at high altitudes. The valve was rebuilt.

Colonel Ritchie had quit thinking about the valve by this time. He hung on to the tanker until the last minute, then dropped off to let Colonel Schilling hook up and get his full load, which he did without difficulty. Colonel Ritchie was almost over Cape Harrison at 36,000 feet when his engine finally flamed out. But he could see nothing but a great white waste of clouds below him. Northwest Territory, mother of storms, had whipped up a dilly to compound his other problems. Overcast extended up to 34,000 feet. He had no sooner established a glide and shut off his dead engine than he was swallowed up by icy clouds as thick as ice cream.

Flying on instruments with one hand, he began to clean house with the other in preparation for bailout. While his battery lasted he sent out May Day messages on his radio. Colonel Schilling was still hanging on to the tanker high overhead, unable to follow him down for lack of fuel even if he could have stuck with him in clouds which got blacker and blacker as the ghostly F-84 lost altitude.

"I figured out later I must have glided a hundred and twenty-five miles on instruments," Colonel Ritchie recalls. "I was in solid overcast from thirty-four thousand feet down to twelve thousand feet. Then I broke out over a good-sized lake. I turned toward shore and held on until I hit three thousand feet. Then I punched out.

"Everything worked by the book. There I was hanging in the harness with a comfortable spread of canopy overhead and a lot of cold water coming up fast below. I pulled on the shroud lines to steer me away from the lake.

"Next thing I knew I was hanging about six feet off the ground. My parachute canopy was hung up on three scrubby trees. I could see the plane hit about in the middle of the lake. It didn't take me long to get down from there, but it took the search party from the base quite a while to find me. They searched the lake first, thinking I had gone into the water. It took me a while to find my way through the timber to the shore of the lake. It was about two hours before they finally spotted me.

"It was getting dark by this time, but the base chopper managed to land on the lake shore and pick me up. I was wearing an orange poopy suit, which helped make me visible, although it wasn't good for much else. I was only nineteen miles from Goose Bay air base.

"I was on my way to New York the next day in a KB-29. I got there about as fast as Dave did. He had to land at Bangor, Maine, when the weather at New York deteriorated. He logged ten hours and thirty minutes. I only got eight hours and twenty minutes. I guess legally I should have logged about fourteen minutes of glider time, too.

"My plane was never recovered, but Dave's plane was sent to Wright-Pat for tests, which revealed the valve stem was the cause of the trouble."

The faulty valve was easily redesigned and gave no further trouble. Colonels Schilling and Ritchie had proved that one-man fighters could span the oceans, and the continents, with the aid of aerial refueling by probe and drogue. They could keep up with the long-legged bombers. Refueling gave SAC's bombers truly global-range, enabling them to reach the very heartland of Russia, or any aggressor anywhere around the world. World War II had shown the necessity for fighters to protect the bombers from enemy attack. SAC had, therefore, insisted on her own fighter force, to protect her bombers. But the advent of nuclear weapons doomed big bomber formations like those of World War II, each of which filled a square mile of airspace and could be destroyed by a single atomic bomb. Bombers would have to resort to lone wolf tactics, attacking singly from different directions and altitudes. Fighter escort was no longer needed. As early as 1952 this evolution was under way. By 1957 SAC's fighter squadrons were being dissolved.

Colonels Schilling and Ritchie had proved the value of the British probe and drogue system of refueling. But SAC, whose primary weapon was bombers, stuck to the flying boom, which was designed especially for bombers, although some experiments with probe and drogue refueling of B-47 bombers were conducted. SAC's F-84s were equipped with receptacles in the right wing for use with the flying boom.

Fox Able 4, the first fighter crossing of the Atlantic, had come at a time when Red forces in Korea were pushing South Korean and United Nations forces into the sea. Refueling was not needed. The Reds made the mistake of striking in a part of the world where the United States had plenty of fighter planes ready and waiting. Within three hours after the order was given, U. S. F-86s were over the front lines in Korea. Within a few days they had cleared the skies of Red aircraft. But refueling would have solved the problems of bringing up reinforcements as the war progressed. New fighter wings ordered to duty in Korea had to be freighted aboard Navy aircraft carriers, a two- or three-week trip for the aircraft, two or three months for supplies and men who came by cargo and passenger vessels.

The British continued development of the probe and drogue system, however. During the Korean conflict the Royal Air Force fitted its Meteor 8s of the 245th Squadron at Horsham St. Faith, England, with probes mounted in the nose, for aerial patrol over England. Six Meteors were used, two on patrol, two refueling from tankers well inland, and two en route at all times. The Meteor, with less than two hours normal endurance, could thus patrol for four hours at a time. The experiment provided practical experience under operational conditions in the field in fair weather and foul, by moonlight and in total darkness.

Meantime, back in Korea, the Air Force by January, 1952, had decided to give the probe and drogue system a full-scale operational test under combat and semicombat conditions. The F-84Es of the 116th Fighter-Bomber Wing were fitted with probes jutting from and feeding directly into the wing tip tanks. Nine KB-29 tankers were equipped with hoses on tail and wing tips. It took more than two months to train 70 pilots who had never seen an aerial refueling. Refueling was then attempted, still over Japan, on a squadron and wing scale. Failures ran about 35 per cent, due to low pilot proficiency as well as mechanical failures.

Five combat missions were finally flown—one combat air patrol over Japan, and four strikes against Korean targets from Japanese bases. Refueling was tried on the inbound leg, on the return leg, and on both legs of the flights. The combat missions showed the need for a single probe from which all tanks could be refueled. The F-84 system required two hookups, one for each wing tank, and did not add enough range to make the operation worth while, since only the tip tanks could be refueled.

Aerial refueling was not vital in Korea so long as the fighter bases could follow the shifting front—and as long as the UN forces controlled the air. But Gen. O. P. Weyland, commander of the Far East Air Force and the most experienced air general in service at the time, foresaw the possibility of loss of Korean bases, either through massive Russian intervention in the air or Chinese intervention on the ground. His experiments were designed to develop a system of effective air operations from bases in Japan.

The first use of aerial refueling in actual combat also set a new endurance record for single-engined, one-place jet fighters. Lt. Col. Harry W. Dorris, Jr., project officer in the FEAF Probe and Drogue Inflight Refueling Project, flew five combat missions in 14 hours and 15 minutes aloft without a landing. He refueled six times in flight in all kinds of weather, by day and night, without ever breaking radio silence.

He took off from Yokota, Japan at 0510 September 28, 1951, with two 500-pound general-purpose bombs, four 5-inch high-velocity air rockets and a load of 50 caliber ammunition for his machine guns. His F-80 Shooting Star, Uncle Sam's first operational jet fighter, was equipped with two 265-gallon fuel tanks, one on each wing tip. Each was equipped with a probe welded direct to the tank. His call sign was "Jungle Jim" over North Korea and "Play Boy" over South Korea. The tanker's call sign was, appropriately, "Bartender."

Colonel Dorris met his tanker, a B-29 with a single hose and drogue in the tail, over Komatsu, Japan, at 15,000 feet, refueled on course, then flew formation with the tanker for 150 miles and topped off his tanks en route to his first target. Clouds up to 20,-000 feet hid the first target at Kilchu in North Korea, but Dorris let down through the overcast, accumulating a heavy load of rime ice, found an opening, hit the deck and continued the attack under a 1,200-foot overcast and light rain. On the first pass he popped both bombs through the second-floor windows of a four-story building housing enemy supplies and saw it go up in smoke before climbing back to 25,000 feet through the overcast, en route to Wonsan, his second refueling rendezvous.

The weather was too rough for refueling here or at the second alternate 40 miles south, but fighter and tanker finally got together at 15,000 feet without breaking radio silence.

Refueling on course, Dorris found a supply dump on the Onjin Peninsula and salvoed his rocket into a building and stacked supplies. Next he strafed a troop bivouac area near Yangdok in Central Korea.

The weather got no better. Each refueling was a game of hide and seek with clouds and rain. Planned targets were hidden by low clouds or thunderstorms, but Colonel Dorris flew weather reconnaissance instead at the request of the Air Control Center, from Seoul to Pyongyang to Wonsan to Chorwon. He had planned the mission at a time when a storm from the north would ground Red Korean fighters.

The last refueling was at night, but Colonel Dorris had no trouble hooking up. He arrived over his home field of Yokota with excess fuel, which he had to burn off at low altitude before landing.

Colonel Dorris didn't report any trouble staying awake on his busy mission, although he got only two and a half hours sleep before takeoff. For one thing, he was too uncomfortable. His old-style seat pack parachute harness "made a deep impression on my posterior" he noted in his official report.

The Mae West life vest, worn on all flights over water, drove him mad. "This became unbearable after five hours and was taken off," he reported. "It hangs around the neck and cuts off circulation . . . causing extreme fatigue."

The helmet in use at that time also cut the back of his neck as he twisted his head to look to the rear for enemy fighters. Luckily he never encountered one. He was flying alone.

Only on the last leg of the flight from Korea back to Japan did Colonel Dorris relax and feel a tendency to doze. Then he was rudely awakened when a Russian broadcast station started jamming the radio station on which Dorris was hopefully homing.

He had one turkey sandwich and four candy bars to eat and a canteen and a half of water to drink. His most unpleasant experience was with the plumbing. The F-80 had a relief tube, but it proved to be stopped up. So was Colonel Dorris when he finally landed.

The flight proved the value of inflight refueling under the most adverse combat conditions even with the underpowered, overloaded F-80.

The test came just in time to be decisive in the debate over boom versus probe and drogue refueling. It also answered critics who said no pilot could stand 14 hours in the cockpit of a jet fighter.

Colonel Dorris is retired now and heads his own aviation consultant firm in Crystal Lake, Illinois.

While refueling played no appreciable part in the Korean conflict, it was finally being adopted as an essential element of both fighter and bomber operations. Fox Peter One (Fighters-Pacific, number one), the first mass movement of jet fighters overseas in July, 1952, marked the coming-of-age of aerial refueling. The 31st Fighter Escort Wing of the Strategic Air Command from Turner Air Force Base, Georgia, equipped with Republic F-84G fighters, first to be factory-equipped for aerial refueling, took off from Albany, Ga., for the Far East, refueling over the Southwest U. S. and again over the Pacific. The 27th Fighter Escort Wing followed in October, 1952.

The first mass movement of fighters over the Atlantic was Operation Longstride. Taking off from Turner AFB, the 508th Fighter Escort Wing flew 4,485 miles nonstop to Lakenheath, England, refueling three times en route and setting a new record for the longest nonstop mass movement of fighters in history over the greatest distance. In the same month, August 21, 1952, the 31st Fighter Escort Wing flew 4,470 miles from Turner AFB to Nouasseur in French Morocco, in 10 hours 21 minutes, with two refuelings en route. Boeing propeller driven KC-97 tankers with flying booms provided refueling.

The Tactical Air Command had been trying officially ever since 1949 to get funds to develop inflight refueling, using the probe and drogue, which was and is preferred by fighter pilots of all services, including the Navy, which officially adopted the system for its special uses. TAC asked that probes be built into the B-66 twin jet reconnaissance bomber and the F-100 and be added to the F-86F. When General Weyland returned to take over TAC on May 1, 1954, TAC had finally acquired two squadrons of B-29 tankers equipped with booms. Only a few F-84Fs were equipped as receivers for aerial refueling. And of these SAC leftovers only the 405th Fighter Bomber Wing was operational, because of lack of communications with the tankers. Attempts to deploy the 388th and 21st Fighter Bomber Wings to Europe in December, 1954, took 72 days. Up to 30 per cent of refueling attempts failed.

General Weyland, with the lessons of Korea still burning in his mind, gave first attention to refueling. He wanted KC-135 jet tankers like those ordered for SAC. His second choice was the fast high-flying C-130 turboprop transport. But he had to settled for the warmed-over B-50 bomber converted to a tanker. This plane had range and could carry the load, but couldn't reach the speeds or altitudes required for safe, efficient refueling of jet fighters.

The first F-84Fs were received by TAC May 12, 1954. By July the first KB-29 Aerial Refueling Squadron had been activated at Langley AFB, Va., TAC headquarters. It was July, 1956, before the first KB-50 tankers with probe and drogue were delivered to Langley; April 9, 1957, before the first KB-50J, with jet engines added under each wing, made its first flight; and January 16, 1959, before the first KB-50J was delivered to TAC. TAC had been promised the KC-135 jet tanker, but none had been received and no delivery date had been set by late 1961.

Refueling had become big business by 1957 and got bigger every year. About 439 F-84s of the Strategic Air Command crossed the oceans between 1952 and 1955, refueling in flight but not always crossing nonstop. The round trip represented 878 crossings. Between 1955 and 1960, inclusive, jet fighters of the Tactical Air Command made about 3,100 crossings. Another 2,100 one-way crossings were made by TAC pilots delivering fighters to U. S. units abroad, bringing the total crossings of the oceans by TAC jet fighters to more than 5,200, a total, including SAC fighters, of more than 6000 crossings.

To show what her supersonic fighters could do with the aid of jet tankers, TAC borrowed a KC-135 tanker from SAC November 26, 1956, and raced the sun from the East Coast to the West Coast, and west to east in Operation Sun Run with a twin-jet F-101 Voodoo fighter-bomber. This reconnaissance plane was then the holder of the world's speed record of 1,201 miles an hour. The fast jet, able to refuel at its best operating altitude—30,000 feet and above—from a jet tanker capable of cruising at twice the top refueling speed of the KB-50, made the dash from east to west in 3 hours 34 minutes and from west to east in 3 hours 5 minutes, a total of 6 hours 42 minutes, non-stop.

Incidentally, the versatile F-101 set another record when ten of the Voodoos set a distance record for a formation flight of 5,953 miles from Austin, Texas, nonstop to Brentwood, England. A lone F-101 flew nonstop from Bergstrom Air Force Base, Texas, to England—6,100 miles in 11 hours 2 minutes on August 23, 1958.

The KC-135 jet tanker would be more than a mere flying filling station. It would be a working member of the TAC team, a command and navigation plane that could take off with the fighters, provide them with multiple navigation service and powerful radio communications of various kinds. It would no longer be necessary to position slow prop-driven tankers at refueling bases far afield in advance of a movement. This factor alone would cut twelve to twenty-four hours off the speed with which a mobile strike force could be launched in case of attack against our allies abroad. The tanker, flying at the same altitude and airspeeds as the fighters, could refuel each in turn without slowing down or descending to the lower altitudes required with KB-50s. This in itself would save not only time, but the fuel required to hang on to the tanker at low altitudes and low airspeeds, plus the additional fuel required to climb back up to jet cruising altitudes.

This "air fleet" system is still TAC's plan for the future, especially with the receipt of the heavier, faster, longer-range Republic F-105. In the more distant future, 1965 and beyond, the FX fighter, now on the drawing boards, will be able to fly the Atlantic without refueling. It will have to be refueled on non-stop crossings of the bigger, tougher Pacific, however.

# 10. Double Trouble

Remember Lebanon?

How could we be forgetting? The fate of nations, the peace of the world, rested in the hands of a few dedicated men that day in July. The future trembled in the balance for many tense hours. It was one of the great gambles of history. Uncle Sam stuck his head in the mouth of the Bear That Walks Like a Man.

"When did you decide we had won the toss?" newsmen asked Maj. Gen. Henry Viccellio.

"When I woke next morning and saw the base had not vanished in a ball of fire," said the commander of TAC's Strike Force in this historic action.

That was the day TAC came of age. After years of trial and error, field tests and exercises, false alarms and empty alerts, TAC had struck with a real Strike Force in a real crisis. And the boy had become a man.

The test could hardly have come at a worse time. The weather over the Atlantic wasn't fit for man nor beast. The route was untried. Plans had to be changed by the minute as the situation changed. But TAC's Tigers bored on to help make history with the fastest flight over the greatest distance ever made under "for-real" conditions.

The movement order called it Operation Double Trouble. And the fates couldn't have chosen a better name. The planners meant "When there's trouble we get there on the double." But the troubles that led up to the Lebanon crisis of July 15, 1958, smacked more of the incantations of Macbeth's witches.

The witches' brew that boiled over on that July of 1958 began to boil generations ago, fired by Russia's lust for the oil of the Middle East, Communist drives for world conquest, and the rising tide of Arab nationalism. Throughout the troubled year the pro-Western governments of Iraq and Lebanon fought off plots, invasions and rebellions fostered openly or covertly by Gamal Abdel Nasser of Egypt and the Communists.

The assassination of Nassib Metna, editor of a pro-Communist newspaper in Beirut on May 8, 1958, brought widespread rioting in Lebanon. United Arab Republic and Communist broadcasts from Cairo, Egypt, and Damascus, Syria, incited the Lebanese to revolt against President Camille Chamoun, his premier, Sami-es-Solh, and their government. UAR and Communist agents joined forces to exploit the friction between Lebanese Moslems and Christians, growing out of a move to amend the constitution to permit Chamoun, a Maronite Catholic, to be re-elected for a second term as president. Hundreds of armed Syrians invaded Lebanon to join rebels in armed clashes against government forces.

Lebanon formally charged the UAR with instigating and aiding a rebellion and appealed to the U. S. for aid. Our State Department announced May 14 that small arms, ammunition, tear gas and gas masks were being sent to aid the Lebanese police. The U. S. Navy announced it would double the amphibious Marine strength of the 6th Fleet and transfer units to the Eastern Mediterranean. Lebanon, on May 21, also appealed to the United Nations Security Council to halt the UAR intervention into Lebanese affairs, but the Council adjourned without acting on the request.

Tiny Lebanon had reason to fear the United Arab Republic. When Iraq had joined with Jordan to form the opposition Arab

Union, February 14, 1958, Nasser had threatened that the rival Arabs would be "scattered like dried leaves before the wind."

On July 14 the "leaves" were "scattered." Brigadier General Abdul Karim el-Kassem led a revolt against the pro-Western monarchy of King Faisal II of Iraq, killing the king, the crown prince and the premier, Nuri as-Said. Within a few hours the new government had joined Nasser's United Arab Republic.

Lebanon was already overrun with rebel bands, up to the outskirts of the capital city of Beirut and the perimeters of the capital's airport. President Camille Chamoun appealed to the U. S. and the United Nations for help. The Middle East was ready to burst into flame.

President Dwight Eisenhower turned in a box alarm for the fire department—the Tactical Air Command. He ordered the U. S. Navy and the Marines to start moving. They made the headlines. But TAC, too, made history. TAC's CASF crossed the Atlantic and raced the length of the Mediterranean nonstop. Seventeen hours later the first TAC units were in place, their atomic lightning aimed at the soft underbelly of the Red fortress. That story, cloaked in military secrecy, remained untold. But there were no restrictions on the Marines. Accounts of their peaceful landing and peaceful occupation of the country, without a shot being fired by U. S. soldiers or a soldier wounded by the elusive enemy, were broadcast in press, radio and television around the world. The story of TAC's pilots, who flew 2,400 sorties without firing a shot in anger—while suffering scores of scars from enemy fire—was never told.

TAC, the silent service, knew it had won its spurs, however. So did skeptics in other branches of the service and in the Government. TAC's response to that box alarm far exceeded even its own expectations.

General Weyland was conducting a briefing that hot morning of July 15, 1958. This was a chore not usually undertaken by TAC's commanding general. But TAC's guest this morning was Etem Menderes, Turkey's Minister of Defense, a relative of Adnan Menderes, Turkey's premier. At 0930 the bell rang. General

Weyland excused himself. It was Gen. Thomas D. White, chief of staff, on the hot line from Washington, D. C. His order was brief: "Trouble in the Middle East. Get there, fast."

General Weyland picked up another phone, the hot line to 19th Air Force: "Activate Operation Double Trouble," he ordered.

Then he returned to resume his briefing. He had been telling Minister of Defense Menderes how a CASF would be deployed to his country in case of emergency. Now, he realized, the emergency had come. The machinery of the CASF was already getting into gear. Turkey's Incirlik Air Base at Adana on the plains of Taurus, just fifteen minutes away from Lebanon by jet, was to be its destination. Here supplies, munitions, equipment and a U. S. "housekeeping force" had been quietly laid down by advance agreement between Turkey and the U. S.

The word spread throughout TAC with the speed of radio. Pilots and airmen of the 354th Tactical Fighter Wing, enjoying their first day off in weeks at Myrtle Beach, saw an Air Police car come racing to the edge of the sand. They rose as a man, kissed the kids good-by and headed for the base. An hour later some of them were in preflight briefings. A reconnaissance jet pilot got the word over California and nearly set a new speed record hitting the assembly base. There the plane, with a fresh pilot hopped off to join the CASF. TAC Troop Carrier planes all over the world got the word in the air, changed course and joined the movement. One crew, flying a load of Very Important People, was contacted over Chicago, made a steep descent and landing, opened the rear doors, unceremoniously deposited the VIP's onto the ramp and rolled off, propellers still whining.

At Langley Air Force Base, TAC headquarters, the B-57 Canberra twin-jet bombers of the 345th Bomb Wing were in the final phases of Operation Swordfish, an operational readiness test —a sort of final exam given to every unit every year. Suddenly they were told they were no longer flying Swordfish missions. Instead they were to island-hop to Adana, Turkey, a base they had never heard of. Even the few top commanders who had need to know about Incirlik Air Base never mentioned the word. The pilots looked at each other and grinned. These inspectors pulled some dillies in their mock war games, but this one was for the bunnies. Many a pilot was well on his way over the Big Water before he was sure that this time it was for real.

Well they might be fooled. No exercise had ever been conducted over that route. No TAC unit had been permitted to test the plans so carefully drawn by General Vic's 19th Air Force staff. Ironically, the exercise scheduled for that very week had been canceled at top government levels because the situation in the Middle East was so critical that any movement of aircraft in strength might aggravate the tangled political situation. Only after repeated pleas had General Weyland obtained permission to put out the tankers which are the key to any overseas movement. The jets can't move until the tankers are in place at Bermuda and the Azores. And not all of these were equipped with auxiliary jet engines. Without this extra thrust they could not carry a maximum load of fuel, which in turn tended to cut down their range and endurance, as well as their ceiling and their speed on the refueling run itself. While Task Force Bravo was under way, plans had to be changed because Morocco and Greece refused permission for flights over their territory.

Night refueling had just been introduced operationally. Not all crews were checked out in night refueling and few had much experience in this most exacting of pilot skills.

"But we really decided this was for keeps," one fighter pilot said, "when we took a look at the weather map at briefing time. Even the big boys wouldn't have given the map a second glance if this hadn't been a cut-the-mustard deal."

To able, vocal Lt. Devol "Rocky" Brett, commander of the 355th Tactical Fighter Squadron, Myrtle Beach AFB, fell the lot of leading the spearhead flight that would make TAC history. None of his squadron had flown the Atlantic nonstop, although some had island-hopped. But all had been checked out on refueling, including a little practice in night refueling. They had just been converted from a Day Fighter Squadron to Tactical Fighters. This was the new squadron's first mission.

Colonel Brett got the green light at approximately 0945 that sunny Tuesday morning. About half of his squadron pilots were standing by on the line for local training flights. The word went out to round up the rest. By 10:30 the chosen pilots were busy finding maps for the 6,400-mile flight, piecing them together, drawing in their routes, figuring speeds, altitudes and fuel, making out their Form 21a navigation logs; assembling their flight gear, and checking their emergency kits. Those who weren't flying drove home to break the word to squadron wives and help pack B-4 bags for an indefinite TDY.

"We couldn't give any clue to where we were going. Everything was classified," Colonel Brett recalled. "But you don't have to tell a TAC wife. They told us. They had been listening to the radio. They knew there was shooting in Lebanon. They knew our job was to stop the shooting."

By 1400 hours Col. Brett's Resort Alfa flight, first wave of the TAC Strike Force, was receiving its go pills in the final briefing. By 1550 the simmering quiet of the hot summer day was torn by the volcanic breath of three flights of four F-100s taking off in tight formation in the turbulent air, 12 tense Tigers all in a hurry. The boss had pushed the panic button and they were raring to go.

Trailing black smoke, each flight of four disappeared in the shimmering mists to the east, climbing steeply on a northeast course. They were nearing their cruising altitude of 30,000 feet as they departed their last point of land, Cape Fear, on a northeasterly course that would take them to Northbank, the first refueling rendezvous, north of Bermuda. At the end of the first hour Colonel Brett managed to contact Duckbutt Charlie Alfa, a C-54 orbiting far below, and got a corrected heading to Northbank. The sun still shone, winds were as forecast. All was copacetic.

Another hour passed. Northbank lay dead ahead. So did a line of towering thunderstorms. The sun was sinking fast behind

Colonel Brett and his 12 Tigers. Now one of the wingmen sounded the tallyho. There was a speck on the horizon, two, three. Where were the rest? The briefing had called for six tankers, one for every two Dogs, so no one would have to fight the tail hose for refueling and there would be plenty of go-juice for all.

But Resort Alfa had run into one of the snafus inevitable in unrehearsed response to all-out orders in an emergency situation. Under the panic pressure of Double Trouble, the fighters and tankers were fifty-two minutes apart in their rendezvous time. The tankers, orbiting on station at maximum range from their home bases, had begun to run out of fuel for their own hungry engines. Gradually one and then another had had to cut and run for home base, leaving only three slow B-50s, and they had turned on course early and were well east and north of the expected hookup point when the fighters finally made contact. By this time all were hurting for fuel. Then troubles began to magnify.

"We managed to get hooked up, three to a tanker, in the clear. Then the tankers bored right into a wall of thunderstorms. They couldn't climb above them. The formation broke up, tankers turning this way and that trying to get out of the turbulent black clouds," Colonel Brett recalls.

The detailed story of the crossing from there on has never been pieced together entirely. Some tankers headed north, some south, some stayed on course. The formation was scattered into two and threes and "loners." The fighter jocks had no idea which way to head when they came off the tankers. About half never did get a full fuel load.

Lts. Shelby Evans and Sidney Ragsdale got a little fuel from the first tanker they contacted, but not much. Lt. Raymond C. Morgan couldn't get a drop for some reason that will never be known. Their tanker was getting low on fuel itself and had to turn back for Bermuda. Evans and Ragsdale headed for their briefed alternate in Nova Scotia. As they got within radio range of the coast they found this field had socked in. But Stargazer,

the coastal radar net, picked them up and vectored them to
Greenwood, an RCAF air base, where they managed to make an
instrument letdown and find the runway under rapidly lowering
clouds.

Lieutenant Morgan, who hadn't got a drop of fuel from the
tankers, was sucking fumes by this time. He, too, had headed
for the briefed alternate field in Nova Scotia, only to learn it
was socked in after he had burned precious fuel heading north.
He, too, was vectored toward Greenwood by Stargazer. By this
time he figured he'd had it. The gauges showed only 600 . . 500
. . 400 pounds of fuel left in the main tank. At 300 pounds—a
scant 50 gallons of kerosene—Lieutenant Morgan stopcocked
the engine and went into a glide from about 40,000 feet.

He was still off the coast, but from that altitude estimated
he could glide 125 miles or more. It was dark now and even the
black Atlantic was hidden by a woolly undercast. Then fate re-
lented for a split second. Morgan spotted a dark hole in the
overcast through which he thought he saw lights. Lights meant
land.

Quickly he hit the air start button, fired up the dead engine
and took off for what proved to be a sure-enough hole in the
clouds. That 50 gallons of fuel, just enough to keep the tank
wet, was all he needed. Once sure he was over land Morgan
tucked in his heels, elbows and chin, and pulled the next-of-kin
triggers. In another second he was spinning through space, revived by the raw air of the Nova Scotia coast. He came down
in the brush unhurt. He made his way through the dark of night
to the beach, where he found an abandoned rowboat which
gave him shelter for the night. In the morning he found a logging road and followed it to a logging camp.

Three were down. Nine TAC Tigers still bored through the
night, wallowing in thunderstorm turbulence somewhere north
of Bermuda. But where?

"When I finally came off the tanker I had two chicks with
me. Three of us left out of twelve. That's all I ever saw until I
got to Lajes," Colonel Brett recalls.

"That was a long night. I was down to a few minutes' fuel when we spotted the tankers at Camp Hobo, the second refueling rendezvous, off the Azores. I took on some fuel, then we ran into extreme turbulence. My tanker was having plenty of trouble. I wasn't getting any more fuel. Finally he couldn't even contact me any more on the radio. So I broke off and took up the heading the tanker was holding. I just hoped to Hell that was the heading to Lajes. There wasn't any way to find out. And I didn't have enough fuel to go on.

"It was about an hour—an interminable hour—before I began to pick up weak signals from Lajes radio on my receiver. I didn't have the faintest idea where we were by that time. The Atlantic is a mighty big ocean, you know, and when you're refueling and the tankers are twisting and dodging this way and that you have no idea where you are, where you've been or where you are going, until the tanker navigator gives you a steer when you drop off. And we never got a steer.

"As the signals from Azores VOR [omnirange] grew stronger I finally figured we were somewhere east, between Lajes and Spain. We turned west and began counting the clicks as the fuel gauges spun around.

"Well, we finally came over Lajes VOR, but the islands were blanketed by their usual bank of clouds. We had to make individual letdowns and come in under about an eight hundred-foot ceiling. One of my planes didn't have any radio transmitter left. But he could receive the VOR and his bird dog [ADF, automatic direction-finding radio] was working. Both wingmen got in all right. I went out and made a sneaky letdown and crept in under the stuff and managed to set my Dog down on the runway."

In the storm, Lts. Clyde Garner and Anthony "Zeke" Zielinski were still lost and alone. Each had dropped off his tanker in the thunderstorm turbulence of the first refueling without receiving the heading to Lajes. Neither could get a peep out of the ADF radio which is the primary—usually the only—navigation aid in the F-100D. Neither could they raise anyone on any radio frequency, except each other on their tactical frequency.

They estimated from their elapsed time that they should be about abeam of Lajes. But should they turn right or left? There was no way of knowing. They could agree on only one thing. They were each down to about ten minutes' fuel. They had to switch back to the universal distress frequencies and make one more bid for rescue. Before switching frequencies Zielinski wise-cracked: "Okay, buddy. If anyone asks which way I went, just tell them I turned left."

Then Zeke switched to guard channel and began calling "May Day, May Day."

Garner, too, throttled back and began to descend through the murky overcast. While the two lost pilots could talk to each other, they had been unable to get together and each had no idea where the other was, except that they figured they were fairly close together, judging by the strength of their radio signals.

As Garner reached 15,000 feet he broke through a hole in the overcast and could dimly make out the black Atlantic below. Suddenly, off his wing tip he spotted a red glow.

There goes Zeke's Dog, he thought. His heart skipped a beat as he wondered whether Zeke had bailed out in time.

Then he spotted another light, a bright pinpoint of light. That would be a ship. At least here was a chance. Time was running out. Desperately Garner buzzed the ship to attract attention, then circled back up to altitude for bailout. As he circled he glanced again at the ominous red glow on the water off his wing tip.

That couldn't be Zeke's plane. It would have made no more than a puff of flame as it exploded, Garner thought.

"That's the Azores volcano," Garner suddenly realized. "That's Flores Island. I've got it made. Lajes is only sixty miles."

Back on tactical channel, Zeke was calling Garner. He, too, had it made. He had picked up Lajes radio and obtained a DF, a direction-finding steer or heading, to fly to Lajes. After their long ordeal Garner and Zeke both landed safely.

Five weary birds now huddled together on the ramp at Lajes. There wasn't enough JP4 among them to fill a cigarette lighter. Half a dozen young Tigers had earned a new lease on life.

Eight Resort Alfa Fighters of Task Force Bravo are now down and out of the race. Four press on. One is a two-place F-100F with Capt. George Branch, twenty-seven, of Waco, Texas, flying the front seat and 1st Lt. Russell Youngblood, twenty-six, of Philadelphia, flying the rear. The others—Lt. Craig Fink, twenty-six, of Wichita, Kan., 1st Lt. Daniel Walsh, twenty-eight, of St. Paul, Minn., and 1st Lt. James Cartwright, twenty-three, of Tacoma, Wash.—are all that remain of Resort Alfa. And they are not together.

Lieutenant Walsh had trouble getting a full load on his first refueling. He stuck to the hose until he could top his tanks. But his tanker made a 120-degree turn with him in the clouds. He dropped off, headed about as far off course as possible. Then he got a heading to take him back on course. But by now he was 150 miles behind the formation, which was no longer a formation. Winds had shifted from the westerly tail wind forecast by the metros to northeasterly, almost on the nose. Delay, storm and turbulence in refueling had cost precious time and fuel. Everyone was sweating out Camp Hobo, the next rendezvous east of the Azores. The weather was still bad, mostly instrument flying. Duckbutt Charlie Bravo never showed up, but the third Duckbutt came on the air with new weather, new winds and a new heading to Camp Hobo.

Captain Branch had no trouble hooking up on the first refueling. But neither he nor Colonel Brett got a full load. Three planes had to split a fuel load intended for two. That left everyone short of fuel by the time they passed the Azores.

Lieutenant Fink had no trouble hooking up, but was thrown off the tanker four times by heavy turbulence and finally filled up on a second tanker.

Lieutenant Cartwright almost didn't make it. Thirteen times he tried to stab the elusive drogue in the dark, fighting turbulence and scud. Twelve times he failed. He was past his bingo when he finally hooked up. Then he held on to the last drop.

Young Cartwright, now a "seasoned trooper," was then a green pilot just out of training school. He had reason to be "all shook up." In the confusion and the panic pressure of this operation he had been late getting the word. He missed the briefing. Arriving at the flight line to see the rest of the squadron mounting up, he suited up and scrambled for his cockpit, minus maps, navigation kit, "discreet radio frequencies" and all the other vital information imparted at the briefing. He didn't even know where the squadron was going.

"Hey Captain Branch, where we going?" he asked as he prepared to mount his cockpit.

His buddies just grinned. No time for banter now. Once in the air he got on the tactical frequency and again asked his flight leader, "Where we headed?" Again no answer.

Wisecracker in the crowd, thought his flight leader. And so Lieutenant Cartwright set out for what he thought was a local scramble, only to see the good old U.S.A. receding farther and farther behind him and the Atlantic growing bigger and bigger under him. By the time he let down for his first refueling, he was thoroughly shaken. "I was nervous as a cat, just plain scared," he said.

As the five remaining pilots in their four sleek fighters bored on to Camp Hobo for their second refueling, most of them began to feel the strain of the long battle with the elements, and went for their go pills. But this wasn't Cartwright's day. As he fumbled for his go kit he dropped his pills in the depths of the cockpit, far out of reach.

The tankers were on station, on time at Camp Hobo. All were lit up like Christmas trees. But the weather was dirty, the turbulence terrific. The tankers lashed their drogue's like a tiger lashing his tail. Trying to hook up in this kind of air was somewhat similar to playing crack-the-whip in a concrete mixer. The turbulence slowed up the tankers, which put the fighters even closer to stalling speed. They had to toboggan to increase speed, and that took them down into worse weather. This was the kind of weather that separated the men from the boys, but they all passed the test.

Walsh, industriously counting his beads for the past two hours, caught up with the tankers during the slowdown for refueling. Both Walsh and Cartwright came off the tankers 2000 pounds light on fuel. They had ridden the tankers for more than an hour and were 'way behind schedule—but had covered about 300 miles in the process.

None had the other in sight when they broke off in the darkness before the dawn. And Walsh couldn't raise anyone on his radio. But the other three planes were able to talk to each other, which was comforting if nothing more. Cartwright was riding Captain Branch's wing now and Captain Branch figured he was pretty well on course. They had pushed the tankers east as far as the B-50s could go and still have fuel enough to return to their base. Even so, Cartwright checked in low on fuel and asked whether he should turn back to Lajes. The weather wasn't too promising there and after a quick mental calculation, Captain Branch figured Cartwright was better off continuing en route. Sure enough, the coast of Spain loomed in the first light of dawn. Now Walsh and Fink could see the coast and determined they were a little south of course. They got a definite fix from a GCI site and were soon joined up in formation. Everything was rosy now. The sun shone bright. The strain of the long night was forgotten. Switching to tactical frequency the five happy pilots sang "Oh, What a Beautiful Morning," and "The Rain in Spain."

The last leg of the flight was a piece of cake. The final refueling was in bright sunlight in quiet air off Marseille, France. For once the tankers outnumbered the fighters. Six tankers had been orbiting at the rendezvous point for more than an hour, waiting for the expected wave of 12 fighters. They were at the limit of their own fuel, but with one fighter per tanker, refueling was quickly accomplished.

Then the pilots pressed on down the Mediterranean, taking time out to nibble on flight lunches as they soared high over the scenes of Ulysses' Odyssey. They had lived through more adventures in ten hours than Ulysses had in ten years. Shrugging off the fatigue of 12 hours and 35 minutes of tension, the fighter pilots tucked their planes into a tight diamond formation for a victory sweep over Incirlik Air Base before landing.

Parking on the sun-scorched dispersal pads far from the base, the weary pilots set about refueling their fighters and arranging for bombs to be slung in place. They carried a full load of 20 mm. ammunition for their guns on all such flights. Within two hours they were ready to fly their first mission.

Lieutenants Fink and Cartwright remained with the planes while Captain Branch reported to the base commander for orders. He was greeted like a man from Mars. So secret was the movement that even the base CO didn't know the planes were coming. The foursome had outrun their support planes. No mechanics were on hand to meet them. Maj. Gen. Viccellio was still en route in his command plane. The field was virtually deserted, except for base aircraft.

"I was pooped and paralyzed," Captain Branch recalled. "I had taken my go pills, but I had so much adrenalin chasing itself around in my blood stream that I didn't need any pills. By this time we all figured this was the real thing."

"I guess we were all kind of keyed up," Lieutenant Fink said. "I was so tired I couldn't think straight. My legs were paralyzed. I knew enough not to jump off the airplane though—we didn't have any ladders when we arrived. I would have collapsed in a heap.

"But I couldn't sleep for twelve hours. I had taken a go pill about an hour before landing, but that wasn't what had me hopped up. We finally slept alongside our airplanes. We didn't know when we would be leaping off again.

"My nose was so beaten up from wearing that oxygen mask for twelve hours that I couldn't bear the sight of it for three days. But aside from that we were all raring to go, after a good night's sleep."

TAC planes were scattered all over France and Italy as plans were changed in mid-air to meet the changing situation. Movement of paratroopers from England to Adana crowded Incirlik Air Base and required diversion of TAC jets in mid-ocean. One jet pilot, refueling in rough air over Corsica, lost his canopy and with it his maps, navigation aids and radio. His wingman steered him safely to land in France. Another developed hypoxia when his oxygen system failed, but his wingman led him down to a safe landing in Italy. The stragglers of Resort Alfa who were forced down at the Azores came through in eight hours with the second wave of fighters.

The first units of the CASF were in business at Adana eighteen hours after the bell rang. Within forty-eight hours after the order was given, 95 per cent of the CASF was in place and ready for action—two squadrons of F-100s, a squadron of B-57s, a reconnaissance squadron, three troop carrier squadrons, a tactical control system and a command headquarters; 100 aircraft, 1,400 people and 1,662,000 pounds of equipment, an air force in miniature with the power to inflict more damage than all the destruction wrought by all means in World War II. Task Force Bravo had set new records for speed without losing a man, despite adverse winds and weather. From Adana the whole of the Middle East lay within combat range of the fighter-bombers of this new form of supersonic peace force. In the next few weeks this force flew 2,400 sorties in the Lebanese theatre without firing a shot.

As planes of all sizes, shapes and speeds began to drop out of the shimmering sky, Incirlik Air Base began to look like a sit-down strike in an aircraft plant. Planes were parked nose to tail and wing to wing at odd angles on every foot of concrete and on the sunbaked plain alongside the taxiways and runways. Flight crews set up their army cots and slept under the wings while mechanics pulled routine maintenance inspections in the sun and the wind. Some 2,400 paratroopers followed the fighters into Incirlik Air Base from Germany. They pitched their pup tents alongside the aircraft, ready to move out on a few minutes' notice.

Supersabre F-100s and B-57 Canberra bombers, F-101 twin-jet reconnaissance planes, C-119 Flying Boxcars, C-124 Globemasters and C-130 turboprop transports almost rubbed wing tips. Men worked to exhaustion pitching their own tents, fueling and servicing their planes, preparing equipment for immediate use, bombing up and establishing emergency alert pads. Bombs were hauled out of storage areas and laid out alongside the F-100 parking mats ready for fast handling if necessary.

Once their most urgent jobs were done, men literally lay down in their tracks and slept on the hard ground. Two slept so soundly they were run over by the heavy trucks which rolled through the night to load and unload arriving aircraft.

The base, built to serve 300, suddenly found itself overwhelmed by more than 5,000. The water supply was quickly drained as temperatures soared over 100° and stayed there. Drinking water was parceled out in Lister bags. There was no water for baths, not even for flushing toilets. Water for shaving was limited to two hours' use in the morning.

The mess hall ran out of food. So did the officers' club. Supplies of food were rushed by air from Europe. Planeloads of trucks, jeeps and Volkswagens were flown in. Planes and men were so dispersed around the big airfield that ground transportation was a necessity. The supply of liquid oxygen for the fighter planes ran low and three oxygen generators had to be airlifted from Europe. The base had a supply of tents, which soldiers and aircrews alike erected near their aircraft.

Then it really got hot. Temperatures rose steadily on the vast plain until it was 110° in the shade, as high as 136° on the runway. Mechanics and pilots alike had to wear gloves to handle tools or work on the aircraft. Favorite sport on the line was frying eggs on the metal surface of the F-100 stabilizers. Eggs actually sizzled and browned before their eyes.

To the fighter commanders there was nothing funny about such runway temperatures. No jet could get off the runway with a load in heat like this.

Each day the number of aircraft on the barren field continued to grow. By the third day some of the transports had to be flown out to make way for the slower B-66 reconnaissance bombers, last of the tactical jets to arrive, and the slower tankers. The base presented a juicier target than ever for a Red missile or bomb, if it were coming.

Within a few hours after the first four Supersabres of the 355th squadron landed from their historic nonstop flight, they were flying cover missions for succeeding waves of fighters and low and high-level reconnaissance missions.

On the fourth day General Viccellio took off in his command plane to lead a formation of C-130s carrying 1,800 Army paratroopers into Beirut, capital of Lebanon, a little more than 200 miles away across the Mediterranean. Lebanese lovelies could be seen water-skiing in the limpid waters of the Mediterranean while Marines washed their skivvies on the beach. It looked like the most peaceful crisis in history. But a transport plane landing just ahead of General Vic's C-130 was hit by ground fire. So was the plane behind his. An F-101 flying visual reconnaissance missions over Lebanon along the Syrian border was hit. Many an F-100 was shot at, but none was hit. The slower B-66s were more vulnerable to ground fire. One returned from a low-level look-see with more than thirty holes in its skin. Fortunately no plane suffered major damage. None fired a shot or a missile, nor dropped a bomb, except on the practice range, during all of Operation Double Trouble. Most of the ground fire was from riflemen. One off the end of the runway at Beirut became known as Annie Oakley—he never missed.

As General Viccellio's plane pulled up in front of the terminal on Beirut airport and cut its engines, a tower of smoke went up from a homemade bomb exploded across the field by rebels. No one was hurt by this or other crude bombs usually made by filling coke bottles with any kind of explosives at hand and detonating the bomb with a punk or a lighted string. Not a paratrooper or a Marine was hurt, nor seriously threatened by these few fanatical demonstrations. The shooting quickly died down. Order was restored in ancient Lebanon by President

Chamoun and his government. The show of force had stopped
the trouble at its source. Flights of TAC's supersonic warplanes
had been seen by thousands as they zipped low over Lebanon
and along the borders of Syria. Vast formations had paraded
along the Iron Curtain, painted bright and clear on Red radar
screens. This was a language Nasser and Khrushchev could
understand. They got the point. The pot quit boiling. The Middle East situation simmered down. The diplomats, speaking
softly in the shadow of the Big Stick poised at Adana and Beirut,
patched up a new peace.

TAC had won its spurs.

The very success of Strike Force Bravo in meeting a crisis
which had all the earmarks of a military and political coup supported, if not engineered, by Moscow, aroused General Weyland to sober second thought.

"Knowing the Communists from years of studying and fighting them, I had a strong feeling this gambit was not finished. I
felt sure the Commies would strike again somewhere at the other
end of the world, either as part of their original plan or in reaction to our show of force in Lebanon," he recalled.

"They were taken aback not only by the speed with which we
could respond, but the weight we packed in Strike Force Bravo.
They would figure that we had shot our wad, that we couldn't
handle any trouble that might break out elsewhere. They would
try something to save face and at the same time to test our reaction time and our strength in depth."

General Weyland was so strongly convinced of his "hunch"
that he began immediately building a second Strike Force, ready
to cope with any brush fire that might break out at "the other
end of the world." He had the men and the planes. But he had
only one 19th Air Force to command an Air Strike Force. To
Maj. Gen. Chester E. McCarty, commander of the all-supersonic
12th Air Force, he gave the job of building a second command
section and organizing a new CASF. The commander of the
new provisional Task Force command section was Brig. Gen.
Avelin P. Tacon. The 19th already had war plans written to

cover almost any situation anywhere, and these plans were in General Tacon's hands.

Within two weeks of the Lebanon crisis, events began to point to the Formosa Straits as the most likely site for the next Communist move. Chiang Kai-shek's commanders reported Communist China was building up its military strength opposite the Nationalist Chinese islands of Quemoy and Matsu. Chiang Kai-shek declared a state of emergency August 6. The ChiComs were reported building up their air strength and the latest model MIG-17s were reported in great numbers. The Communists had declared they would capture the islands and conquer Formosa.

On August 23 the Chinese Communists attacked Quemoy and Little Quemoy with an artillery barrage of more than 50,000 shells in two hours, and continued daily shelling. ChiCom planes strafed the islands on August 24. The U. S. Seventh Fleet, which had been patrolling Formosa Straits, reinforced its patrols. The reinforcements included 1,600 Marines from Singapore. But the shelling continued.

Then, on August 29, the fire bell rang again. President Eisenhower acted under the Mutual Defense Treaty of 1955 which gave him the authority to defend the Republic of China with "any armed forces he might find necessary to protect Taiwan [Formosa] and the Pescadores." The resolution specifically authorized the President to protect the offshore islands of Quemoy and Matsu if considered necessary to the defense of Formosa.

This time TAC was fully prepared. General McCarty's provisional staff had anticipated the command. The 388th Tactical Fighter Squadron from Cannon Air Force Base, New Mexico, had been standing by at George AFB for days, ready to take off. Its Flyaway Kit was already loaded aboard C-124 Globemasters ready to go. The tankers and movement control teams were already in place across the Pacific. Communications had been established, operations and weather officers placed at island control points and the command team, headed by General Tacon, was in the Philippines. They were following a trail well blazed in a practice exercise, Operation Mobile Zebra, November and December, 1957.

The Pacific's greater distances, adverse winds and scarcity of island steppingstones make the 9,500-mile route an exacting test of man and machines. Taking off August 30 from George AFB, the first squadron of fighters refueled twice en route, landed at Hickam Field, Hawaii, overnight, then continued on to Guam, where they were delayed by typhoons for two days before completing the hop to the Philippines. The 9,500-statute miles was covered in 16 hours 31 minutes flying time.

Here, within fighter range of Formosa Straits, most of the planes of the Task Force remained until September 5 and 6 when the spearhead of F-100s took off with loaded cannon and live GAR-8 Sidewinder air-to-air rockets for the Chinese air base on Formosa which was their final destination. Other units were dispersed to other bases on Formosa, Okinawa, Japan and the Philippines. More squadrons were deployed as the tension grew in Formosa Straits until the total strength exceeded that of Task Force Bravo still in Lebanon.

The movement was marred only by the loss of a C-124 Globemaster of the Military Air Transport Service which disappeared in the ocean west of Guam, with a crew of five and twelve enlisted men of the 388th TFS; and by a night landing accident which wiped out an F-100 and injured the pilot on the last leg of the flight to Formosa.

While heavy guns boomed in Formosa Straits, the most serious threat to the CASF in the first hours of its arrival in Formosa was snakes. First task of the air crews was to cut the tall grass alongside the parking ramps and alert stands where deadly snakes bred in abundance. The Chinese divided them into three varieties—50-pacers, 100-pacers, and 200-pacers. You could walk 50 paces after being bitten by the deadliest variety; 100 paces and 200 paces by the more sickly species.

Within an hour after landing, the fighter-bombers of the CASF were ready to take off on a few minutes' notice. Their assigned job was to aid in the defense of Formosa against aerial attack. But their basic mission was to make a show of force. While they never fired a shot in action, the F-100Ds, with GAR-8 Sidewinders prominently displayed under their rakish wings, flew low over Quemoy where our Chinese allies could see physical evidence that Uncle Sam kept his word when he signed a treaty of mutual defense.

They also flew high and fast across the radar screens of the Chinese Communists. So did the F-101 Voodoos, capable of 1,200 miles an hour in level flight. So did the F-104 Starfighters of the Air Defense Command, which were flown over later in C-124 transports to add their world-record speed and altitude capabilities to the Chinese Nationalist defenses. Sight of this "Missile with the Man Inside" zipping across their radars at 1,400 miles an hour could not fail to impress the Communists.

The final persuasive touch was lent by mechanics of the CASF who invented means of hanging the deadly new GAR-8 Sidewinder, the rocket with the college education, on the wings of the F-86 Sabres flown by the Chinese air force. The Chinese pilots, trained by U. S. instructors, were among the sharpest in the business, after years of skirmishing with the Communists. They had been more than holding their own against the MIG-17s of the Chinese Communists, despite the superiority of the Russian fighter plane. With the heat-seeking Sidewinder they quickly knocked down half a dozen MIGs. After that the Reds weren't so eager to tangle with the ChiNat F-86s. Meantime, a team of F-100 Supersabre pilots from George Air Force Base was busy checking out pilots of the Chinese 4th Fighter Bomber Wing in F-100s.

As the shelling of Quemoy and Matsu continued, the Chinese were unable to supply their troops on the island by ship. Chinese pilots flying C-46 Commandos undertook to supply the besieged garrisons by air, kicking supplies out the doors of the C-46s on repeated passes over the island. To speed up the airdrop, a number of U. S. C-119 Flying Boxcars were turned over to the ChiNats, and their pilots were checked out in the big cargo plane built especially for dropping up to ten tons on a

single pass. U. S. Army riggers and drop specialists were flown
in from Japan with cargo parachutes, drop platforms and other
equipment to help load and rig the Boxcars for the airdrop.

As the strength of the CASF continued to build up on bases
in the Philippines, Formosa, Okinawa and Japan, ringing the
threatened Formosa Straits, the shooting and the air activity
began to die down.

The U. S. Army had bolstered its strength in the Pacific area,
including a battalion equipped with the Nike Hercules anti-
aircraft missile sent to Formosa. U. S. artillery capable of reach-
ing the Chinese mainland and striking back at the Communist
guns was supplied to the defenders of Quemoy. Eight-inch how-
itzers and a fleet of U. S. tanks were added to Chiang Kai-shek's
forces. U. S. Marines landed on Quemoy to train the ChiNats
in the use of their new weapons.

Still the facts speak for TAC's nuclear strike force. All the
ships of the Navy and all the soldiers of the Army and the
Marines could not stop the shooting. But it stopped when TAC's
supersonic atomic air force appeared on the scene.

General Weyland put it this way:

"In both the Middle East and the Far East, the Composite
Air Strike Force proved its point. Such a force, properly trained
and equipped, could operate successfully either independently
or in conjunction with theater forces. To exert the influence it
did in two military areas of the globe where military forces
previously known to be in position did not deter trouble, the
CASF must have a firm military basis. Obviously the potential
enemy was well aware of its capability."

By October 6, 1958, Communist China ordered a one-week
cessation of the shelling of Quemoy. On October 25 the Communists announced they would cease to bomb the islands on
even-numbered days of the month. The shooting gradually
tapered off to a few token, face-saving shots. TAC's CASF
began the long flight home in December. Every Tiger was home
by Christmas 1958 from both ends of the earth. They had played
a decisive part in preserving the uneasy peace of the world for
another year.

# 11. Home of the Tigers

If Britain's battles are "won on the playing fields of Eton," the free world's air battles are won on the ranges and in the classrooms of Nellis Air Force Base, Las Vegas, Nevada.

This is the College of Tactical Knowledge, the Oracle of Air Battle to all the free world. This is the Home of the Tigers, Mother of Aces, where the skills of all U. S. fighter pilots are honed to that razor edge which makes the difference between victory and death in air battle. Here they get that "platinum finish" which distinguishes the professional, returning every year for a fresh polish. Here come fighter pilots from all our allies to acquire the same high polish and to keep up with the rapidly changing new weapons, techniques and tactics.

The cream of the crop of fighter pilots come from all the world to get their degrees as fighter-instructor pilots in intensive postgraduate courses. Fighter commanders from all over the world bring special problems to be solved by the Nellis air oracles. Here new tactical weapons and devices are tested and evaluated, and TAC's Research and Development experts dream up and test new tactics and improve old techniques. Here R. and D. experts develop tactics for use of new weapons. Virtually all the NATO fighter pilots who flew MIG Alley during the Korean war got their final training or retraining at Nellis. Their 14-to-1 kill ratio in Korean skies is Nellis' proudest boast. It is also one of the prime reasons why her graduates have since been able to win a succession of cold wars without firing a shot. Outnumbered, outgunned and outclimbed by Red MIGs, the Nellis Tigers in their early Sabres nevertheless shot down 801 MIG-15s for a loss of only 58 Sabres.

In any future conflicts, big or small, Nellis alumni will play a decisive part. For one of the major missions of the Tactical Air Command is to supply trained pilots to all the United States tactical air forces and to supply training to key pilots from the air forces of our allies.

Nellis is also home to the Thunderbirds, the USAF demonstration team of jet pilots who tour the world impressing friend and foe with the near perfection of their flying skill. Here, too, the best of the nation's fighter outfits from all the world compete in the biennial USAF Fighter Weapons Meet, the World Series for fighter outfits. Here the top guns are chosen in a series of contests simulating combat conditions.

Las Vegas is world-renowned as a city of "sin, sun and fun." Millions flock to "Lost Wages" to lay millions on the gaming tables. "The Strip," glitter and glamour street, lights the sky at night like a forest fire. Las Vegas means "the greens" or "the meadows" in Spanish. But there was only dust, rattlesnakes and horned toads to mark the site of Nellis Air Force Base when it was established March 28, 1941. Western Air Express had smoothed out a dirt runway nine miles northeast of town for its DC-3s and had dug a well. For this Uncle Sam paid $10. In true Las Vegas style this investment was quickly parlayed into the world's biggest and busiest Air Force base.

Actually it was the very dust and the gila monsters that attracted the Air Force. They spelled cloudless skies, almost perfect flying weather. And to the north and west lay the bad-lands, a barren waste of dry lakes and mountains writhing in the heat. Fire-red slag heaps and mountains of fresh cinders create the illusion of hellfire. No wonder Uncle Sam was glad to turn over three million acres of this Devil's dump yard for testing man's most devilish devices. The A-bomb and related weapons then under development were tested here, including the AEC's Frenchman Flats testing grounds. Las Vegas, then a town of 8,422, is now a fun capital of 150,000.

The Air Force was still the Army Air Corps in those days and the desolate bit of desert was desired immediately for a "flexible gunnery school," for instruction of aerial gunners. The pressure was on, as usual, with the usual snafus. One of the first carloads of supplies for the new desert base, marked RUSH, URGENT, included a canoe, mule carts, hayrakes and three power lawn mowers, fit playthings for the base's first mascots—a family of horned toads which occupied their own cactus garden at the headquarters of Col. Joe Mason, first base CO.

The canoe was about as useful in the desert dust as the first base fire engine—a Model-T truck, vintage 1918, which boasted 200 feet of hose, darned and patched like a pair of socks—which didn't much matter as there wasn't any water anyway. The tires were held onto the cracked rims with wire.

"The fire truck had its points, however," Peggy L. Penney, wing historian, notes soberly. "It could go anywhere it was pushed."

The few motor vehicles that didn't require pushing had more urgent missions—like the restroom run which rushed clerks and stenographers of the fair sex from the new base, which lacked plumbing, to the nearby civilian airport which boasted modern "facilities."

Pride of the Army was its rifles. But none reached Las Vegas in those early days. Sentries walked their posts with lead pipes and shotguns for lack of other weapons. It was during these days of tension following Pearl Harbor that a newly assigned young lieutenant mistook the whistling snore of his roommate for the gas alert signal and rushed forth into the night, clad only in his gas mask and his natural dignity. Next day there was a new regulation—against sleeping in the raw.

This confusion continued right up to the end of World War

II when two supervisors met in the mess hall at what was by that time Las Vegas Army Air Field.

"What's your crew doing here?" asked one.

"We're closing the barracks," said he. "What's your crew doing?"

"We're opening up the barracks."

Both were right. LVAAF was inactivated, reactivated, and inactivated again within a three months' period before going on "standby status" in 1947.

One of the hardships of service at Las Vegas Army Air Field in those early days was the mail service. At first no one got any mail. It was missent to Las Vegas, New Mexico. No one had heard of Las Vegas, Nevada. Today Nellis, named for 1st Lt. William Harrell Nellis, Las Vegas pilot killed in combat, is one of the best-known air bases in the world. It claims the title of the world's busiest. A plane takes off or lands on its busy runways every thirty seconds. Some 300 planes fly more than 10,000 hours per month over its complex of ranges, burning more than five million gallons of fuel. More than 1,200 pilots per year graduate from its multiplicity of courses.

It is undoubtedly the most popular Air Force base. About 1000 transient planes land here monthly to RON—remain over night. How many of them actually remain overnight on the base itself is open to question. Most are "navigational training flights," required of all pilots. And where can more heavenly bodies be found in nightly orbit than in the glitter and glamour palaces of Las Vegas' famous Strip?

During World War II, LVAAF did a booming business in gunners, turning out 600 gunnery students and 215 copilots in B-17 Flying Fortresses every five weeks. In March, 1945, the base converted to a B-29 gunnery school. In 1949 the base was reactivated as a single-engine advance pilot training school. It came into its own when the Reds roared down on South Korea in June, 1950. By July 17 the first class of pilots was getting refresher training in the Combat Crew Training School, which operated six days a week, twenty-four hours a day, to turn out 4 new fighter pilot replacements for our Korean air forces every month.

"Nellis is the answer to a fighter pilot's prayer," said one of the early returnees from MIG Alley.

Most of the MIG-killers who distinguished themselves over Korea won their spurs at Nellis, including Capt. Joseph Mc-Connell, Jr., the top-ranking Korean ace. McConnell, like many another Korean fighter jock, was a "retread," having been turned down for pilot training in World War II and tossed into the navigator hopper. After many missions as a navigator he finally won his pilot's wings in 1948, one of the first group to check out in jets—the F-80s.

McConnell, then thirty-one, had a further fight on his hands to get assigned to Korea, but finally made it in the fall of 1952, with the 51st Fighter Interceptor Wing. By January 14, 1953, he got his first Red MIG. A little more than a month later he shot down his fifth MIG to become an ace. By April he was a double ace. May 18 he shot down three MIGs in a day to become the first "triple jet ace" in history. McConnell was killed August 25, 1954, when the F-86 he was testing at Edwards Air Force Base crashed and burned.

He typified the goal of the Nellis College of Tactical Knowledge—to turn out fighter pilots who "could hit any target from any angle"—the fighter pilot's accolade for a pilot with the widest possible education in fighter tactics and the skill to kill.

*Every Man a Tiger,* was and is the motto of Nellis. The Tiger spirit is that divine rage which makes giants of men and turns the tide of battles. It is the spirit of the hunter, the killer, the difference between the lion and the lamb, the tiger and the housecat. It is this spirit that makes a man an ace—that extra spark of divine fire that sharpens a pilot's senses, giving him the gift of sensing the presence of the enemy, picking him out of the blue by the merest glint of light from enemy wings in the uncertain depths of high altitude, and sending him hurtling to the attack. Victory goes to the attacker in the air. The defensive fighter may not lose, but he cannot win.

But there is more to air combat today than mere "fighting." Fast jets, swimming through the unreal atmosphere of 50,000 feet or more at high speeds in tactical formations, are operating in a new world, a world with more than three dimensions. To survive and shoot down the enemy in this other-worldly atmosphere requires a thorough knowledge of aerial maneuvers as intricate and complex as Einstein's theory. In fact, to understand them as they are explained in the classrooms at Nellis, TAC pilots have to have a considerable knowledge of mathematics. If they are to live to fight another day, they must be able to catch a glimpse of the enemy twisting and turning in the blue-black sky and see the whole picture of the maneuver the enemy is attempting and the countermaneuver required to send him down in flames.

The study of aerial tactics is like chess in three, or more, dimensions, played on a board with no top, bottom or sides. The pieces are very much alive and shoot back. The stakes are life or death.

The instructors in this College of Tactical Knowledge are not necessarily aces, but they *are* ace-makers. It takes a rare combination of genius to make an instructor in this life-or-death school. It takes men like Maj. Frederick C. "Boots" Blesse and Capt. John R. Boyd, called "the best fighter pilots in the business." Col. Arlie J. Blood, commander of the Combat Crew Training group, pointed out that Boyd, for example, is more than a fighting fighter pilot. "He also has the rare ability to figure out how he achieved victory over the best of opponents, analyze his maneuvers mathematically, diagram and explain them, set them down on paper and then teach them to others. He has written some of our best manuals on air tactics."

The manuals themselves are closely guarded secrets, but simplified explanations published in the Fighter Weapons School *Newsletters* read like Greek to pilots without fighter training. Captain Boyd's "Air Combat Maneuvering Guide," for student fighter pilots, was written with the aid of a mathematics major.

"But it was most often Captain Boyd, not the math major, who would finally come up with the explanation for new maneuvers he invented," Colonel Blood said. "Sometimes the solution to a new tactical problem would come to him in his sleep."

The F-100 "Lead Sled" wasn't designed for dogfighting—or "gunfighting," as TAC's Tigers call it. But Captain Boyd could outfight anything in the sky with it. He could make that Dog do everything but sit up and beg, his buddies recall. He could also do some things the airplanes couldn't do.

Once in the summer of 1960 he got in a tight spot in a gaggle. To get out, he suddenly applied full rudder and full aileron while burning the paint at maximum Mach. The violence of the maneuver ruptured both main and spare hydraulic control systems. With both control systems gone there was nothing to do but bail out. Boyd, a legend among fighters, later left TAC for the Air Research and Development Command.

Major "Boots" Blesse, also a legend, wrote not only technical manuals for throttle jocks, but *No Guts, No Glory*, a fighter pilot's fighter book for the layman.

Is dogfighting, or gunfighting, passé in this day of supersonic fighters, rockets and missiles?

Opinions differ among fighting men. But TAC still teaches the intricate art to all fighter pilots. They still learn how to hold tactical formation. How to hold position in maximum G turns. How to cut the turn to stay with the leader. How to keep him covered at all times, at all costs. How to feed in the back pressure on a hard turn to throw the attacking enemy to the outside of the turns. How and when to make a "hard break" or sudden violent turn. How to "scissor" from side to side to force an attacker to overshoot. How to defend against a scissor if you are the attacker. How to "Yo-Yo" at high speed to avoid overshooting your target on attack and at the same time trade airspeed for altitude to stay behind and above the target. How to maneuver for a head-on attack. How to follow through after such an attack. How and when to use a high speed, high G barrel roll to literally roll around your attacker and wind up on his tail. How and when to go into a defensive spiral, a high G roll underneath, a Lufbery circle. How to perform a defensive split. How to maneuver against a defensive split.

It's a whole new language. It's learned first in the classroom, then practiced on the range. And this is but a cross section of one sample of what it takes to make a TAC fighter pilot.

SAC reflex air crews stationed at Moron Air Base, near Seville, Spain, wear red caps and leather jackets with big red circles painted on the backs. In the circle, painted in big white letters, is each crewman's title: PILOT, COPILOT, NAVIGATOR, RADAR-BOMBARDIER, ECM OPERATOR (electronic countermeasures), or AERIAL ENGINEER.

TAC fighter-bomber pilots assigned to the same base silently eyed the SAC decorations. Next day the TAC pilots walked into the mess hall in their flight suits, wearing leather jackets with big white bull's-eyes on the back, each bearing in modest lettering his crew duties: PILOT-COPILOT-NAVIGATOR-BOMBARDIER-RADAR OPERATOR-AERIAL ENGINEER.

The placard was no exaggeration. Each lone TAC pilot has to do the work of a six-man crew and keep his skill razor-sharp in each of his multiple duties.

"You need three heads, two pairs of eyeballs, five hands and nine lives," as one young captain put it.

The average TAC pilot spends the first 18 months and 350 hours of his Air Force career learning the fundamentals of flying, navigating, bombing, strafing, and rocketry. He used to start in propeller-driven T-34 and T-37 training planes, then make the jump to T-33 jet trainers before flying operational fighters like the F-100. Now he starts directly in the T-33 jet and flies jets the rest of his military life. He starts with a class of 180, which has been weeded out to about 120 by graduation time. By this time the 60 best suited by temperament and ability for fighter pilots have been selected and assigned to TAC. The rest go to multi-engined bombers or transports.

The typical tactical student pilot has had about 20 hours of practice in delivery of nuclear bombs when he comes to Nellis.

He has practiced air-to-air combat and air-to-air gunnery, but has never fired a shot at a "live" target; has simulated delivery of rockets, but never fired a real one. He is a pilot with wings and a commission, but no guns. At Nellis he has three months in which to win his "guns." He will pound the books in more than 100 hours of classroom instruction, then fly 50 hours in F-100Ds to put classroom theory into practice. He will fire live 20 mm. ammunition at ground and air targets, shoot live rockets at ground targets, drop live napalm bombs, practice aerial re-fueling that isn't just practice, and fly an actual deployment within the ZI (Zone of Interior), combining tactical formation, refueling by night and day, bombing and return to base.

The only phase of his training that isn't live is the delivery of nuclear weapons. This is the most exacting phase of a TAC Tiger's training, but "shapes" are used simulating the size, shape and weight of the real weapon instead of the cocked weapon, for obvious reasons. The care and handling of "the weapon" is a major study in itself.

Dropping the biggest bomb that could be hung on a fighter or light bomber plane in World War II or Korea was no problem. A pilot either dived on the target, or skimmed in low over the ground, popped his pickle in the barrel and went on about his business. There was a bang and a cloud of smoke and flame, but the pilot was far from there by that time. Even the biggest bombers of World War II and Korea could, when the situation demanded, drop down to treetop height, lay their eggs and escape without damage. These techniques are still used with conventional bombs in close support of ground forces.

But an atom bomb that could blast a city like Hiroshima could also "atomize" the fighter plane that delivered it by conventional methods. Even SAC's bombers at 40,000 feet have to run from the blast of their A-bombs. TAC's answer is LABS—Low Altitude Bombing System. Actually there are five LABS maneuvers designed to place the nuclear or thermonuclear bomb on its target and still give the fighter-bomber pilot a chance to escape the lethal core of the blast.

One is a shallow dive maneuver for use with "low yield" nuclear bombs of limited destructive power. The second is a true LABS maneuver during which the nuclear "weapon" is tossed at the target from a distance of several miles at a low angle and low altitude, while the fighter-bomber continues to climb upward in a loop, rolling out on top of his loop at about 10,000 feet above the ground and streaking for cover. A timing point on the ground at a known distance from the target is required for accuracy. Speed and altitude during the bombing run are also critical.

The third and most exacting maneuver in the book, for fighters or bombers, is the High Angle LABS maneuver—essentially the old World War I Immelmann. This "idiot loop" can be executed anywhere, any time, at almost any altitude by any fighter-bomber pilot who can sneak under the enemy's radar line and find his target. As he passes directly over his target he pulls into a loop, tossing his bomb up and over his shoulder as he nears the top of his loop. The bomb continues to soar up and back with the speed of his flight, then falls back onto the target. By this time the pilot has rolled out of his loop and is making for cover.

Sounds simple. But it requires the most exacting knowledge, skill and precision.

At 1100 hours you get your orders:

"Plant the M-1 at 116 degrees 18 min west long.: 37 degrees 33 min north lat. T.O.T. 1435 hours local."

That means your bomb is to hit the target at 2:35 P.M., just 3 hours 35 minutes from now. You are given a circuitous route to fly, which turns out to be 370 nautical miles. At 426 knots true airspeed, 492 miles an hour, that will take 52 minutes.

You plot the course on your navigation chart. The red course line cuts straight across desert ridges and dry washes. You have three sharp turns to make at more than a right angle. The F-100 at 426 knots won't turn a right angle. But it will turn on a dime. And that is what you use. The radius of your turn at this speed is five miles. Instead of being on your new course line when you complete the turn you will be five miles beyond it. Sometimes you can't see five miles when you are skimming over rough terrain in poor visibility at 492 miles an hour. You're lost. So instead of trying to cut a square corner, you lay a dime down on the map and draw your course line around it. That's where you will actually be when you try to turn sharply onto your new course line.

How are you going to see your target at such speeds, much less hit it on the nose with a million dollar bomb within plus or minus 30 seconds? This is precisely the problem that will confront any TAC pilot if the bell ever rings. Find the target, figure out the route that will dodge known hazards, escape detection and fool the defenders. Figure the best angle from which to make the final delivery pass. Then start figuring backwards to takeoff time, fuel load, gross weight and performance data.

The target folder shows photos of the target from various angles. It proves to be an old mine shaft and miner's cabin. Fairly easy to spot. An arroyo with dry lakes of distinctive shape provide a final check point before the bomb run. Temperature over the target is forecast to be 24 degrees Centigrade (75° Fahrenheit), wind at 13 knots from 210 degrees. Wind from the right will drift the plane to the left during delivery. Head wind will also affect the accuracy of the drop. The Batori computer shows you must offset your course 270 feet to the right. You figure 72 mils of correction is required on one LABS indicator gyro and 62 mils on the other. You open the panel behind your cockpit to correct the gyros with the aid of a tiny mirror and a screwdriver. They will make your corrections for you. Now you have only to fly the needles on your LABS indicator in the cockpit.

You would have similar target photos and forecast weather data behind enemy lines. The temperature and wind might not be as forecast when you got there, but you know a lot of tricks to correct for this "fumble factor," at the last minute.

Now all you have to do is strap on the airplane and fly the mission. That you can do in half the time it took you to do your preflight planning. Normally you would have twelve hours or more to study your target folder. You start your engine at 1315 hours, and call Godson Control:

"This is Oak Leaf Thirteen. Request clearance to Range Five, T.O.T. one-four-three-five."

"Oak Leaf Thirteen. Cleared to Range Five. Report Southbound."

Godson Control is a special radio net controlling the vast gunnery and bombing complex which extends for 150 miles to the northwest, 80 miles wide, including the Atomic Energy Reservation, which is restricted to flight below 20,000 feet. Godson Control operator sits behind a big map of the range complex at Combat Crew Training headquarters in front of a blackboard showing flight plans from all aircraft scheduled to use each range during the day and the time blocked off for each. Like a railroad dispatcher in a busy switching yard he checks to see if he has any conflicting flights going or coming. Then he instructs the fighter pilot to switch to Range Five Control.

But on this CPM—Combat Profile Mission—you will be flying too low to be heard by radio. All the more reason why your navigation has to be precise and your timing exact. Godson Control will allow you ten minutes' leeway over the range for your safety. If you can't make it in that time you'd better stay off the range. Once you get up off the deck, Angel's Peak radar, a part of the national radar net, set on a 10,000-foot peak thirty-five miles northwest of Las Vegas, will pick you up on its screen and vector you home or steer you around other traffic. Until then you hug the deck, a lone wolf, unseen, unheard, unnoticed, sneaking in under the radar screen.

You start taxiing at 1336, take off in a cloud of heat waves at 1340, climb 1000 feet, then dive low over Dry Lake, a tiny speck on your map, the assigned starting point of your mission, precisely at 1343. The trick is to hit the point precisely, hold your compass heading of 353 on the nose and hit your stop watch as you cross the dry lake, no bigger than a midget's girdle on the dry plain alongside the highway.

Nothing but barren hills ahead, a ridge looms above you as you hug the ground. You are navigating by the clock now. Three minutes. You're crossing Highway 93, climbing with the rising ground to cross the ridge tops which lie like a row of slag heaps as far as the eye can see, which isn't far. Another ten minutes, another highway. Right on the nose. This is duck soup. Now down itno a barren wash for eight minutes, rocking and rolling in the shimmering heat waves boiling off the hot desert. Distance is measured in minutes, not miles, when you are down on the deck: 7 nautical miles, 8 statute miles every minute, 666 feet every second, about the speed of a .45 caliber pistol bullet. No time to study landmarks, which don't look like their portraits on the map, anyway, from this down-under angle. Only roads, railroads and dry lakes can be recognized. Nearby features blend into a brown blur at this speed. You can whip by a town two miles off your wing and never see it. Your watch is your best friend. It says 22 minutes 30 seconds. Time to turn. Sure enough, there's the key railway.

The wing seems to plow the gravel of the desert valley as you whip your lead sled over into a steep bank. More mountains, more rough air. You're crossing them now. No more roads or railroads. You're turning into the home stretch now. Still on the money. Forty-five, forty-six minutes. Still no sight of the dry lake which marks the key turn onto the bomb run. It's hidden by an 8,000-foot ridge. You dive to the valley floor, over the dry lake, whip into your turn to heading 197. Bombing switches on. Hit the deck. Looks like the correct hill ahead. Forty-nine, fifty minutes. Now you can see the mine shack. Clamp down on the "pickle button," the bombing trigger. Hold it. Over the mine shaft.

Now! The afterburner cuts in with a kick like a mule. Pop the stick back fast, but smoothly. Four Gs in 1.5 seconds, the book says. Makes your guts want to crawl into your boots. The old iron Dog is clawing for the sky, higher, higher, straight up. Now over on your back. Keep those LABS needles centered. The vertical needle to keep you straight on course, the other to keep this idiot loop tucked in tight, 4 Gs all the way. Loosen up the back pressure on the stick and you get an error at twelve o'clock. Your bomb falls beyond the target. Tuck it in too tight and it falls behind the target at six o'clock. If you don't stall out.

The LABS black boxes know when to let go of the bomb. There it goes now. A flick of the needle, a flicker of the light on the bombsight and it's away, soaring up and back over your shoulder. Only you aren't there any more. You're over on your back. Ease off on the back pressure now. The old Dog is burbling on the edge of a stall. And this is no place to go into an inverted spin.

Eyes still glued to the crossed needles on the LABS indicator you can still see the horizon coming in view over the nose. Time to roll out. Get off your back into level flight. Here you are at 15,000 feet MSL. You've reversed directions. The bomb is behind you. Only this is a 25-pounder with just enough powder in it to throw a little plume of white smoke. You whip around in a turn to see where it hits. Takes it 1 minute 10 seconds from the moment of release to make its fall at your indicated airspeed of 500 knots, true airspeed of 565 knots, 650 statute miles an hour almost the speed of sound, if you figured everything right—including temperature, dew point and weight of the airplane. You started out weighing 34,900 pounds, 17½ tons, with two 275-gallon fuel tanks on your wings and three practice bombs slung under your belly. Your metal mole drank fuel like a hog, 6,700 pounds an hour on the low-level run, another 1,200 pounds during the 60 seconds of the idiot loop. You're down to 3,700 pounds of fuel.

Time to hit for home. Your bomb has plopped in short at about 300 feet. A pretty sharp hit, considering the bugger factor you had to throw in at the last moment when you had to relax the back pressure a little to prevent a stall on that Immelmann. A pitiful little puff of dust on the desert floor. But the air would be rent by a ball of fire and a blast that would rock if not tumble your bird if this had been the real thing. And what's 300 feet to a weapon that could utterly destroy everything within couple of miles in a nuclear nightmare such as you hope the world will never see again? In your annual LABS flight tests a bomb within 1,500 feet is considered a bull's-eye.

Pilots learning the LABS maneuver make their passes over Dogbone range, number two, where they can be coached from a control tower and their pattern checked by electronic devices which also score the drops precisely as the spotting charges burst over an elongated dry lake shaped like a big bone.

Here, too, pilots are instructed in two new methods for delivery of nuclear bombs, the "laydown" and the "retard" methods. In the laydown delivery the bomb is lofted into the target from a low-altitude approach. The "weapon" has a spike in its nose which is designed to stick in the ground or the roof of a target building. A time fuse delays detonation of the bomb until the TAC fighter can escape from the blast area. In the "retard" or "drogue retard" method, the bomb is delivered by the standard LABS maneuver, but its descent onto the target is delayed by a ribbon drogue parachute or metal "dive brake" to give the delivery plane more time to escape the blast.

The Strategic Air Command tried some of these LABS maneuvers with its B-47 bombers, but encountered difficulties. Bombers aren't built to stand 4G pullups.

Aerial gunnery training used to consist of shooting at a tame banner towed 2000 feet behind a towplane. The banner was a sitting duck. It couldn't twist or turn or dodge like a real, "live" target. Neither did it register on the radar sights with which TAC fighters are now equipped. In an effort to provide a realistic target, TAC came up with the Dart, 16-foot, three-winged device shaped like a paper dart, with a 6-foot "wingspread." Made of corrugated paper covered with aluminum and braced with wood "spars," the Dart flies like an angry angel. Towed on a 2000-foot cable behind an F-100 it will twist and dodge and snap around the tightest turns, following the towplane like a silver shadow. Fighter pilots who have seen combat say it is like the real McCoy.

The Dart is fastened to the wing of the towplane, like a bomb. Over the range it is released to fall back behind the towplane as the cable unwinds from a reel mounted under the belly of the plane. The aerial gunnery range is only ten minutes flight from Nellis. There the towplane flies tight figure-eight patterns while four planes each make four passes at the elusive silver shape. The 20 mm. bullets of each fighter plane are painted a different color to permit scoring of the target, which is dropped by a small parachute, cable and all, alongside the runway at Nellis at the end of each hour's "class."

Rocket ranges, bombing and strafing ranges are equally handy to Nellis, where planes take off in a constant stream every few seconds day and night during the training week. A new range is being installed for more realistic training in the primary cold war role of the fighter-bomber pilot—close support of Army forces in the field. Tanks, trucks and heavy guns will be placed on the range, disposed as they would be in an actual enemy advance. Combat controllers on the ground will then contact fighter pilots in the air over the range and call for strikes on specific targets with specific "loads," such as napalm, high-explosive bombs, rockets or conventional cannon strafing.

"War" rages almost continuously over the Nellis complex, from Las Vegas to Tonopah and from Alamo to Gold Point. Sonic booms mingle with the muffled boom of napalm and fragmentation bombs and the occasional rip of machine-gun fire. Clouds of smoke sprout out of the target valleys and contrails are carved in the sky.

Yet in the midst of all this shot and shell and supersonic excitement, "poachers" are occasionally sighted inside the thoroughly posted borders of the ranges. Pilots stationed at Nellis make a practice of looking for the telltale trails of dust from sand buggies driven by desert prospectors who can't resist another look at long-abandoned diggings in the danger area. There is even a little wildlife left in the midst of the deadly hail of bombs and bullets that falls over the Nellis complex. In fact, there is a brief open hunting season in one corner of the complex for a species of wild sheep.

Three types of students are found on the cactus campus at Nellis.

Thirty-five lieutenants with shiny new wings report to Nellis every three months for 90 days of training. These are the "freshmen." Two classes are in residence at all times, about 600 students a year. Each gets 54 hours of flying time, 50 in F-100s and 4 in T-33s, plus 100 hours of classroom academic instruction.

The Fighter Weapon School, a "graduate school," puts a super polish on a dozen gunnery instructors every 11 weeks, turning out 60 pilots of flight commander status with "masters degrees" in weapons delivery every year. They get 50 hours of flying and 120 hours of intensive academic instruction, requiring at least 3 hours of study each night. They learn all the latest theory, then "drop everything we can hang on the airplane."

There are few aces on the faculty of this postgraduate school for fighters. But most of the instructors, like Maj. W. L. Creech, operations officer of the Fighter Weapons School, have years of experience in the most exacting of precision flying. Major Creech served two years with the Thunderbirds, four years with the Skyblazers and is the author of a book on air tactics. Of the 41 officers in the faculty of the Combat Crew Training group and the Fighter Weapons School, 5 have flown on demonstration teams. Only one, Maj. Ralph "Hoot" Gibson, in group headquarters, is a fighter ace.

"An ace has to be sharp, but there's a big element of chance there, too," as one professor of air tactics put it. "The best pilot in the world will never make ace unless he happens to be in the right place at the right time."

Biggest business at Nellis is the postgraduate "Rotational Training" of TAC squadrons. Every tactical fighter squadron in the Tactical Air Command spends three weeks at Nellis every year, catching up with the rapid progress of the art and honing pilot skills in a dozen different complex maneuvers with live bombs, rockets and ammunition. Twenty-four squadrons a year, about 600 pilots, zoom through Nellis, two squadrons at a time, collectively logging 11,000 hours of jet flying time, 1,800 hours' academic time.

A flight instructor from the Fighter Weapons School in a two-place F-100 leads the squadron through its first passes, explaining and demonstrating new techniques and tactics, then watches and scores the squadron pilots on their runs. Each pilot also gets 28 to 32 hours of academic instruction on new developments in all tactical fields.

Where do these new developments come from? TAC's missions have increased with the years. So have the tools of the trade. The TAC sextuple-threat pilot has become as busy as a one-man band with the seven-year itch. To help solve his problems TAC has established its own Training, Research and Development section (TR & D) at Nellis Air Force Base. Here veteran fighter pilots with practical knowledge and experience in the cockpit take new guns, new bombs, new rockets, new developments of all kinds and make them work.

Here the Dart tow target was developed to its present state of practical, realistic perfection. Here the mechanical problems of fitting the GAR-8 (Guided Air Rocket) Sidewinder to the F-100 and firing it were solved. Here research pilots worked out the best tactics for use of the Sidewinder by TAC fighters against other fighters and bombers. The Sidewinder, named after the desert rattlesnake and just as deadly, was developed by the Navy and adopted by the Air Force for TAC and the Air Defense Command. It measures 9 feet in length, weighs 155 pounds, is cheap and easy to build, and is capable of destroying supersonic aircraft at altitudes from sea level to 50,000 feet or more. Biggest problem, one not yet solved under some combat conditions, is to identify a target as friend or foe at the great distance from which the air-to-air rocket is normally fired. The Sidewinder is deadliest in the very combat situations where guns are useless, the researchers found. The Communist MIGs, which used to soar tantalizingly 10,000 to 15,000 feet above the top ceiling of the F-86s over Korea, would have been sitting ducks for the

Sidewinder. No longer is the top dog necessarily the top dog. With the Sidewinder the preferred attack is from below and behind the enemy. This is his blind spot. Yet he is outlined brightly against the sky like a clay pipe in a shooting gallery. TR & D pilots work out the best formations and formation tactics for use of the new rockets as well as the best individual tactics.

The Sidewinder does have limitations and these are fully explored in all combat situations by TR & D pilots. For one thing, the GAR-8, a heat-seeking missile, will not fire when it is hot. Pilots claim the heat-seeking wafer mounted in the nose of the missile behind a glass lens is so sensitive it will sniff out the infrared rays from a cigarette. But as the temperature of the photoconductor cell increases, its sensitivity to infrared radiation decreases. When cool, the heat-sniffing missile is accurate enough to enter the tailpipe of a jet target drone. The supersonic missile can outmaneuver the best of planes and pilots. By the time a pilot sees the missile it is already too late to escape, even by bailing out. TR & D's job includes testing missiles that can be used as targets for testing Sidewinders and for training pilots in firing the GAR-8s. One of the biggest problems is spotting a target missile at supersonic speeds in the uncertain visibility of high altitudes and shooting it down in the few seconds available.

The newest and most challenging problem for the Research pilots was the Bullpup, the missile that minds. The GAM-83 (Guided Air Missile) can be launched by the mother plane at any altitude, then can be guided to its ground or air target. It was originally developed by the Navy for use against small ground targets such as tanks, trucks, bridges, railroad tracks and trains, pillboxes and supply dumps. The Bullpup is a relatively inexpensive, solid-fuel missile 11 feet long, weighing about 750 pounds and capable of mounting a nuclear warhead.

How was a lone pilot to navigate, calculate, fly his single-engined fighter and at the same time fly a missile he could barely see to a target equally elusive? The four-dimensional mathematical problems involved were enough to puzzle an Einstein. The "eyeball engineers" of the TR & D section made a few practical passes with the missile and came up with the answer to this supersonic chariot race.

They built a simulator, mounted a control stick on the left side of the cockpit and found they could fly the F-100 with the right hand and the missile with the left. Once the missile is launched, the pilot has to keep his eyes glued to the Bullpup as it snorts toward its target in a ball of fire, "flying" the Pup with a small radio control stick in his left hand, while flying his F-100 blindly with the other. To TAC's two-headed six-handed pilots the feat proved no feat at all. The device was then used for a training device to save firing the expensive missiles themselves.

The Bullpup, equipped with a nuclear warhead, can be launched straight ahead, rocket-boosted to supersonic velocity, about Mach .8, then turned far off to the side, where the pilot can see to line it up with the target yet be far away when the dread mushroom clouds begin to sprout. In most cases the obedient missile can be launched while the vulnerable fighter is well above the effective range of most ground fire. While details of the Bullpup's performance are classified, pilots report that under some conditions the maximum slant range of the missile is limited only by the altitude that can be attained by the fighter plane and the distance at which the pilot can see to hit his target. TAC's jet jocks call it "The Fighter Pilot's Equalizer." First public demonstration of the radio-controlled Bullpup came at the 1958 World-Wide Tactical Fighter Weapons Meet at Nellis.

Each of the dozen hard-working research pilots works alone on anywhere from one to four projects at a time, with the aid of expert mechanics and ground crews. Few projects are as dramatic or spectacular as the Bullpup testing; most are hard, inglorious, exacting work. In experimenting with new and improved methods of delivering the new nuclear bombs retarded by drogue parachutes, the project pilot was soon out of suitable practice bombs. Uncle couldn't afford practice bombs with real ribbon parachutes. Practice bombs with metal "speed brakes" on the tail fins were used instead, until the project officer ran out of them, too. He tried picking up used bombs off the range and found that by adding a nose plate to absorb the shock he could use the "hand-me-downs" again and again.

One research pilot, struggling to find an accurate formula for delivering an M-1 nuclear bomb by diving and then pulling up at about 13,000 feet above the ground and tossing his bomb into the target, flew 125 sorties or flights, tossing about 600 practice bombs plus 50 live 750-pound bombs, 30 500-pound bombs and 6 "shapes" or dummy nuclear bombs—all to assure deadly accuracy when and if the bomb ever has to be delivered in earnest.

One of the latest major projects is a system of dropping bombs on a tactical target at night or by instruments completely in the blind. Research pilots have clobbered targets they never saw on missions flown entirely "on the gauges." Control is supplied automatically by radar from the ground. The MSQ equipment sends visual signals to the pilot in the cockpit directing him to the exact bomb release point, which he never sees. As usual, details are restricted. But it works. The possibilities, for use on the battle front in fog, night or foul weather, are obvious.

The TR & D pilot's job is never done. As fast as he solves one problem he is handed another. As fast as he harnesses one weapon and puts it to work someone invents another. And with each new aircraft added to TAC's stable of war horses he has to do the job all over again, adapting each weapon to the new fighter-bomber.

Climax of the work year at Nellis for all hands is Operation William Tell, the USAF World-Wide Fighter Weapons Meet, held at Nellis every two years. Here come the top guns from all USAF tactical fighter outfits throughout the world for a shoot-out to choose the fastest guns in all departments of the fighter's trade.

Each team of five pilots fires his guns against the Dart target, his Sidewinders against a "live" target, and matches his skill in dive bombing, skip bombing, low-angle strafing; drops napalm, conventional bombs and strafes realistic ground targets in close support of Army ground units at the direction of an air control officer on the ground. He releases nuclear practice bombs by LABS maneuvers—including the retarded and laydown method for the first time in 1960.

The TR & D pilots climax the world-wide turkey shoot with a demonstration of virtually all TAC weapons except the atomic bomb.

Nellis' "School Teachers" have won every meet, to clinch their claim to the title of "World's Best." The margins were narrow—and the "Teachers" were, of course, competing on their home grounds.

# 12. They Also Serve

"These TDYs [Temporary Duty Tours] are a little like dying," this TAC wife was saying quietly.

"The parting is just as hard. You'd think a TAC wife would get used to it after a while. Some do. But me, I die a little every time he takes off for another TDY.

"In some ways the overseas rotation tours are the worst. You know they're coming for a month or two in advance. It's like a last illness. The tension builds up slowly. You talk over final arrangements, make your plans, revise your will, make out a new budget, try to anticipate all the household problems for a half a year ahead, grab a week's vacation together, if you're lucky. But it still hits you just as hard when the moment of parting actually comes.

"The kids are too old or too young to feel it coming, until a day or two before takeoff. A rotation date means nothing to a baby of eighteen months, or even a boy of four. But the day comes when Buddy asks why Daddy can't take him swimming Saturday and you tell him Daddy won't be here. Then the tears begin to flow. He's too sleepy to know what's going on down at the flight line for takeoff before dawn. But when Daddy doesn't come home for lunch, Daddy's boy goes into a tailspin.

"In some ways the homecoming is even worse, for John. The kids don't know him. Four months is a long time in the life of a baby of eighteen months, now two and a quarter. Jill just stared at that strange ape in the monkey suit, with his hands full of flight gear, and hid behind my skirts. That leaves scars no amount of time will heal, when your own kids don't know you."

This is a pain as old as man, as old as battle. But TAC wives live in double jeopardy. They know their husbands will be gone at least five months out of the year on regular TDYs, four months or more "rotational training" on alert at bases in Italy or Turkey, and another month on TDY at Nellis sharpening up their shooting eyes to stay combat ready.

In addition, the threat of a sudden alert hangs over the heads of most TAC pilots—and their wives—every day and every night of the year, especially in those squadrons which are maintained on ready status for CASF duty.

"Every time that phone jangles in the middle of the night, I jangle with it. I wake up quivering like a gong that has just been struck with a club. And that's the way I feel," one TAC commander's wife said. "My stomach ties itself into knots. I listen for Pete's answer. 'On the Double,' means he's off again and I'm out of bed to help him pack and brew him a cup of coffee. Gives me a chance to dry my tears before he's out the door on the run."

TAC wives seldom know where their husbands are going or when they will return on one of these alerts. They don't even know if it is for real. They never know when or whether their men will return even from a routine day at the base.

July 15, 1958, started out as just another dull Tuesday to the wives of TAC's 355th Tactical Fighter Squadron at Myrtle Beach. Their men had reported for a day of routine training. They didn't come home for lunch. They didn't come home at all. Their wives didn't see them again for weeks. Squadron buddies came to pick up their clothes and their shaving kits. Their husbands were taking off. Period. No one could tell them exactly when, or where, or why, or for how long, or whether this was another practice alert, or the real thing. They knew soon enough. The radio was already blaring out news of the crisis in Lebanon. The Middle East was about to catch fire and their men were hired to put out fires.

For Mrs. Jim Cartwright this was to be a red-letter day. She was in the base hospital with a new baby. This was the fourth day and the doctor had said Jim could pick her up this afternoon and take her home. She was so excited she couldn't eat.

Jim never came. His baby was months old before he saw his daddy.

"This is TAC," the colonel's wife comforted her. "It could be worse."

She was thinking of that morning in May when her husband took off with his squadron for Aviano. In the dark before the dawn one flight of three took off with afterburners searing the velvet darkness, disappeared in low clouds—and were never seen or heard from again. No trace of them was ever found. The best guess is that the leader lost control of his heavy-laden F-100 and dived into the ocean, followed by his wingmen. The rest of the squadron was already halfway across the Atlantic before the three were determined to be missing. Who was to comfort the widows? One had been married only six weeks; one for six years. She was due to have her first baby in a month. The third had a month-old baby in her arms when she got the word.

The squadron wives, TAC's hidden reserve force, rallied around the widows. TAC wives at squadron level are a strength unto themselves. They have to be. They lean on one another for support during the long, long days and weeks and months of the endless TDYs. They baby-sit for each other, visit and party together, share joys and troubles—and live on letters, one a day, like vitamin pills.

"When things get too rough we think of the wives of the tanker and the troop carrier crews. They have it even worse. I know one captain who was never home more than two weeks at a time last year. He was gone forty-seven per cent of the time."

"We try not to yak about it, but we die a thousand deaths,"

said one capable TAC wife, mother of three. "When Dan is in Aviano and trouble begins to bust out in the headlines in Hungary, and Suez and Algeria or Morocco, then I really begin to clunk. I read the headlines and check the map. Hmm. Only forty minutes from Aviano.

"And those big lugs just shrug and say, 'That's what we're here for.' The world's on fire and they've got to put out the sparks. Yeah, but who's going to save the women and children? Strike that last remark. Who cares about the women and children? It's Dan I care about. Of course he says he's safer than we are if it comes to all-out war. And I guess that's right. But who wants to be safe and alone?

"Our youngest didn't even know him the last time he came home. That big C-124 opened its mouth and spit him out like Jonah from the belly of the whale. That scared little Joan. She started crying. She's older now. Last night she broke into tears when I tucked her into bed. She had just begun to realize Daddy was going away again. She'd heard us talking about it for a month, but it didn't sink into her little noggin until just the night before he was to leap off. She'll be in school when he comes back. That will help take her mind off her daddy.

"Some wives can take it. Some can't. I don't know whether I can or not. The first time Dan went to Aviano—that was for six months then—I was all ready to follow him. I had it all figured out. I had my bags packed and the kids ready to go. I sat down and wrote a twelve-page letter explaining how I had it figured out. I was about ready to take off when I got a wire from Dan saying 'Are you crazy? Stay home.' He didn't even say he loved me, or missed me, or anything. Just a panicky 'Stay home.'

"I was so mad I kicked holes in the walls. They were pretty flimsy walls. Then I would wring out my hanky and kick some more holes in the walls. Then I bundled up the kids and drove all the way back to South Carolina.

"Come to find out, he wasn't even in Aviano. He had got stuck with a sick bird in Prestwick for thirty days. I would really have been in a clank if I'd turned up in Aviano and no husband, no place to stay and, of course, no government transportation. Now that I think of it, Dan must have been suffering as much as I was about that time."

True, lady, men bleed, too, when you prick them. They aren't allowed the luxury of tears, not in TAC, but they hurt when the time comes that they must say good-by to their families.

"My nine-year-old had been awful quiet for a week before leap-off," a young, lean major recalled. "Nothing much to say. Boys aren't supposed to make a fuss at that age, but the night before takeoff he broke down and cried. Why did I have to go away for four long months? What would you have said? I've always believed in telling kids the truth, as much as they are able to understand. Why did Daddy have to go across the Big Water and sit on the end of a runway in Italy with a bomb strapped to his bottom?

"I told him it was necessary to preserve the peace, to protect the Free World. It was a job no one wanted to do. But someone had to do it. It was Dad's turn and Dad had to do his duty. He could understand that. Just like in the Boy Scouts.

"My older boy was beginning to show signs of the impertinence which is considered smart in the Smart Sixteen set. I sat him down and explained he would have to take my place and help his mother and not give her any guff. I explained that, the way the world was, someone had to be ready to fight. If you wanted peace you had to fight for it, and Dad was trained for the job and proud to be able to do something for his country. And that seemed to get under his skin.

"But what do you tell a woman? Nothing, really. They know it all anyway. It would be a comfort to the wives if we could talk to them once in a while when we're away. But we don't have any MARS [Military Amateur Radio System] station at Aviano and who can afford to pay fifteen dollars for a trans-atlantic telephone call? But lots of the boys do. Sometimes it's worth it."

These long separations are more than a heartache. They are

a headache to TAC commanders. They know that family happiness is the most important element of morale. The wives are TAC's secret weapon. They are the source of strength, or weakness. More good pilots have been shot down by unhappy wives than by the enemy.

"If a pilot really likes to fly, nothing will stop him, except his wife," one veteran commander put it. "Push them too far and they will leave TAC, and take their husbands with them."

"The Strategic Air Command had a big flap over this problem," one TAC wife, who was formerly married to a SAC commander, pointed out. "The divorce rate rose to alarming heights. SAC started a backfire. They put SAC wives through orientation and 'phasing.' I was one of the 'phasers.' But TAC has taken the most effective action, I believe. They've cut down the rotational tours from six to four months. They've given certain bases a 'vacation' from this overdose of TDYs.

"My husband was gone eight and a half months out of the past year. Two rotations, a couple of TDYs. That's too much. There's a limit to what anyone can take. Now his outfit has been relieved of its overseas commitment for a year. That takes an awful weight off your shoulders. You know you can settle down for a year and work out some of your family problems, live a normal, settled, relaxed life. You can get a lot of living done in a year. It's the best cure for TACitis.

"Then maybe we'll be ready to face the eternal TAC tension again. Maybe by that time I'll be able to hear the phone ring in the middle of the night and not go into a ring-tailed spasm."

TAC pilots are some of the handsomest men ever made. They marry some of the prettiest, smartest and most stable women to be found anywhere. Most of them know what they are getting into when they marry. Few understand TAC and their husband's role as does Mrs. L, a strikingly beautiful brunette with Hollywood eyes and a brain like a quiz kid.

"I love my husband. He loves to fly. He loves TAC. He loves his job. Therefore, I love TAC, too," she declared. "I wouldn't trade my career as a TAC wife for anything. And it is a career.

I make it my job to know as much as possible about Link's job. I know there are some things he can't even talk about. It makes him mad when I read them in the magazines after he's been pledged to secrecy.

"It's true that a TAC marriage can be only half a marriage if you don't work at it, since you are only together as a family half the time. You have to have a good marriage to start with. You have to feed it and take care of it like any living thing. We do that by writing every day when Link is away. We grow in understanding.

"I have four children and love them all. But I can't stand them all the time. I have to get out of the house. I have to broaden out or I'll become kitchen-minded. You can't be a good wife if all you can talk about is babies and formulas and household problems. Once a year we try to take a week's vacation together. Then we pick up the children and visit relatives. That is their vacation. They're two, four, six and eight.

"I have no desire to pick up and go overseas with Link. We have a fine home here, a fine base, nice people. This is home."

Not so Mrs. W.

"Why don't they take us with them? Why not go PCS—permanent change of station? It would be cheaper to fly us all over there and leave us two or three years than to fly the whole squadron over and back every four months. I could have choked that general who said it was 'hard on the men' to have their families with them, that they were always concerned about their family problems when they had their families with them, that they need their 'minds free.'

"Doesn't he think they don't worry about us when we are separated by 7000 miles? That's when the furnace breaks down, the TV gets the jitters, the automatic washer goes into automatic breakdown and the plumbing goes to pieces.

"My husband never worries about household problems anyway," she added scornfully. "Besides, we could be ambassadors of good will abroad and show our allies we feel the country is really safe and that we aren't too uppity to associate with them.

"We followed Dave to Nouasseur, lived at Rabat in a native-type house and thoroughly enjoyed our year. Dave had to drive sixty miles to the base and back every day over practically a goat trail. But we did get out and meet the natives, went to their huts and sat on the floor and drank strong tea with mint and raw sugar boiled together, and made a lot of friends for Uncle Sam."

This is an issue that has been argued since the days of Caesar, although there wasn't much to argue about in those days. Every army had its camp followers who simply fended for themselves.

Supersonic camp followers face a whole new set of problems. Seldom can they pick up and follow their husbands on their own initiative. They don't have that kind of money. Private transportation isn't available to some military areas and government transportation isn't authorized unless specified in orders for permanent change of station. Suitable housing is not to be found in some areas, scarce in others. Sometimes dependents aren't welcome for political or military reasons. For these and other reasons dependents are forbidden to follow their men overseas unless specifically authorized on orders. The number authorized overseas doubled, however, in the decade between 1950 and 1960, while the number of military personnel stationed overseas was being cut in half.

The whole question of dependents overseas has been debated by all the services ever since the end of World War II. The cost of transporting and maintaining dependents is astronomical. Total cost for all armed forces overseas is about three billion dollars a year. The direct cost of the dependents program for all services was estimated at about 500 million dollars annually in 1960. Not only do the dependents and their furniture have to be transported at government expense, but military families have to be provided with housing, commissaries and PXs (post exchanges or base exchanges), clubs for officers and airmen, swimming pools, tennis courts, gymnasiums and golf courses, schools and recreational programs. Wherever they go, a little bit of America has to be transplanted with them. It takes about seven service people to support and supply every American living abroad. It takes 1,300 base support people to "keep house" for two squadrons, 400 strong, on rotation at Aviano. If they brought their families, the base would be loaded with another 1,200 persons, facilities would have to be doubled and support personnel redoubled.

All of which may be worth the cost in the increased efficiency and high morale of men serving two- and three-year tours of duty abroad. It is also argued that if even half these dependents were shipped home it would cost Uncle Sam just as much to build more housing, commissaries, PXs, clubs and golf courses to care for them at home. TAC provides Uncle Sam with the answer to all these controversial questions. By limiting tours of rotational squadron duty abroad to four months, TAC reduces hardship to the men and their dependents to a minimum. The families would see little of their menfolk if they could follow them abroad. They are confined to the base on alert most of the time.

"One squadron on rotation is worth two at home," one veteran TAC commander explained, "for many reasons. In the first place, a man with a family abroad is working for two masters. He has to have the afternoon off to fix the roof, or take the kids to the doctor, or put in some plumbing.

"When he's overseas alone he works twice as hard—and twice as long. The more he works the better his morale. For one thing, he can see he's contributing to an important mission. He takes pride in doing his part to make his outfit not only the best, but the best able to protect him and his family if the bell rings.

"Second, he takes pleasure in showing what he can do on his own. Overseas, under field conditions, red tape is cut to a minimum. Supply channels have to be followed, of course. But there's less of the paper work that is the bane of all hands. If a part or a tool isn't available, a good mechanic takes pride in improvising, making his own tools and parts on the spot."

At Moron Air Base, Spain, mechanics of TAC's 476th Fighter Squadron found themselves suddenly faced with the necessity of removing the engines from all the squadron's F-104 Starfighters and making a difficult modification on the turbines. To do so required special tools which weren't available outside the United States. To send a special crew of mechanics with the proper tools from the U. S. would have cost thousands of dollars and would have required weeks. The mechanics made their own tools, invented their own method of making the modification and did the job in a fraction of the time and cost of doing it "through channels." The mechanics volunteered to work through the year-end holidays to finish the modification and "keep 'em flying." Periodic overhauls of the F-104s take two weeks in the States. It took the squadron mechanics, working on the open ramp in rain and sun, only three days. Not a plane was AOCP (out of commission for parts) during the squadron's tour of duty.

"This business of working on weekends and holidays is not unusual during overseas duty," the colonel continued. "For one thing, the men enjoy working at their own pace and their own convenience. For another thing, there isn't anything else to do at most of these outposts.

"Another thing, only the best men go overseas. We eliminate the bane of 'the thirty missing men' that drives the squadron CO nuts back Stateside. The sick, the lame and the lazy we have always with us. That's about two or three out of one hundred— Squadron strength is more like one hundred twenty-five, but we're never up to strength. About ten per cent are always on leave. Another ten per cent are lost to KP [kitchen police], mess check, bed check, CQ [charge of quarters], promotion boards, inventory, fire drill, or other details—or TDY on schools and boards. That leaves about seventy men out of one hundred ready, willing and able to try and get some work done, when they aren't training.

"Overseas you can skip most of these housekeeping chores and hurry up to get the job done so you can get back home."

SAC has been hard hit by loss of overseas bases and the threatened loss of more on which millions of U. S. dollars have been spent. Under nationalist pressure from Morocco the U. S.

is pulling its bombers out of the four air bases built there as a deterrent and retaliation force against any attack on the Western world. Uncle Sam has agreed to evacuate all Americans by 1963.

Nine squadrons of tactical fighter-bombers were withdrawn from France when President DeGaulle insisted upon the right to veto use of nuclear weapons in 1959. The future of air bases in Japan, Turkey, and even England is in doubt as Khrushchev continues to threaten our allies with ICBM attacks if they harbor U. S. aircraft and missiles. Heavy reliance has been placed on 80 U. S. bases in 25 lands and territories, plus right to stand-by use of some 170 other air and sea bases.

TAC offers an effective answer to all these problems. TAC doesn't need to maintain strong forces abroad. TAC can get there from home bases overnight with any strength required, anywhere in the world. Only small service detachments are needed abroad, ready to provide fuel, munitions, supplies and housing for TAC strike forces when, as and if required. This is not only an economy measure, but sound strategy. It maintains a reserve of air power which can be quickly applied wherever it is needed. And the men and planes are there only when needed, at the invitation of the host country. They aren't there in periods of peace to irritate the national pride of the host nation and give the Commies more propaganda ammunition.

Over a third of the USAF's total tactical air strength is maintained in TAC's "ready reserve." Less than a third is needed in place at permanent posts in Europe and England to hold the line against Communist pressure. Another force is maintained in the Far East, to protect that defense line from Red Chinese aggression. Here permanent bases must be maintained. These units cannot be diverted to other parts of the world, lest they leave gaps in the free world's defenses which might tempt the Red aggressors. The problem of dependents at these bases by late 1960 had posed an economic problem that overshadowed military considerations.

The whole problem of dependents abroad was projected into the political-economic arena in November, 1960, when President

Dwight Eisenhower, in the final days of his administration, ordered the number of dependents abroad cut from 484,063 down to 200,000. Of this total, the Army had 248,788 dependents abroad; the Air Force 197,438; and the Navy 37,837. Announced object of the cut was to reduce spending abroad by some 500 million dollars immediately, to reduce the flow of American gold abroad and strengthen American finances. The order, effective December 1, was to reduce the number of dependents by 15,000 a month.

President John F. Kennedy, after a review of the dependent problem, revoked the Eisenhower order, leaving the picture unchanged.

# 13. Drop Everything

Air power is no better than the airlift power which is its lifeline. The fastest of fighters is no faster than the transport planes which bring up the spare parts, the supplies, the mechanics and the ground equipment to keep them flying on CASFs.

That's where the troop carrier transport wings of the Tactical Air Command come in. They are TAC's truck drivers. But these are "fire trucks," Lockheed C-130 Hercules turboprop transport planes, powered by four jet engines turning propellers, capable of carrying 37,000 pounds of cargo or 92 passengers 3000 miles or more at cruising speeds of 400 miles an hour. This high-flying pressurized beauty provides TAC for the first time with a command ship that can almost keep up with the jets. On longer deployments, where the jet fighter pilots are required to make overnight stops, the C-130s, with double crews, are able to outrun the fighters to provide the kind of forward control required in critical situations. Where more warning time is available, both the command ship and the en route support planes take off twelve to twenty-four hours ahead of the fighters, to be in place on the ground when the jets land. The support teams, carrying spare engines, wheels, tires, cockpit-cooling units, jet starters, hoists and 1000 smaller items, are the "flying field hospitals" that keep the tactical fighters flying, making repairs overnight while the pilots sleep.

TAC currently has 110 C-130s, never enough to provide full support for all TAC's missions. For additional en route support TAC calls on the Military Air Transport Service for C-124 Globemasters. The waddling Globemaster, driven by four conventional reciprocating engines, can carry 100 troops, or more than ten tons of cargo up to 3000 miles, but at speeds of 250 miles an hour, or less.

MATS Globemasters also transport the STRAC troops of the Strategic Army Corps which follow the CASF by twenty-four to forty-eight hours to support the armies of our allies in the field.

One of TAC's major jobs is to move Army troops within the combat theater and supply them, both by airdrop and air landings. For this specialized battlefield taxi service the twin-engined Fairchild C-123 Avitruc was developed. Designed like a glider with wheels added as an afterthought, the Fairchild can land in rough, unprepared fields with up to 60 soldiers, or with jeeps, trucks, field guns or up to eight tons of supplies. Quickly fitted with litters, it can fly out the wounded from fields or rough landing strips in the forward zones. A rear door that opens like a tail gate in flight makes an ideal platform for dropping equipment or paratroopers. This rough-and-ready workhorse of the battlefield is used extensively in the routine training of paratroopers and in constant maneuvers with airborne and other Army troops in the States.

In the fifties, TAC also experimented with the use of helicopters for "vertical envelopment" of the enemy on the battle line, for reconnaissance and general use as "aerial cavalry." Both the Sikorsky H-19 single-rotor 'copter and the Vertol H-21 Workhorse, with its twin engines mounted at each end of the "Bent-Banana" fuselage, were employed for years in joint exercises with the Army before all helicopter squadrons were deactivated in 1961.

In addition to their primary duty—training paratroopers and

moving Army troops on joint maneuvers—the troop carrier units constitute the commandos of the Air Force, helping to push back the frontiers of the Arctic and the Antarctic and other remote corners of the earth. If there is a transport job that can't be done, they do it.

The Air Force and the U. S. Weather Bureau encountered such a problem in the spring of 1952 when Uncle Sam agreed to help the Danish Government establish a forward weather station at the Nord site on the northeast coast of Greenland. No ship had ever been able to push its way through the hard-packed sea ice to the eastern coast of Greenland so far north of the Arctic Circle. The Army attempted to cross the 700 miles of the high Greenland Ice Cap from Thule to the Nord site with weasels and caterpillar tractors, but failed.

Finally two C-119 Flying Boxcars succeeded in landing on the sea ice about 60 miles from the Nord site in Crown Prince Christian Land in April, 1952, to unload bulldozers, which were to clear a landing strip at the site. The heavy bulldozers bogged down in the sandlike snow. It took the cat train two weeks to make the trip and then the seven-ton bulldozer proved unable to carve out the required landing strip.

The 435th Troop Carrier Wing was called to the rescue, with the aid of the 1st Aerial Port Operations Squadron—experts in rigging and dropping anything anywhere by parachute or free-fall. Their orders, under the name of Project Parkway, simply called for the aerial delivery of the weather and radio station to the site.

To drop the 180 tons of prefabricated building materials required about 50 tons of rigging, padding and platforms, which had to be flown 5000 miles, from the squadron's base at Donaldson A.F.B., South Carolina, to Thule, Uncle Sam's northernmost base in the Arctic. To deliver the more delicate items of equipment by parachute, 620-pound steel platforms or pallets worth more than $2,100 are used. Kapok padding scientifically designed to absorb the required foot-pounds of landing shock is placed under the load, which is fitted with two or more cargo parachutes with 100-foot canopies atop the load. To extract the load from the plane with the speed and precision required for accurate delivery, a 16-foot ribbon parachute is rigged to the load, attached to a smaller nylon pilot parachute. A 16-pound sandbag is attached to the glider release at the rear of the open-ended C-119 Flying Boxcar. When the pilot pulls the release, the sandbag falls, pulling the pilot parachute, which pulls the extraction parachute, which jerks the load out of the airplane, then opens the main cargo parachute.

Two such parachutes were required to deliver the 5000-pound weasel for the Nord job. Two were employed on the 7000-pound scraper for leveling out the permanent runway on the frozen gravel of the site. One was sufficient for the 4,200-pound tractor, one for the grader, one for the ubiquitous jeep without which no project could prosper; and one for most of the 5000-pound loads of materials and supplies, which were loaded on rollers in the ample belly of the winged Boxcar and dropped two at a time.

Heavier individual drops have been made, both before and since, but this was the first operational experience for the troop carrier squadrons in the Arctic—in the face of savage weather and savage geography. Every flight had to climb to 7000 feet or higher and skirt the highest humps of the Ice Cap, which rises to 12,000 feet. Every flight approached the maximum range of the Boxcar with its rear doors removed. In fact, once past the Point of No Return the crew had to drop its load to have fuel enough to return to Thule. There was no alternate airfield.

Having proved their ability to operate in the Arctic, TAC's troop carrier planes returned year after year to fly supplies to Thule, to support the Army's Cat Trains on the Greenland Ice Cap and to help resupply U. S.-Canadian weather stations throughout the Arctic.

In March, 1954, TAC's 62d Troop Carrier Wing, Larson A.F.B., Washington, equipped with C-124 Globemasters, flew the 11th Airborne Division troops to Thule in the northernmost Army-Air Force maneuver on record. In March, 1956, both men and equipment were dropped in Operation Arctic Night.

This arctic experience was valuable training for the biggest and most complex airlift ever attempted in the polar regions— the crash project to build the DEW Line, the Distant Early Warning radar line that was to stretch 4000 miles from the Aleutian Islands to the east coast of Greenland. The decision to launch the crash project was announced in November, 1954, before the final location of the radar sites north of the Arctic Circle in the U. S. and Canadian Arctic had even been decided. The arctic coasts of Alaska and Canada were blocked by ice except for a month or two in summer—and most of the sites lay in the Barren Lands of the Canadian interior, far from any shipping lane, road or railroad. They could only be built by air. And the job had to be started in the dark of the winter night in the worst weather of the year.

The 18th Air Force, then TAC's airlift force, commanded by Maj. Gen. Chester E. McCarty, deployed 80 transport planes to the Arctic, mainly C-124 Globemasters, starting in February, 1955. Every available commercial plane also was assembled for the airlift, a motley fleet of about 200 planes of all kinds. But the Globemasters were the only aircraft big enough to haul the larger pieces of equipment and building supplies and with range enough to cover the vast distances involved.

Flying without landmarks, accurate maps or navigation aids of any kind, often on instruments in or above the clouds, the troop carrier pilots landed on the ice on remote lakes and ocean bays to unload the bulldozers required to carve permanent runways out of the frozen tundra. Machinery as big as the 21-ton tractors and scrapers required for site construction were landed on freshwater ice of unknown thickness by Globemasters overloaded to gross weights of more than 180,000 pounds.

"Try it. If your hat floats the ice is too thin," was General McCarty's instruction to his pilots in the first days of the urgent airlift.

Not a life was lost, but arctic whiteouts and landings on rough sea ice took their toll. Three C-124s were washed out in the Canadian sector that first year.

Unsung heroes of the DEW Line project in the far Canadian Arctic in those tense early weeks when every day counted were the officers and men of the 314th Troop Carrier Wing and the 2d Aerial Port Operations Squadron, from Stewart Air Force Base, Smyrna, Tennessee. No clear ice could be found for C-124 landings in this area. Bulldozers big enough to scrape landing strips on the rough sea ice and through the drifted snow had to be dropped from the C-119 Flying Boxcars. To carry the fuel required for the 1,400-mile round trip flights from Frobisher Air Base to the sites, hauling cats weighing 17,500 pounds, meant taking the groaning Boxcars off the runway overloaded by as much as 15,000 pounds. There was trouble with the rigging and the parachutes on some of the first drops. Some of the first bulldozers dropped right on through the five-foot ice. But 17 cats were dropped successfully in record time to assure start of the historic project on schedule. Altogether the Troop Carrier pilots landed and dropped 18,600 tons of freight and equipment during that first season and continued to fly in special equipment until the DEW Line—an engineering feat which has been compared to the pyramids or the Great Wall of China—was completed in July, 1957, just two years and eight months after it was started in the dead of winter.

The DEW Line airlift is still the biggest polar airlift of its kind, but TAC's 18th Air Force made more history in Operation Deep Freeze—the joint Navy-Air Force-Army-IGY conquest of the Antarctic continent during the International Geophysical Year, starting in 1956. The aerial assault on the antarctic was the biggest airdrop operation in peacetime history. Conquest of the South Pole itself could not have been achieved except for the special training, equipment and ability of TAC's 18th Air Force. The Troop Carrier Globemasters were the only aircraft in the world at the time capable of lifting 14-ton loads of equipment and supplies from a runway on the floating sea ice, climbing to 12,000 feet, flying 900 statute miles to the South Pole and parachuting the prefabricated buildings for construction of the scientific station at the Pole. Rear Admiral George J. Dufek, commander of the Navy's Task Force 43 in Operation Deep Freeze, acclaimed the Air Force achievement as "the most unique, difficult and hazardous in peacetime history."

During the forty-five critical days of the brief antarctic summer—which starts in October and ends in February—TAC's Globemasters succeeded in parachuting 1,012 gross tons to the South Pole and other scientific stations in 86 sorties. Another 34 round-trip flights were made over the 2,587 statute miles of Antarctic Ocean between the rear base in Christchurch, New Zealand, and the antarctic supply base at McMurdo Sound, delivering 250 tons of high-priority cargo and 200 passengers. Together the eight Globemasters involved flew about 2,500 hours and covered about 500,000 miles.

The Antarctic, grimmest, most remote and inhospitable area on the face of the earth, presented the most formidable challenge man or plane had ever encountered. Sudden blizzards, almost unpredictable, frequently whited out the lone runway on the floating sea ice at McMurdo Sound. Wind and weather on the 2,587-mile flight from New Zealand was unpredictable, the ocean ice-locked and untracked. Once past the Point of No Return there was no place to land but McMurdo Sound. There is no alternate airfield in the Antarctic for wheeled aircraft. Three Globemasters were damaged on the rough ice strip at McMurdo during Deep Freeze II. Many others had hair-raising escapes when blizzards blanked out McMurdo. Four Globemasters and a Navy R-4D8 (C-54) were able to land safely on the sea ice at Cape Hallett, 250 miles north of McMurdo in early October, 1958, when they were caught out by such a blizzard.

Six men were killed and two injured when their Globemaster crashed on an uncharted peak while letting down to drop supplies to Cape Hallett Station, October 16, 1958. No one would have survived the high winds and temperatures of 50 below but for a series of coincidences which enabled passing Globemasters to hear the faint SOS sent out by the seven survivors on a pocket survival radio, and the heroism of a Navy pilot who flew his helicopter through the lingering darkness to locate and rescue the men in the scattered wreckage of the plane.

The price of victory is very high in the Antarctic. The roll of the dead of all nations now tops fifty since the first explorers set foot on the shifting ice. The victory was worth the great sacrifice, however. The honor of the nation and the fate of the IGY hung upon completion on schedule of the scientific station at the South Pole.

General McCarty made the first Air Force flight over the South Pole on October 26, 1956. He is one of the first "bipolar" pilots in history, having flown over the North Pole September 21, 1956, on an operational flight from Thule to Fairbanks, Alaska. He was the first in history to make an operational parachute drop of supplies at either pole. The five-ton load of arctic diesel oil for use of the scientists at the South Pole served as a navigation aid to subsequent flights and a test of the density of the wind-packed snow, which proved to be almost as hard as concrete.

The first polar parachute jump was made November 25, 1956, by T/Sgt. Richard J. Patton, of the First Aerial Port Operations Squadron, assigned to the 52d Troop Carrier Squadron for the project. Sergeant Patton, a trained and experienced drop zone controller and senior parachutist with thirty-one jumps to his credit at the time, was needed to diagnose troubles encountered with the rigging on the drops of heavy equipment and supplies at the Pole. The next day he helped direct the successful dropping of a 13,500-pound D-2 caterpillar tractor, the largest item ever dropped from a C-124.

"Join the Troop Carriers and see the world," was the boast of the 18th Air Force in the fifties. One crew of the 62d Wing flew around the world twice in three weeks. In the spring of 1954, the 62d's Globemonsters, as the pilots affectionately call them, dashed to France to pick up 1,300 French paratroopers and fly them halfway around the globe to Indochina to reinforce the doomed fort at Dien Bien Phu.

In August, 1954, TAC's 52d squadron airlifted 150,000 pounds of medical supplies from the U. S. to Pakistan for relief of flood victims.

In July, 1955, in Operation Gyroscope, the 63d Wing, aided by the 62d, airlifted 7000 Army troops a total of 1,014,484 plane miles halfway around the earth. The Army's 508th regimental combat team was flown from Kentucky to Japan to relieve the 187th airborne regimental combat team, which was flown back to the States.

In five years the 18th flew more than 83,000,000 plane miles, 391,000,000 passenger miles and 241,000,000 ton miles. Some 407,000 tons of high priority cargo was airlifted for the Army and Air Force. Late in 1957 all heavy transport wings of the Tactical Air Command were transferred to the Military Air Transport Service.

TAC's remaining troop carrier squadrons continued to help push back the frontiers of the world. In the spring of 1957, TAC's huge C-124 Globemaster transports landed on floating ice floes 550 miles north of Point Barrow in the Arctic Ocean, within about 300 miles of the North Pole, to establish the first U. S. scientific station of its kind for study of sea ice, currents and weather.

When the ice floe broke up in November, 1958, cutting the 5000-foot runway in two, the C-123 Avitrucs were called to the rescue, this time equipped with skis. The assault pilot succeeded in sliding his plane in for a landing on the short strip at Station Alpha in the dark of the winter night with the aid of flares and torches outlining the runway. The twenty marooned scientists and Air Force personnel were quickly loaded aboard, with some of their scientific gear. To get off from the short runway, the overloaded transport was equipped with jato.

In May, 1959, the station, now called Station Charley, was re-established on a new floe about 400 miles northwest of Point Barrow, some 600 miles from the North Pole. In January, storms again broke the ice floe in two, cutting the runway from 5000 feet to 3,700 feet. Again the C-123J, this time equipped with two jet engines on its wing tips in addition to its conventional engines, flew to the rescue, removing twenty-nine scientists and Air Force "housekeepers" in two trips.

C-124s were used to establish scientific station Bravo during the IGY on T-3, Colonel Fletcher's Ice Island, 800 miles north of Thule, within 120 miles of the North Pole. Landing on a frozen lake on the 4- by 9-mile ice island, the C-124s delivered a heavy bulldozer and a number of trailers to provide housing for the scientists.

A new dimension was added to TAC's air pioneering in January, 1959, when the Lockheed C-130 Hercules four-engined turboprop transports first received, in 1956, were equipped with retractable skis as well as wheels. They proved the ideal answer to the heretofore impossible task of delivering heavy equipment and building materials to the Greenland Ice Cap for an extension of the DEW Line, where no prepared runways were possible.

In January, 1960, seven of the "Ski-130s" made the first landings in the Antarctic, where they revolutionized the problem of supplying more than 1000 tons of food, fuel, supplies and equipment annually to the South Pole and Marie Byrd Station. Landing on the hard snow at the Pole, the Ski-130s were able quickly to unload heavy steel beams and bulky equipment that could not be dropped by parachute.

Resupplying the remote stations by air-landing rather than vertical delivery saves up to $1,000,000 annually in parachutes and rigging alone, not counting the saving in time and the inevitable losses in paradrop operations. On the 900-statute-mile flight from McMurdo to the Pole, the Ski-130s are able to carry up to 15.5 tons and climb to 20,000 feet, high above antarctic storms, in pressurized comfort.

The C-130BL Hercules worked so well that the Navy bought four of the big skiplanes and took over the air-landings with their own pilots in 1961, while the MATS Globemasters hauled high-priority cargo and personnel from New Zealand to McMurdo.

Integration of the services has long been a goal of the Department of Defense. With the Tactical Air Command, integration is a fact. Close co-operation with the Army is one of TAC's primary missions. While the Army and the Air Force do not always agree on questions of strategy and tactics at the policy level, TAC and the Army work together as one in the field.

This is no accident. It is the result of long experience at the operating level, experience which is embodied in the training of both Army and Troop Carrier units. To provide the close co-ordination necessary in close tactical support on the battlefield, and airlift support in peace and war, the Air Force in 1950 established the Air-Ground Operations School, AGOS, now at Keesler Air Force Base, Mississippi.

This "University of Co-operation" is commanded by an Air Force officer with a joint Army, Air Force and Marine Corps staff and faculty. Key officers of the Air Force, Army and Marine Corps here learn uniform doctrines and procedures for planning and conducting troop movements, aerial resupply and close fighter-bomber support on the battle line. Specialized courses train Air Force officers specifically for air liaison, intelligence, reconnaissance, or operations, and Army officers for ground liaison officers, intelligence and air officer jobs. Experience acquired in Europe and Korea in use of Air Force fighter-bombers as combination artillery and reconnaissance is embodied in the training of Air Force pilots as forward air controllers to direct air strikes against surface targets from forward ground observations positions.

TAC's on-duty strength in men and planes does not appear too impressive, compared to other air commands. But TAC has hidden resources that would double her effective strength in time of emergency. For TAC relies on Air Force Reserve and Air National Guard units more than any other command. Some fifteen troop carrier wings of the Air Force Reserve, and about half the country's Air National Guard wings, are assigned to TAC for training and inspection and would be under TAC's command in time of war.

They are called "the ready reserve," and with TAC that means exactly what it says. TAC's weekend warriors are as ready as the regulars. The first crews, trained and ready for any duty, can respond within an hour, as shown by repeated readiness tests. They fly as many hours a year as the regulars, or more. They meet the same qualifications, are governed by the same regulations and exhibit an *esprit de corps* that challenges the regulars. They engage in annual maneuvers with active duty units of TAC and the Army and compete in annual proficiency contests. Starting in 1957, Reserve air crews flew official freight and passengers throughout the continent on regular Air Force missions in Operation Swift Lift, making a record comparable to active duty units.

Air Reserve crews regularly fly over water to Alaska, Panama and Puerto Rico, participating in joint operations with the Army and the regular Air Force. Reserve crews have flown halfway around the world, delivering planes to India and ferrying planes from France to the United States.

The C-119 Flying Boxcar, a flying truck with two 3,500-horsepower engines, a range up to 2000 miles, cargo capacity up to seven tons of freight or sixty-two troopers, makes them a favorite of airborne troops. Some Reserve squadrons are being equipped with C-124s, but the Boxcar will be the workhorse of the Reserves for some time to come. Some 650 are assigned to 12 Reserve wings, ready when the bell rings. The strength and composition of the Reserves changes from time to time, however.

TAC also has one wing of about fifty C-123 Avitruc assault transports which would beef up its combat theatre support forces in event of mobilization.

Strength of ready reserves alone is about 23,000 officers and men trained and ready for any emergency. On M-Day, TAC could count on as many as 70,000 Guardsmen and Reservists to more than double its peacetime strength of about 51,000 regulars. TAC's reserves operate on the theory that it is the forces ready now that will count in case of an atomic attack. They are ready now.

# 14. The Sword and the Shield

No one can foretell the future, but TAC and the tactical forces of USAFE, PACAF and the Navy are sure to play an increasingly important role in that future. There is no end in sight in the struggle between Russia and the rest of the world. Communist Russia and China are openly committed to extending their power by any means, including violence, wherever they think they can succeed. Tactical air forces will continue to be the primary defense against such limited wars, in conjunction with local ground and air forces.

The SUSAC, the Soviet Strategic Air Command, and America's SAC, find themselves in the role of giants each holding a vial of nitroglycerin in his hand. Either can destroy the other—and the whole stage setting—by merely dropping the explosive. One thing gives him pause—he, too, may perish in the holocaust. But these giants are armed not with mere nitroglycerin, but with a power so cataclysmic it defies description, a power that might literally destroy the world.

Russia's SUSAC some years ago boasted it had a hydrogen bomb capable of melting all the ice in the polar regions in a flash. In January, 1958, the Rockefeller committee investigating the state of U. S. defenses reported that a 20-megaton thermonuclear bomb—equal in explosive power to more than 20 million tons of TNT—was "by no means the largest available."

The British in May, 1957, detonated such a small hydrogen bomb in a laboratory test" which released 16 million degrees of heat. The surface of the sun is hot, but doesn't exceed 10,000 degrees. The British blast, presumably the smallest the British scientists could devise at that time, still seared whole forests in a single flash, and set fire to the very sand of the island two miles from the center of the blast, melting and fusing the earth into molten glass.

Even the fission bomb, the old model-T A-bomb of the type used on Hiroshima, is now produced in yields equal to 20 million tons of TNT. Each bomb is capable of killing or maiming more than a million people, perhaps many more, and wiping a major city off the map. This is nearly double the number of Americans (600,000) killed in all the wars in U. S. history. Some scientists believe there is literally no limit to the destructive power that may be built into an H-bomb, the fission-fusion-fission bomb. This is an "open-end" bomb. It is detonated by an "atom bomb," atomic fission which acts as a fuse or detonating cap, producing the terrific heat to start a hydrogen "fire." This fusion "fire" will burn as long as more hydrogen atoms are added, growing bigger by what it feeds on until, in the ultimate weapon, fusion may "burn up" the whole atmosphere and destroy the earth and everything in it.

Dr. Edward Teller, father of the H-bomb, advisor to the Air Force, professor at large in the University of California at Berkeley, does not believe this is apt to happen in the present "state of the art." He doesn't believe the human race can actually be destroyed in one fell blast by A- or H-bombs today. "Anyone who attempted to do so today would be met by enormous and unsolvable technical difficulties," Dr. Teller told the press in San Francisco in October, 1960.

"The human race could be destroyed by bacteriological warfare. But this will not be undertaken on this side of the ocean.

The Russians don't want to undertake it either. This isn't human nature."

Some scientists and strategists believe the Russians may launch an all-out nuclear attack "at any time they think they can sweep the board clean," as one general put it. Until that time each stands with his nuclear weapons held at the head of the other, finger on the trigger.

The Communists have one fearful advantage—the advantage of surprise, the advantage of attack. They will be first to draw. And they know it.

The aggressor has always had an advantage in any fight, whether with fists, spears, slings, guns or bombs. The bigger the weapon, the bigger the advantage. But the United States has managed to survive a score and more attacks in its comparatively peaceful history, partly because it had friends who bore the brunt of the first attacks while Uncle Sam gathered his overwhelming strength. This time there will be no intervening oceans and no intervening armies and navies to protect us from that first deadly blow. And the blow will be of such unimaginable power that it can't be stopped by any means available today. How much it can even be blunted is a matter of debate.

Faced with such a situation, some theorists argue that the best chance of survival is to strike first, fight a defensive war. This has been proposed. But it has always been rejected, and always will be. If we knew Russia would strike tomorrow, this nation would not, could not, strike first.

"It is wrong, it is immoral, it is impractical," to quote Dr. Teller. It is also impossible under our democratic form of government. The nation would never vote for it—and the war would be over before we could call an election.

This puts the United States—and all the free world which depends upon her strength—in the perilous position of exposing herself to the first blow. The implications of this Biblical posture go far deeper than the layman is apt to realize. This is something like taking on the world's champion chess player—

and giving him your queen before you start. It is like fighting a duel with a top gun, giving him the first shot.

By this deliberately publicized posture we are guaranteeing the Communists all the time they need to prepare their attack, free from aggression or fear of aggression. Behind their curtain of secrecy they can not only devise new and devilish devices to hurl against us with all the advantages of surprise—which are often decisive even in conventional battle—but they can at their leisure put all their commanders, all their key reserves, all their important missiles and missilemen and large chunks of their population underground on the day they choose to attack.

We face the desperate necessity of absorbing that first massive, carefully calculated, precisely planned surprise attack—and surviving. Estimates of the deaths in the first nuclear attack run as high as 50 million people. But in the dedicated eyes of those who have to fight such a war, people "don't count," on either side in that first flash attack. Nothing counts but airfields, airplanes, missile sites and missiles. The principal hope for the survival of the populace in that first attack is the assurance that the first nuclear missiles will be aimed at missile bases, SAC air bases and nuclear weapons stockpiles. For the Soviets know they cannot survive if they cannot knock out our nuclear power in the first blow. They know that if we can survive that first blow with enough nuclear striking power remaining to knock them out, then they will have lost the war. If they can knock out enough of our Counter-Strike force with that first blow, they can quickly knock out the rest and capture or destroy us at their leisure.

The full extent of the advantage that lies with the aggressor in nuclear war, on whatever scale, came as a shock even to military commanders who observed or participated in Operation Sage Brush in the fall of 1955, one of the most important—an least known—military exercises in history. Conspicuous for lack of sage brush, it was the first and only large-scale test of nuclear war tactics under the most realistic conditions possible short of actual war. The "laboratory war" was fought by 30,000 airmen,

850 aircraft of varied types, tactical missiles and 110,000 Army troops spread over seven southern states. This was the first big "free play" exercise. Field commanders were given realistic battle orders and a limited number of small, tactical nuclear weapons—simulated, of course—and allowed to fight the campaign as they would in actual combat, not following any script written by armchair directors. The progress of the battle and the results of the action were recorded and assessed by more than 4,000 observers and umpires in the field, who instantly flashed their reports to the maneuver control center over an elaborate radio net.

Various combat situations were simulated during the 45-day exercise, under the direction of Gen. O. P. Weyland. But no matter who shuffled the deck, or how the cards were dealt, no matter who had what limited weapons or how he used them, the aggressor always won.

The one paramount lesson of the exercise was plain. Whoever attacks with nuclear weapons wins. He wins not in days, or even hours, but in minutes. Within seconds after the attack was launched, strike reports flashed on the central control board showed the defender's airfields destroyed one after another, his aircraft, his missiles and his nuclear weapons with them. Even without the advantage of surprise, even when the defender was expecting the attack, he could not stop any substantial part of it.

The battle always proved to be a battle of bases. Opposing aircraft passed each other in flight without firing a shot, each intent on knocking out the other's base. He who first knocked out the other's bases, swept the board clean, controlled the air and ruled the battlefield. Radar nets, ground fire, and air defense fighter forces all proved ineffective.

Many commanders learned many different lessons from this 10-million-dollar "war," the biggest since Korea. But the paramount lesson was this: No nation will live to turn the other cheek in an atomic war. He may absorb the first blow, but he will have to knock out the aggressor before a second blow can be launched.

As long as Russia is convinced we pack that kind of a wallop, she won't attack. There was no doubt of our power prior to August, 1949, when Russia detonated her first A-bomb. But Russia has been building up her nuclear power rapidly ever since, concentrating on production of operational Intercontinental Ballistic Missiles. Some military strategists say Russia will have sufficient nuclear power to risk an all-out attack on the United States early in the 1960's. She may have it now.

Dr. Teller in October, 1960, said: "The Russians today and for many years can outbuild us, and as long as this is the case there is no reason for complacency and no justification for economy."

In late 1960 the Strategic Air Command considered the possibility of an all-out nuclear attack increasing to the point where a third of SAC's bombers should be airborne at all times to escape destruction and assure the free world of a retaliatory force to strike back against such a surprise attack. Congress was sufficiently convinced to vote the President the authority to authorize such an airborne alert if and when considered necessary. Airborne command posts took to the air in 1961, together with a limited airborne alert.

The bigger the stockpile of nuclear weapons, the surer the prospect of a continued crisis and tension. The question of which nation has the biggest stockpile of nuclear weapons becomes purely academic.

"It is of little consequence that we have the nuclear stockpile capability of destroying Russia several times, if Russia simultaneously has the capability to destroy us just once," writes T. F. Walkowicz of the Institute of the Aeronautical Sciences, advisor to the Department of Defense.

What lies at the far end of this long, dim avenue of atomic stand-off? Nuclear disarmament is the professed hope and the official doctrine of the U. S. and her allies. This seems the only defensible goal, impossible as it appears of practical achievement. Yet, the final irony in our policy is pointed out by such practical strategists as General Weyland.

"We can't win. We can only lose," General Weyland argues.

"Nuclear disarmament would appear to be the final solution. It would be final all right—for us. As long as we have our nuclear arms we are as big as the world. No one can be bigger. But once we lay down our nuclear arms we are naked before the world. We are right back where we started. We don't have a chance. The Reds could whip us with bows and arrows, or war clubs. The Communist hordes of Russia and Asia could roll over us like the seas. We can never match their masses of manpower on the ground with any weapons except nuclear."

While strategists, moralists and statesmen debate the ultimate outcome, TAC prepares for its expanding role in the immediate future.

"The cold war will get colder, although the possibility of hot war cannot be dismissed," says Gen. Frank Fort Everest, who took command of the Tactical Air Command in August, 1959, while commanding the United States Air Forces in Europe.

"To survive we must be strong. The weak can only beg. Only the strong can negotiate. Our diplomacy is no stronger than the arms that back it up," he declared.

"Between 1945 and 1950 the Soviets took control of nearly half a million square miles of territory and some 90 million people without committing a soldier or an airman to battle. The role of the tactical air forces, in TAC and in PACAF and USAFE, is to keep the peace, to prevent such unprincipled seizure of territories and peoples from our allies, or from neutral nations to whom we have extended our protection. The tactical forces of the free world play a primary—although little-known—role in holding the line against further Communist aggression.

"The deterrent value of SAC has been widely publicized. The complementary role of tactical air forces is not as well known, except by the Communists. . . . It is significant that they have maintained their tactical forces at World War Two levels, far outnumbering the tactical forces of the free world, and have updated their TAC with modern jets.

"Having given the Communists the advantage in quantity, it

is imperative that we maintain a decisive edge in quality of weapons. We must constantly keep pace with progress. New inventions and scientific improvements make today's aircraft obsolete tomorrow. We must replace our force about every five years. If war is forced upon us, we must fight, not with tomorrow's dream weapons, but with what we have today."

By this definition the F-100, first of the Century series, is already obsolete. The F-100, which revolutionized tactical air warfare, is being replaced by the Republic F-105 Thunderchief. The F-105 takes up where the F-100 left off. It can take off in less space, carry about twice the load almost twice the distance, return and land at lower speed. All initial testing of the F-105 was done by the 335th TFS at Eglin AFB, Florida. This was the first time a regular fighter squadron was given the job of "debugging" a new aircraft from the first production model to squadron use.

The Thunderchief is a pilot's dream, but an electronic nightmare. It has an "Iron Copilot" that can do almost anything the pilot can do and do most things better. It set a new world speed record of 1,216.48 miles an hour over a 100-kilometer closed course with Brig. Gen. J. H. Moore, commander of the 4th Tactical Fighter Wing, at the controls, in December, 1959.

"The Chief will make Mach 2.75—1,500 miles an hour—and kick up to that speed in nothing flat," pilots of TAC's new 26th Cobra Squadron at Nellis will tell you. It is their job to tame the new beast and break it for squadron pilots, at the same time they are putting it through Phase III testing. Squadron pilots at Seymour-Johnson AFB, South Carolina, are simultaneously putting it through Phase II testing to speed up the long time-lag between production and operation.

"This monster is not for kids," the Cobra pilots say. "It's a man's airplane. The day when you can hand a new plane like this over to a squadron and tell them to go ahead and check themselves out in it is past. From now on they'll all be checked out here by the best pilots in the business. We're picking senior pilots, instructor pilots and squadron operations types for the course here. We can't afford to risk a three- or four-million-dollar airplane in the hands of amateurs.

"This one is a sizzler. No telling how fast she'd go if we could let her out. Mach 2.75 is the limit right now—because the windshield and canopy begin to melt like wet waffles beyond that speed. We're getting into the heat barrier.

"The Chief's so long she might snap in two on sharp turns and hard breaks at her top speeds. We've got the rudder movement restricted to keep her from breaking her back.

"She's got not only AB [afterburner], but ADI [antidetonation injection of water-alcohol] for takeoff, which kicks her up to 23,000 pounds of static thrust for takeoff. That's like riding Mt. Vesuvius during an eruption.

"She's stuffed full of idiot boxes. Her gizzard is crammed with miles of wires. She can do almost anything a pilot can but eat. She's got an automatic pilot that is really automatic. First one that really works. You can just sit there and watch George do the work.

"George can be coupled to the ILS [instrument landing system] and fly an actual touchdown, or a takeoff, hands-off. She's got a dream box that enables her to sniff her way through the fog or the dark of night cross-country. All you have to do is to feed in the right data and she'll follow airways to your destination and even make a letdown.

"What's more, she's designed to do the same thing on the deck. You can crank in a 'map' of the route and she'll put her nose to the ground and sniff her way along, eight hundred feet above the ground, navigating herself by check points like roads, rivers and bridges, pulling up when her radar shows mountains ahead and then diving down the other side.

"She's even designed to recognize the IP [Identification Point], then the target and pull up into an automatic LABS maneuver and pickle her own bomb when the time is ripe. She'll do everything but pick your teeth for you. Of course, the boys are still a little leery of sitting there and letting those black boxes feel their way over the mountains and down the valleys at speeds like

that in the dark, but this is not dream stuff. She's actually done
it all."

At such speeds nuclear weapons can't be hung on the outside
of the airplane like washing on a line. They would get hot at
top speeds. And the drag would be terrific. So the F-105 is designed to carry nuclear bombs—and eventually airborne ballistic
missiles—in its long bomb bay. A 450-gallon fuel tank can then
be hung on the belly outside the bomb bay, plus two more 450's,
one under each wing. With this four tons of fuel, plus the supply in internal tanks, the Chief can fly about 2000 miles without
refueling. She can also be refueled in flight. The refueling probe
folds neatly away in the nose of the airplane on the left side,
just ahead of the cockpit during cruise. When needed, it extends
out like a big pitot tube in the pilot's line of vision where hookup is simple.

The external bomb bay tank would have to be jettisoned, of
course, before the internal bomb could be dropped. For maximum range all external stores might be dropped. The Chief is
armed with the Vulcan electric cannon, 20 mm. "Gatling Gun"
that fires an incredible 100 rounds per second, 6000 rounds
per minute. This stream of explosive lead is poured through
revolving barrels. A single barrel would melt under the heat.
The Vulcan, also installed in the F-104 Starfighter, is the answer
to combat at supersonic speeds, where you may have the enemy
in your sights for only a fraction of a second. You can tear him
apart with an almost solid stream of explosive bullets even in
the split half of a second with the Vulcan.

The F-105 also can carry a wide array of conventional missiles,
rockets and bombs, including the 2.75 HVAR (high-velocity air
rocket), the Sidewinder, napalm fire bombs, or a half ton and
two 750-pound bombs. A single F-105 can pack more wallop
than a whole squadron of World War II bombers.

The F-105, coupled with the KC-135 jet tanker, could constitute a "wolf pack" that could range the world to strike terror
into any aggressor who attacked our allies anywhere in the world.
The KC-135 and four or five F-105s could take off together,

climb and cruise in formation with none of the intricate planning and co-ordination now required for jet fighters to rendezvous with slow, piston-powered KB-50J tankers at the mercy of the weather over thousands of miles of land and ocean. The two jet aircraft have the same economical cruising speeds and altitudes common to such jets. Refueling would be a simple matter. Whenever the fighters needed fuel they would simply slide in behind the tanker at the normal cruising speed and take a drink, then slide out again into loose formation. There would be no complex, hazardous rendezvous requiring a descent into turbulent weather, no slow-up to dangerous near-stalling speeds where fuel consumption increases to a maximum and safety and controllability are marginal. There would be no expensive climb back to cruising altitude, burning precious fuel, and no sweating over navigation problems with limited navigation and radio equipment. The KC-135 jet crew, in their comfortable cabin equipped with all the latest navigation and radio gear, could provide precise navigation for the whole flight. If plans were changed en route, as they inevitably are in an emergency situation, there would be no scrambling of tankers to refuel the thirsty fighter planes, no urgent aborts with flameout landings at emergency airfields. The wolf pack would simply change course as a unit and go on its way. When they got there they would have tanker service ready when the fighters were ready for the next mission.

With reliable auto pilots and airborne radar the fighter pilots would be "fat." They could open up into en-route formation, relax and let "George" do the work. This could make the difference between arriving over the target exhausted or ready for action.

This buddy system for TAC jets cruising with KC-135 tankers has been requested by TAC commanders for many years. Many hours of tests with the old reliable F-100s, F-104s, and F-101s has proved it feasible and valuable. The tactical value of this wolf-pack plan was proved November 27, 1957, in Operation Sun Run, when TAC RF-101s raced the sun across the U. S. from

east to west and west to east, setting three new speed records—
west to east in 3 hours 5 minutes at an average speed of 781.74
miles an hour; east to west in 3 hours 34 minutes at 677.7 miles
an hour; and round trip in 6 hours 42 minutes at 721.7 miles an
hour—refueling at top cruising speeds from KC-135 jet tankers
borrowed from SAC.

All TAC needs is the tankers. So far she doesn't have them.
SAC still has the priority. But this development is one of the
inevitables of the future as TAC continues to shoulder a bigger
share of the burden of defense in the era of the Atomic Stand-
off.

The first F-105s are programmed to be in operation with TAC
squadrons "Tomorrow"—by late 1961 or early 1962. But General
Everest is already looking forward to Day After Tomorrow. By
1965 he expects to have a new all-around miracle plane in service designed especially to excel in all TAC's multiple missions,
up to 1975. The general specifications of this new FX tactical
fighter-bomber, as revealed by General Everest in October, 1960,
read like witchcraft. The "Witch" will fly at once faster and
slower than any jet to date, fly further and carry greater loads. It
will be able to operate from "backwoods" airports, flying further
with bigger loads than heretofore dreamed of. It will be able to
compete as an Air Defense interceptor plane and could even
operate from the deck of an aircraft carrier, General Everest
hinted.

But the FX "Witch" is no dream. Preliminary studies requested by TAC have established the possibility of building such
an airplane today, a fighter that can fly the Atlantic ocean nonstop without the complicating necessity of refueling, and "reduce refueling needs in the Pacific"; a fighter that can bore over
or under enemy defenses at supersonic speeds, carrying loads
that would have broken the back of a World War II bomber; a
fighter with a doctor's degree that will make the most sophisticated of modern-day spook boxes look like the village idiot.

But, above all, the FX will be "light-footed," like nothing

built today. TAC's jets today can go anywhere in the world *where modern high-speed runways are available.* But TAC's primary role is to keep the peace in the far places of the world, where only primitive runways may be found. The "Witch" will be able to take off and land from such second- and third-class runways, and hit aggressors at supersonic speed—or "loiter" for hours at low speed on patrol to prevent enemy attacks.

While details of the design specifications are restricted, aircraft companies say they can produce such an FX fighter capable of taking off from a 3000-foot runway, with a full combat load and landing on such a runway at speeds in the air-liner range, "loitering" on patrol for up to eight hours, or cruising for 5000 miles at 500 miles an hour, yet, capable of twice the speed of sound either on the deck or at 50,000 feet.

This smacks of magic—two kinds of magic, the variable-sweep wing and/or BLC (Boundary Layer Control). Both these new developments in aerodynamics promise all this and more. By taking off with wings swept forward the wing area can be increased to compare with that of an airliner. In this configuration a jet fighter could loiter something like a sailplane. When the need for speed arose, the FX could fold her wings like a falcon until they were swept back 45 degrees. Now she could burn the wind like the F-105, which she might well resemble. For landing she would slow up and sweep her wings forward like a sea gull, with the same stabilizing effect.

Boundary Layer Control doubles the performance of a plane by sucking air from the surface of the wing through tiny knife-blade slots and blowing it out to increase the jet thrust. This vacuum cleaner sucks in the turbulent air which burbles over the wing, thus removing a major source of aerodynamic drag. BLC can double the range and greatly increase the speed of a plane for a given engine power. BLC is used on the F-104 Starfighter to reduce the landing speed and to increase top speed. Which method or combination of methods is used in design of the FX depends upon the winner chosen in the design competition. Funds for preliminary development of the fighter of Day

After Tomorrow were assured in the fall of 1960. A further congressional appropriation was expected in the 1962 budget, to assure award of a contract for construction of the prototypes.

TAC's arsenal will include new tactical ballistic missiles in the not-too-distant future for use against fixed targets along the frontiers of the free world. A new mobile TBM or TBX missile designed specifically for use by tactical fighter forces was under consideration in 1961 to supplement the Matador and the Mace. The Matador, TM-61, a long-range "artillery" missile, has been in service since 1954. It is a subsonic missile with a top speed of about 650 miles an hour and ceiling of 35,000 feet. Powered by an Allison J-33-A-37 engine, it is launched from a mobile launcher by means of a rocket booster. It is 9 feet in diameter, with a wingspan of 28.6 feet and is 39.6 feet long.

The Matador is being replaced by the Mace TM-76B, a more sophisticated missile, with better low-altitude performance and a range of more than 1,200 nautical miles. The Mace is guided by a self-contained brain called ATRAN that enables it to follow a map, turning and twisting until it finds and clobbers its target. It was first based abroad in 1959.

Such missiles are cheap, quick means of knocking out certain tactical targets that cannot be readily moved or sufficiently fortified to resist this type of bombardment. They are valuable adjuncts to fighter-bomber forces, especially where airfields are scarce, since missiles can be launched from mobile carriers or fixed launching pads.

Missiles, big or little, cannot begin to carry the weight of explosives—nuclear or conventional—that can be carried by a tactical fighter-bomber, however. Even the much-vaunted ICBM can pack in its warhead only a fraction of the destructive power that can be delivered by the least of the tactical fighters.

And missiles don't have minds. They can't think. They can't be recalled. Once launched they can only follow instructions, blast the spot on the map for which they are aimed. Under the secrecy imposed by the Iron Curtain countries, that "spot" may not be there when they arrive, or there may be many more lucrative targets demanding higher priority. Only a missile with a man in it can see, think, decide, improvise and strike most effectively—or return to home base if the enemy attack proves to be a false alarm. Every tactical fighter is such a missile-with-a-man-in-it, a missile capable of doing more damage than the biggest of ICBMs.

One of TAC's urgent needs for the immediate future is a greater variety of tactical nuclear weapons, cut down to battlefield size for use against ground and air forces in the battle zone, so "clean" they will pose no threat of mass destruction to civilian populations, whether friend or foe. This, of course, is out of TAC's hands, in view of the existing ban on nuclear testing.

The farther you look into the future the more apparent it becomes that the traditional distinction between "fighter" and "bomber" planes has already vanished. Bombers in the beginning were built big because they had to carry enough bombs large enough to knock out the enemy's tanks, guns, bridges, highways, railways and industries. Today a single TAC fighter can deliver a nuclear weapon with more destructive power than all the explosives packed by all the Allied bombers that took off from England in World War II, prior to Hiroshima. The ancient F-100 can do the job of a whole fleet of bombers of World War II vintage. The F-105 can outbomb the bombers even more effectively.

Only SAC's B-52s can strike the heartland of Russia, or any other aggressor, with the biggest of hydrogen bombs. But TAC's fighters of Today and Tomorrow can hit everything else—50 per cent of all the war targets in Russia, for instance, just as effectively.

"You buy aircraft by the pound," one officer pointed out. "A TAC fighter-bomber weighs a fraction of a B-47 or a B-52 and costs a fourth to a tenth as much. The TAC fighter can be used not only to fight in a general, all-out war, or a small brush war, but for shows of force, and shows of flag to reassure our allies. Our allies may believe that SAC can lick the Russians

from U. S. bases far across the ocean, but they still like to have
U. S. forces based in their homelands as visible proof of our support, to reassure them as they face the ever-present threat of
enemy attack across their immediate frontiers."

Intermediate Range Ballistic Missiles like the Thor and
Jupiter help give this reassurance. The threat of the Polaris
missile will also be helpful. The Polaris can be fired from sub-
marines under water. It, too, can reach about 50 per cent of the
war targets in Russia when its range is extended from the present limit of 1,200 miles.

But TAC's fighters can hit any target these missiles can hit,
and hit it harder. This the Russians know full well. This explains their concentrated efforts to force us out of our overseas
bases. They know that before they can knock out the United
States they must knock out every tactical fighter deployed in the
European-African theatre, if they expect to escape our crippling
blows in retaliation. And such an attack would give us time to
launch our own ICBMs and SAC bombers from U. S. bases.
They know that if they first launched their ICBMs against the
United States, they would be giving our TAC fighters sufficient
warning to take off and knock out major Russian military installations before the Red ICBMs could hit their targets.

"The damage which could be inflicted by a handful of our
fighters with nuclear weapons might in itself be too high a
price to pay for starting a global war," General Everest points
out.

Hence the co-ordinated attempt to dislodge us by political
means from some eighty U. S. bases in twenty-five lands and
territories overseas. TAC maintains squadrons on alert on only
two such overseas bases at present. In past crises the small nations threatened by aggression have been eager to make bases
quickly available for TAC forces.

But a more complete answer to the growing threat of Russian
attack, as well as to the continuing loss of overseas bases, was
proposed by General Weyland just before his retirement as TAC
commander:

"SAC's only answer to the growing threat by Red ICBMs is the airborne alert. SAC bases cannot be hardened. B-52s can't be protected from nuclear blast. It's true the only way to assure the survival of an effective number of B-52s in case of all-out nuclear attack is to have them in the air ready to go.

"But this is tremendously expensive. So much so that Congress, although convinced that the airborne alert might become necessary, wasn't willing to spend the money for the astronomical amounts of jet fuel, spare parts, maintenance and additional air crews required. They authorized the President to spend the money only if the need, in his judgment, became critical.

"The same deterrent power can be achieved at a fraction of the cost by placing two thirds of the tactical fighters overseas on 'hardened alert.' We already have the proven ability to launch F-100 fighters, fully armed and bombed, by ZEL (zero launch), firing them from mobile launching pads by rocket boosters.

"We have also proved we can fire them like missiles from fixed launching pads which can be protected by concrete and dirt walls and roofs against damage by anything but a direct hit from an enemy nuclear missile or bomb. One third of our overseas tactical force could be maintained on the ZEL pads ready for instant launching, while one third was undergoing maintenance in hangars also protected from nuclear blast. One third would be required for training and other purposes on unprotected airfields.

"This whole program could be accomplished for less than the cost of maintaining SAC on airborne alert for a single year. And the cost of the hardened ZEL program would, of course, be a one-time cost.

"Russia would then be confronted with the almost impossible necessity of expending enough nuclear missiles to be sure of direct hits on all our hardened ZEL sites before she could hope to escape devastating retaliation. That would mean about ninety missiles against each deployed squadron. This is the cheapest and most effective of deterrents and is available immediately.

"Mounting these tactical fighter-bombers in protected ZEL pads would add to their power to deter all-out atomic attack, without in any way reducing their value for other limited uses," General Weyland contends.

General Frank F. Everest, TAC's current commanding general, believes the mobile ballistic missile will do the job more effectively.

Whatever the shape of things to come, the winged sword of TAC, with lightning—the first truly all-purpose air force in history—casts an ever longer shadow over the future.

# Appendix

FIGHTERS

NORTH AMERICAN F-100D SUPER SABER, weight 39,750 pounds maximum, top speed more than 1000 miles an hour; service ceiling over 50,000 feet; range over 1,000 miles; Pratt & Whitney J-57-21 engine, 10,000 pounds of thrust; nuclear capability; inflight refueling; backbone of TAC fighter-bombers.

McDONNELL F-100 VOODOO, weight 40,000 pounds; speed over 1,200 MPH; 2 Pratt & Whitney J-57-13 engines, 4 20-mm. cannon, Falcon missiles; nuclear capability; inflight refueling.

LOCKHEED F-104 STARFIGHTER, weight 17,000 pounds; maximum speed ultrasonic; service ceiling, 60,000; General Electric J-79 engine; T-71 20-mm. cannon; missiles, rockets, nuclear capability; holds record for climb to 98,424 feet in 15 min., 4.92 seconds, and continued climb to 103,-395, Capt. J. B. Jordan at the controls.

REPUBLIC F-105 THUNDERCHIEF, weight 40,000 pounds; maximum speed 1,300 MPH; General Electric J-75-5 engine; rocket and nuclear capability; inflight refueling; 20 mm. cannon, Sidewinder missiles; set record of 1,216.48 MPH Dec. 11, 1959, for 100 kilometer closed course, Brig. Gen. J. H. Moore at the controls.

DOUGLAS B-66 DESTROYER, weight 78,000 pounds, two Allison J-71-13 engines; service ceiling 45,000 feet; 2 20-mm. cannon in tail; nuclear capability; range, 1500 miles plus; inflight refueling.

MARTIN B-57 Canberra twin-jet reconnaissance and weather plane, weight 50,000, range 2000 miles or more, speed 600 MPH or more, two Wright J-65-5 engines; 7,200 or more pounds of thrust each.

## TRANSPORTS

LOCKHEED C-130 HERCULES, weight 108,000 pounds; four Allison T-57-1A turboprop engines; cargo capacity, 36,900 pounds or 70 litter patients, 64 equipped paratroopers, or 92 soldiers; range, over 2000 miles; service ceiling, 30,000 feet, key CASF support planes.

FAIRCHILD C-123 PROVIDER, weight 60,000 maximum; maximum speed 245 MPH; service ceiling 23,000 feet; range with maximum load 1,470 miles; 2 Pratt & Whitney R-2800-99W piston engines; 60 fully equipped troops, or 50 stretcher cases; or 16,000 pounds of cargo.

BOEING KB-50 TANKER, maximum gross 173,000 pounds; ceiling 35,000 feet; top speed over 400 MPH; range over 2,000 miles; four 3,500 horsepower Pratt & Whitney piston engines, 2 jets of 5,620 pounds thrust; a converted Super-fortress.

## TAC MISSILES

MATADOR TM-61, tactical missile, subsonic speed (650 MPH), made by Martin company, first operational missile (March, 1954); 9 feet in diameter, 39.6 feet long, 28.7 feet wingspan; ground launched by a rocket booster, powered by

Allison jet engine, electronically controlled from ground, nuclear capability; TM-61C carried in Germany, Korea and Taiwan.

MACE TM-76, Near sonic speed, ceiling over 40,000 feet, range over 600 nautical miles, launched by booster, 22 feet, 10 inches wingspan; 44 feet, 3 inches long, self-contained navigation system; nuclear capability; designed to fly low under radar net.

## TAC COMMANDERS

Maj. Gen. Elwood R. Quesada, March 21, 1946 through Nov. 23, 1948.

Maj. Gen. Robert M. Lee, Nov. 24, 1948 through July 7, 1950.

Maj. Gen. O. P. Weyland, July 7 through 16, 1950.

Maj. Gen. Glenn O. Barcus, July 17 through Jan. 24, 1951.

Lt. Gen. John K. Cannon, Jan. 25, 1951, through March 31, 1954.

Gen. O. P. Weyland, May 1, 1954 through July 31, 1959.

Gen. Frank F. Everest, Aug. 1, 1959.

# Index

WOLFGRAM LIBRARY, WIDENER COLLEGE
CHESTER, PA.